AUSTRALIAN BIRDS

Dark Phase

EEF HERON 23in.

PIED HERON 19in.

WHITE-FACED HERON 24in.

PINK COCKATOO 16in.

WOMPOO PIGEON 19in.

WHITE-HEADED PIGEON 16in.

TOPKNOT PIGEON 17in.

NUTMEG PIGEON 13in.

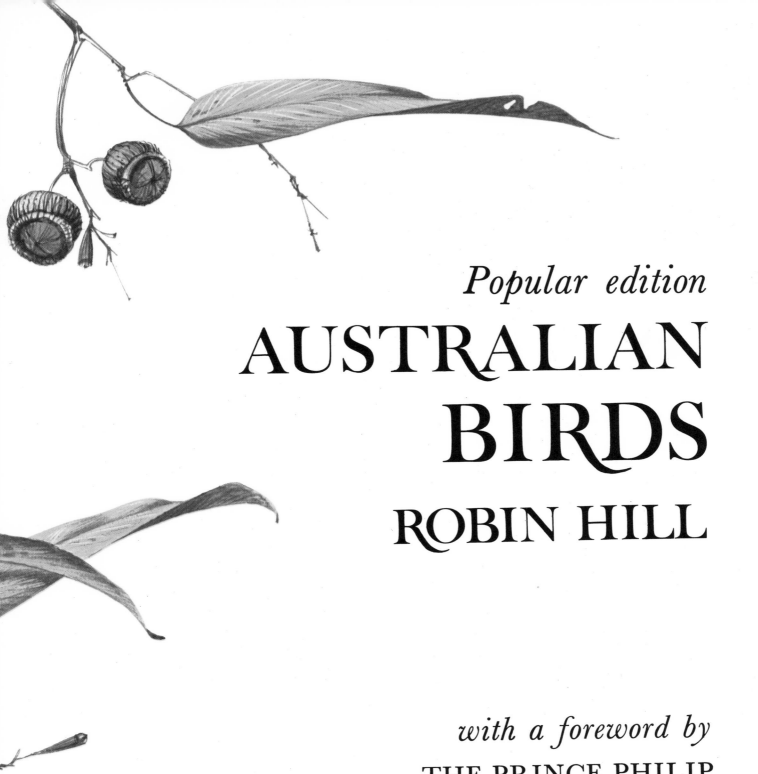

Popular edition

AUSTRALIAN BIRDS

ROBIN HILL

with a foreword by

THE PRINCE PHILIP
H.R.H. THE DUKE OF EDINBURGH

NELSON

GREAT-BILLED HERON
41in.

WHITE-NECKED HERON
30in.

THOMAS NELSON (AUSTRALIA) LIMITED
19-39 Jeffcott Street West Melbourne 3003
104 Bathurst Street Sydney 2000
and in Brisbane Qld, Adelaide SA and Perth WA

THOMAS NELSON AND SONS LTD
36 Park Street London W1Y 4DE

THOMAS NELSON AND SONS (CANADA) LTD
81 Curlew Drive Don Mills Ontario

© Thomas Nelson (Australia) Ltd 1967
Reprinted 1968
This edition © 1970
Reprinted 1972, 1973, 1975
ISBN 0 17 001704 4

Printed in Hong Kong by
Dai Nippon Printing Co. (H.K.) Ltd

DIVING PETREL 8in.

For my parents: Russ and Blue
Qui semper confidebant nuper animum confirmabant

Brief details of birds
illustrated in the preliminary pages

Page 1: PIED HERONS are found in northern Australia from the Wyndham district to north-eastern Queensland. REEF HERONS are found mainly in northern coastal regions. WHITE-FACED HERONS are common to most parts of Australia. See page 20.

Page 2/3: PINK COCKATOOS are perhaps the most beautiful of the Australian cuckoos. One of the least common, they are, however, thriving in the Wyperfeld National Park.

Page 4: GREAT-BILLED HERONS are found in coastal districts across northern Australia and down the Queensland coast as far as Broad Sound. WHITE-NECKED HERONS are not particularly common, but are to be found throughout Australia.

Page 7: Australia's two introduced doves: INDIAN TURTLEDOVES are found largely in the east, SENEGAL TURTLEDOVES are confined to Western Australia. See page 46.

Page 9: BLACK-SHOULDERED KITES are delicate birds found throughout Australian coastal regions.

Page 11: INLAND DOTTERELS are nomadic birds and are seen in middle Western Australia, Northern Territory, western Queensland south to north-west Victoria and inland South Australia. KOELS are the cuckoos of the forest and big brush country, and are found from north-west Australia across the continent and down the eastern states to north-east Victoria.

SENEGAL TURTLEDOVE 9in.

INDIAN TURTLEDOVE 13in.

CONTENTS

Foreword by H.R.H. The Duke of Edinburgh — 9

Author's preface — 11

CASUARIIFORMES—Emus — 15
  Emus — 15

PODICIPEDIFORMES—Grebes — 16
  Grebes — 16

SPHENISCIFORMES—Penguins — 16
  Penguins — 16

PROCELLARIIFORMES—Tube-noses — 17
  Albatrosses — 17
  Shearwaters — 17

PELECANIFORMES—Pelicans and Allied Birds — 19
  Pelicans — 19
  Cormorants — 19
  Gannets — 19

CICONIIFORMES—Herons and Allied Birds — 20
  Herons — 20
  Bitterns — 20
  Egrets — 20
  Ibises — 23
  Spoonbills — 23

ANSERIFORMES—Ducks, Geese and Swans — 24
  Shelducks — 24
  River Ducks — 24
  Pochards — 24
  Perching Ducks — 25
  Stiff-tails — 25
  Swans — 26

FALCONIFORMES—Birds of Prey — 27
  Eagles — 27
  Kites — 28
  Goshawks — 28
  Falcons — 30
  Ospreys — 32

GALLIFORMES—Fowl-like Birds — 33
  Mound-builders — 33
  Quails — 34

GRUIFORMES—Cranes, Rails and Allied Birds — 35
  Cranes — 35
  Waterhens — 35

CHARADRIIFORMES—Waders, Gulls and Allied Birds — 37
  Painted Snipes — 37
  Oyster-catchers — 37
  Plovers and Dotterels — 37
  Sandpipers and Allied Birds — 39
  Stilts and Avocets — 41
  Gulls — 43
  Terns — 43

COLUMBIFORMES—Pigeons and Doves — 46
  Ground Pigeons — 46

PSITTACIFORMES—Parrots and Cockatoos — 48
  Lorikeets — 48
  Cockatoos — 48
  Cockatiels — 52
  Aprosmictus Parrots — 52
  Long-tails — 53
  Rosellas — 53
  Ringneck Parrots — 56
  Psephotus Parrots — 56
  Neophema or Grass Parrots — 56
  Budgerygahs — 58

CUCULIFORMES—Cuckoos and Allied Birds — 59
  Cuckoos — 59

STRIGIFORMES—Owls — 61
  Barn Owls — 61
  Typical Owls — 62

CAPRIMULGIFORMES—Nightjars and Allied Birds — 63
  Nightjars — 63
  Frogmouths — 63
  Owlet-nightjars — 65

APODIFORMES—Swifts — 65
  Swifts — 65

CORACIIFORMES—Kingfishers and Allied Birds 66
    Kingfishers 66
    Bee-eaters 68
    Dollar-birds 68

PASSERIFORMES—Perching Birds 69
    Pittas 69
    Lyrebirds 69
    Larks 71
    Swallows 72
    Martins 72
    Cuckoo-shrikes 73
    Trillers 74
    Drongos 74
    Crows and Ravens 76
    Mudlarks 77
    Choughs 77
    Magpies 77
    Butcher-birds 78
    Bower-birds 78
    Birds of Paradise 80
    Australian Treecreepers 81
    Sittellas 82
    Babblers 83

    Quail-thrushes 8
    Shrike-thrushes 8
    Thrushes and Blackbirds 8
    Old World Warblers 8
    Old World Flycatchers 9
    Whistlers 9
    Pipits 9
    Wood-swallows 9
    Starlings 100
    Mynahs 100
    Honeyeaters 10
    Shriketits 11
    Whipbirds 11
    Chats 11
    Pardelotes 11
    Mistletoe-birds 11
    Silvereyes 11
    Old World Seedeaters 11

Location Map 118

Bibliography 120

Index of Common Names 121

Index of Scientific Names 124

BLACK-SHOULDERED KITE 12½in.

FOREWORD

Painting wild animals, and particularly birds, is the most exacting branch of the art. Photography cannot compare with the work of an accomplished artist, and the discipline of faithful yet aesthetic presentation of the subjects demands a very special talent.

Robin Hill's work is in line with the great bird painters of the world and it betrays the same painstaking research in the field and inspiration in the studio.

Australia is fortunate to have such an artist working at this time when there is a growing interest in the natural history of the continent and particularly in its very rich bird life.

I hope this splendid book will have the success it deserves and help to encourage even more Australians to appreciate the scope and variety of the natural background to their lives.

H.R.H. THE DUKE OF EDINBURGH

INLAND DOTTEREL 8in.

KOEL 18in.

PREFACE TO POPULAR EDITION

The tremendous success of *Australian Birds* has encouraged, and indeed made possible, the production of this popular edition. Broadly speaking, I have chosen species that will be found from South Australia to about Cairns. The book now deals with 310 species; all that the average bird-watcher might expect to see in the eastern and southern states.

The people I have had in mind in compiling this book fall into two main groups: children, and all those people who go out of doors for recreation and who have at least a passing interest in the natural world. At about a quarter of the price of the complete edition, it is hoped that children will be able to use it more freely to help them in their birding—to knock it about, take it on picnics, holidays, make notes in it—in short, to treat the book with a healthy lack of respect.

This book is also for those who fish, garden, golf, hike or indulge in any other activity that might bring them into contact with birds.

By selecting the species most bird-watchers are likely to see—getting the 'process of elimination' well under way—I hope I have made the book much easier to use for bird identification.

As a result of my travels since the first edition appeared and my greater familiarity with the subject, fifteen plates have been repainted, covering thirty birds. The text for each species has also been revised in its syntax and punctuation and placed, where possible, on the same page as the related illustration. As an aid to finding the notes on each bird, the first appearance in the text of the bird's name is printed in a contrasting type.

A very few of the species included are rare or non-existent in the geographic area covered. This has been unavoidable as it was impossible to break up some of the plates and, to keep the retail cost of the book down, not practical to repaint them.

I should like to thank the number of people who have written to me offering criticism and advice. We go on learning. Some of what I have gleaned from the public is incorporated in this volume; more will be found in the revised complete edition we hope to produce in the not too distant future.

1970

Dark Phase

AUSTRALIAN BIRDS

REEF HERON 23in.

PIED HERON 19in.

WHITE-FACED HERON 24in.

EMU
♀ 78 in.

14

CASUARIIFORMES

Emus

mus, *Dromaius novae-hollandiae*, are the second largest birds in
e world, standing about three feet high at the 'shoulder';
further two feet of neck gives the birds considerable stature.
is a happy chance that the emus, which are represented on
ustralia's coat of arms, also head the classification of our
rds, thus giving them a double claim for starting this book.

Australians have not treated their official bird kindly.
hen white men came to this continent there were three,
d perhaps four, forms of emu; all except the mainland
rd are now extinct.

Sealers on the islands and settlers in Tasmania wrought
voc amongst these flightless birds. They were hunted for
od and for their very clear oil, which was used in lamps and
edicinally. Emus were also persecuted in self-defence by
storalists. Control was no doubt justifiable, but hardly
termination.

Emus are still persecuted in parts of Australia, sometimes
th a bounty being paid on their heads, but they are
parently in no danger of extinction. They are distributed
roughout the continent, and they pair off when breeding
t otherwise travel in flocks.

A large male weighs up to 120 lb and may stand six feet
ll; the female is slightly smaller. They are quite flightless,
ving only the merest rudimentary wings, but run strongly
speeds up to 30 mph for short distances. They can also
im well.

If unmolested, emus are inquisitive and even friendly, and
ey are frequently tamed on outback stations.

Although they eat caterpillars and grasshoppers when
ailable, their diet is mainly herbivorous; consequently
ey suffer greatly during droughts. The call of the female is
deep, resonant drumming sound and the male utters belly-
unts and low rumblings when disturbed or excited. The
xes can also be distinguished by the brighter blues on the
ck of the male.

CRESTED GREBE 24 in.

Winter

LITTLE GREBE 9¼ in.

Summer

PODICIPEDIFORMES

Grebes

Every major land mass except Antarctica has its grebes; and in Australia we have three species. The most handsome of these are the CRESTED GREBES, *Podiceps cristatus*, with their regal chestnut and black collars and bifurcated dusky crests.

They are fairly common in eastern Australia, moving latitudinally with changes of season. In the west they are confined to the south-west corner and are not so common.

Like most grebes they swim with their chicks on their backs and even dive with the young birds securely tucked under their scapular feathers. The plumage is close and velvety and was once in great demand for the trimming of women's hats.

Grebes have the unique and inexplicable habit of eating their own feathers; they also feed them to their chicks.

Although they sometimes visit brackish or salt-water to feed, the Crested Grebes breed only on fresh-water. They build a floating nest from weeds and other aquatic vegetation, and anchor it to other nearby growth.

Having their legs placed so far back for greater efficiency in swimming, Crested Grebes are clumsy on land and seldom venture more than a few yards from water.

Although they can fly they have difficulty in taking off on their short wings; to escape danger they more usually resort to diving, although they seldom stay under for more than about 30 seconds.

Like other grebes, the Cresteds have the ability to expel

air from their body and feathers thus increasing their specific gravity and enabling them to sink slowly beneath the surface. When suspicious of danger a grebe will often swim with only its head periscoped above water.

LITTLE GREBES, *Podiceps novae-hollandiae*, found throughout Australia where suitable habitats exist, usually inhabit fresh water, although they do visit salt-water to feed. Large parties gather in the non-breeding season but in the spring they pair off, although even a few acres of water may contain many breeding pairs.

SPHENISCIFORMES

Penguins

Penguins were established in their present form and over much of their present range 50 million years ago, and their ancestors lost the power of flight about 100 million years ago. So the penguins are among the most primitive and ancient of birds.

Their loss of flight has been compensated by their extraordinary swimming powers. Some species' under-water speeds are in excess of 25 mph, and they can shoot themselves up from beneath the surface fast enough to land on a rock or ice-floe five or six feet above the water.

Penguins' bodies are a perfection of streamlining. Their hard inflexible flippers which move only at the shoulder are ideal for propulsion under water and their plumage is also highly adapted for an aquatic existence. The feathers grow thickly and uniformly all over their bodies, forming an insulating coat with a shiny waterproof surface.

On land the penguins are ungainly and awkward, although they sometimes travel long distances from the sea to their nesting sites. They breed in vast colonies, sometimes numbering in the region of half a million in the common species.

LITTLE PENGUIN, *Eudyptula minor*, are Australia's penguins and are favourite with many people. Some Little Penguin rookeries are readily accessible and are frequently visited by the public. The 'penguin parade' starts at dusk, and at one place at least—on Phillip Island in Victoria—the beach is floodlit for the benefit of spectators.

Little Penguins range around our southern coasts and islands from around Fremantle in the west to as far north as Moreton Bay in Queensland. They are also common around Tasmania. They frequent local seas throughout the year and can often be met, singly or in small parties, swimming out at sea. In Western Australian waters they are much less commonly seen in daylight and are more timid of man.

LITTLE PENGUIN 18 in.

PROCELLARIIFORMES

THE TUBE NOSES

Albatrosses

hese huge sea-birds have been woven into the tales and aditions of the sea ever since men sailed the southern ceans. Coleridge's poem about the Ancient Mariner is erhaps the best known reference to the bird.

Their long narrow wings, so effectual for gliding, are efficient for flapping flight in still air. This explains why batrosses are confined mainly to the windy southern oceans the world. The doldrums—windless areas about the quator in the Pacific and Atlantic—are effective barriers hich neither the southern nor the few northern species oss in any significant numbers.

BLACK-BROWED ALBATROSSES, *Diomeda melanophris*, are erhaps the commonest albatrosses in our seas, especially off e south-east coastline. They are distinguishable by their llow bills and are usually seen between May and November. hey nest in the sub-antarctic and like all other albatrosses ild large mound nests of grass and earth cemented together ith their own droppings.

BLACK-BROWED ALBATROSS 33 in.

SHORT-TAILED SHEARWATER 14 in.

WEDGE-TAILED SHEARWATER 17½ in.

Light Phase

SOOTY SHEARWATER 18 in.

FLUTTERING SHEARWATER 14½ in.

Shearwaters

IORT-TAILED SHEARWATERS, *Puffinus tenuirostris*, are the well-own mutton-birds which are 'farmed' commercially in ass Strait. The centre of the industry is the Furneaux roup where thousands of young birds are taken from the rrows each season and sold, either fresh, or salted and cked for transport. Great flocks of shearwaters invade the ass Strait and other southern Australian islands each year out the end of September. The birds nest in burrows, ying one white egg.

WEDGE-TAILED SHEARWATERS, *P. pacificus*, in contrast to uirostris, appear to be more or less resident in our oceans. ch spring they nest in large rookeries on various islands off r coastline—particularly along the Barrier Reef. Their eeding habits are much the same as the preceding species, d islands where the birds are nesting are loud with their lls throughout the night. Like the other shearwaters they ed on krill and small fish such as schools of anchovies.

SOOTY SHEARWATERS, *P. griseus*, are found in the seas ound our south-east coastline, and are the commonest utton-birds of New Zealand. They also breed on Brough-n Is., N.S.W., Tasman Is., and probably other Tasmanian ands where they could easily be confused with *tenuirostris*. hey are a migratory species, moving up through the Pacific the non-breeding season.

PELICAN 60 in.

LITTLE BLAC[K]
CORMORAN[T]
24½ in.

BLACK CORMORANT 32 in.

LITTLE PIED CORMORANT 23 in.

PELECANIFORMES

PELICANS AND ALLIED BIRDS

Pelicans

Australian Pelicans, *Pelecanus conspicillatus*, are among our largest flying birds; they can weigh up to 17 lb with a wing-span of 6–7 ft.

Pelicans live on fish and use their large gular pouch, which can hold up to three gallons of water, as a 'dipper' for catching their prey. The fish are not stored in the pouch, but the water is strained out and the fish are then swallowed or carried crosswise in the bill.

These birds are of very ancient lineage and fossil remains have been found that are 30 to 40 million years old. The fossil pelicans are so similar to the present birds as to be placed in the same genus.

Although powerful flyers and good swimmers, pelicans are clumsy and slow on land, having their feet placed far back for swimming efficiency. They also have trouble taking off, and on a windless day have to run flapping a considerable distance over land or water before becoming airborne.

They nest in colonies and tend to be sociable even out of the breeding season. The colony may be close to either fresh or salt-water. The nests are usually a mere hollow scraped in the ground, each bird sitting just out of pecking distance of its neighbour.

Cormorants

BLACK CORMORANTS, *Phalacrocorax carbo*, are the largest of this group. They are quite common birds and are found on both fresh and salt-water. They breed close to the water in colonies which are sometimes very large mixed gatherings of various cormorant species. These are the only cormorants which are significant predators on 'commercial' fish, and then only in fresh-water habitats.

The nests are bulky and made up of whatever materials are to hand. The three or four eggs are greenish when new but soon become coated with lime. Black Cormorants, like others of the genus, swim well and usually pursue their prey under water.

In Western Australia they appear to be more common on inland waterways, whereas in Tasmania they are recorded as being frequenters of estuaries and sheltered bays. In any case, like all cormorants, they are seldom found far from land.

They are often seen sitting with their wings held open to dry in the sun and wind. This is because they do not have the waterproof plumage usually associated with aquatic birds. Indeed, they can become so saturated that flight becomes difficult or impossible until they have dried out.

LITTLE BLACK CORMORANTS, *P. sulcirostris*, are more estuarine or fresh-water birds and are seldom found on open coasts. They hunt in large flocks; contrary to the belief of many fishermen, their prey is usually 'non-commercial' fish such as anchovies, smelt and other small rough fish. They are found throughout the continent but in Tasmania have been recorded only as non-breeding visitors. They nest in colonies, often in association with their Little Pied and Black relatives. The nest and eggs are similar to those of other cormorants.

LITTLE PIED CORMORANTS, *P. melanoleucus*, are probably the most commmon of the genus in the east; in Western Australia, however, the Pieds would appear to be more numerous. Like all cormorants they are rare along the wild, steep coastlines of the Bight.

There is some variation in their plumage, some specimens having partly or wholly grey underparts. The nesting and other habits are similar to those of other cormorants.

Gannets

GANNETS, *Sula serrator*, are fairly common birds within their Australian breeding range, becoming less common westwards and northwards. Five breeding colonies are Laurence Rocks, Black Pyramid and Cat Island in Bass Strait, and Pedra Branca and Eddystone Rocks off Southern Tasmania. They also breed in New Zealand, and in the winter migrate to our warmer south-eastern waters. Gannets are handsome and striking birds and may often be seen fishing in parties. They hunt by flying above the water until a school of fish is spotted. The birds then plummet down from as high as 100 ft or so and dive more or less vertically beneath the surface, usually staying under water only a few seconds. Gannets have been found trapped in fishermen's nets as much as 90 ft down. If a fish is caught it is swallowed under water.

They start nesting in the early spring, laying their eggs in solidly built nests, which are cones of earth and guano lined with weed, twigs and other material.

Immature

AUSTRALIAN GANNET 32 in.

CICONIIFORMES

HERONS AND ALLIED BIRDS

In Australia this order is represented by six genera of fairly similar looking birds. They vary considerably in size, however, ranging from the Great-billed Herons which stand about three feet high, down to the mere fifteen inches or so of the Pied Herons.

All the 'true' or pond herons are long-necked, long-legged birds which spend most of their time in or near water or swampy land. Their principal food is fish and small aquatic animals such as frogs, yabbies and eels.

The necks of herons are made up of unequal vertebrae, causing that typical kink. This is probably helpful as a form of leverage—enabling the birds to dart their heads forward with great rapidity at moving prey.

Linked with the herons are the bitterns. These birds tend to be stockier and shorter necked than the herons and are usually more complexly patterned in mottled browns and buffs.

Both herons and bitterns have a marked development of powder-down patches. These are found in paired areas on the breast, rump or flanks. The powder-down is never moulted and is made up of feathers which crumble into a powder used by the birds in cleaning their plumage.

The oil and slime adhering to the feathers after a bittern or heron has struggled with an eel or other slimy creature, is absorbed by the powder. It is applied in some cases by means of the bill, or the bird rubs its head through the powder patch. After the powder has done its job of absorption, it is vigorously scratched and combed out, mainly by means of the serrated 'comb-claw' on the middle toe. Once cleaned and combed, oil is rubbed in from the bird's preen gland to waterproof the plumage.

WHITE-FACED Herons, *Ardea novae-hollandiae*, are the common herons in most parts of Australia and Tasmania. Erroneously known as 'blue-cranes' by many people, they can be seen on waterways and swampy areas even in and close to cities. Flocks of twenty or thirty birds are quite common although solitary birds are also often seen standing sentinel over a pond or swamp. They also frequent sea beaches, hunting along the tide-line and shallows for food.

They nest as a rule in tall trees, not necessarily near water, and sometimes a small number of birds will build in the same vicinity, although hardly forming a tight colony.

NANKEEN NIGHT-HERONS, *Nycticorax caledonicus*, are bittern-like birds found throughout the continent and Tasmania.

They are in the main nocturnal, fishing in the shallows of swamps, lakes and streams for yabbies and other aquatic life. Sometimes they can be seen wading into deep water up to their 'shoulders'. If disturbed they will fly off on broad slow wings, with a grating croak of alarm.

Nankeen Herons are well known for their visits to city parks, and have been known to roost in busy places, quite undisturbed by people and traffic. Every year the Botanic Gardens in Melbourne has a wintering colony that has been in existence since before the gardens were started. A few non-breeding juveniles also stay throughout the year.

These herons build in colonies, constructing slight nests of sticks at varying heights up to one hundred feet or so, and usually over water.

Bitterns

LITTLE BITTERNS, *Ixobrychus minutus*, are shy birds of the reed-beds and swamps. They seldom fly when disturbed but prefer to depend on remaining stationary and unobserved. They will sometimes stretch up to their full height in a typical bittern-reed-pose: alternatively, they may crouch and puff their feathers out into a ball. They are so loth to fly that they may sometimes be taken up in the hand or caught by dogs. If they do take off they fly low over the reeds with slow laboured wing-strokes. In spite of being so wary they have been recorded in large city parks that contain a suitable habitat.

They construct slightly built nests of pieces of reed, grasses and other aquatic plants. There are usually placed a little above the water in a reed-bed. Sometimes a few nests will be built near each other by separate pairs of birds. The usual clutch is four white eggs which are laid about October or November.

Little Bitterns are found in south-western Australia and eastern and south-eastern Australia. They are not recorded for Tasmania.

The range of the BROWN BITTERNS, *Botaurus poiciloptilus*, is similar, although they are recorded further west, as far as the Adelaide plains. They are also found in Tasmania where their numbers are said to be dwindling.

Brown Bitterns may be seen singly or in pairs haunting reed-beds and other sedgy areas. Haunting is an apt word as their weird booming call is a most mysterious sound and is thought to be one of the sources of the Aborigines' tales of Bunyips. In fact, they are more likely to be heard than seen as their booming call is repeated through the dusk and into the night.

Brown Bitterns will sometimes stand out on an exposed mudbank, heads in the air, perfectly resembling mottled rotting stumps of wood.

They nest in the densest parts of swamp, bending down the reeds and flags and interlacing them into a hollow platform. Four or five olive-green eggs are laid during October or November, as a rule. The bittern's food is yabbies, small eels and fish or any other aquatic life it can catch.

BLACK BITTERNS, *Dupetor flavicollis*, are largely birds of the mangrove swamps. They roost by day in the trees and fly down to feed at dusk.

If disturbed on the ground they are very elusive, running over the mud under the mangroves for a great distance before they will be flushed. If startled, they will assume the bittern pose, stretching upright and pressing their feathers close to the body.

It is recorded that if these bitterns are robbed of their eggs they will immediately lay again in the same nest or build another close by. They feed on water-insects, fish, frogs and other aquatic life.

Their nests are platforms of sticks built in the branches of a tree, usually overhanging the water. The three to five eggs are white and the breeding season is September to January.

Egrets

LARGE or WHITE EGRETS, *Egretta alba*, are tall graceful birds that may be seen stalking small aquatic animals and fish in suitable localities throughout the continent. They are the only egrets common in Tasmania.

WHITE-FACED HERON 24in.

WHITE IBIS 30 in.

GLOSSY IBIS 25 in.

STRAW-NECKED IBIS 28 in.

ROYAL SPOONBILL 29 in.

YELLOW-BILLED SPOONBILL 28 in.

LARGE EGRET 30 in.

CATTLE EGRET 21 in.

23

In their breeding plumage the birds' yellow bills become largely black and they grow long filamentous plumes on their backs. It was for these plumes that they were once hunted. There was, of course, a far greater mortality than that caused by the adult being taken; with the parent birds gone, eggs and young were left to perish in the nests.

These egrets breed in colonies, often in association with similar species and cormorants. The nests are platforms of sticks built at varying heights in trees in or close to water. They usually breed from November to January and lay three to five greenish-blue eggs.

E. intermedia is the middle-sized PLUMED EGRET. These birds, as well as developing the nuptial plumes on the back which project well beyond the tail, also grow ornamental feathers on the fore-neck and something of a head crest.

They are similar in habits to their larger relative but not as extensive in their range. The species *intermedia* is not recorded for south-western Australia or Tasmania.

Out of the breeding season they will be seen singly or in pairs or small groups foraging through swampy land. They feed on yabbies, frogs and anything of a similar nature that they can catch.

Like the other egrets they nest in colonies and usually in association with various other species of egret and water birds.

Their nests are flattened platforms of twigs and sticks, often with a few leaves interwoven. From three to five eggs are laid between October and December or later, depending on local conditions or rainfall and water levels.

LITTLE EGRETS, *E. garzetta*, are found in suitable habitats throughout northern and eastern Australia and Victoria. They are seen occasionally in South Australia but very rarely in Tasmania. Throughout their range in this country they are nomadic and rather rare, although they may occur in some numbers in certain localities from time to time.

During the breeding season a few plumes develop on the backs of their heads and long lanceolate feathers grow on the fore-necks. There are also great developments of the beautiful train of plumes growing from the birds' backs, and two six-inch-long plumes from their napes. The females are smaller and their plumes are developed to a lesser extent.

They forage in swamps and other wet places in the usual egret manner—stalking slowly forward for a few paces and then stopping quite still, sometimes for minutes at a time. They stare down into the water and if some tit-bit comes within reach, the rapier-bills are shot forward on the long springs of the birds' necks. They are usually successful in snapping up what they aim for. These egrets are wary and if disturbed the birds circle high into the air and fly off to some more secluded spot.

The usual platforms of sticks and twigs are built in trees growing in or near water. They nest in colonies, often in association with other water birds. Three to five pale blue-green eggs are laid from October onwards, depending on the locality and prevailing conditions.

CATTLE EGRETS, *Ardeola ibis*, were introduced into the Kimberley area in 1933 with some idea of counteracting cattle-tick. It may be that these died out, although some time later cattle egrets were seen in the area. Since then their numbers have been increasing, whether from the original stock, or by a natural spread of birds from South-east Asia is not really known. However, these handsome egrets are now firmly established and have been found breeding as far south as northern N.S.W. As a visitor they have also been recorded in the south-west of the continent, and there are sight records for Tasmania.

In non-breeding plumage these egrets are white, but in their nuptial dress they develop a bright yellowish-ochre wash on the head, breast and part of the back. They also grow head, neck and back plumes, the latter not being as long as the Little Egrets'. The nest is a saucer platform of twigs and sticks built in a tree in or close to water. The three to six eggs are bluish-white. As with the other egrets they breed in the spring and summer.

PLUMED EGRET
24 in.

BROWN BITTERN 24 in.

BLACK BITTERN 21 in.

LITTLE EGRET 22 in.

LITTLE BITTERN 10 in.

Ibises

In general the most common ibises are the STRAW-NECKED IBISES, *Threskiornis spinicollis*. They are found throughout the mainland, though rarely visiting Tasmania. They may be seen in various numbers from single birds up to large flocks hunting along the edges of swampy land or out in open pastoral country. They have even appeared on some occasions in the dry interior to feed on grasshopper swarms. In this respect, they are one of Australia's most useful birds, eating many insects that are harmful to crops.

They are wide-ranging and banding has shown that some birds travel the length of Australia.

They build a nest of trampled-down bushes, reeds, or other vegetation, with sticks and herbage added to give the nest substance. They are colony breeders and in some favoured localities gather in thousands, often mixing with other ibis species. The breeding season is about September to December, but may vary under different conditions. Three to five dull white eggs are laid which soon become nest-stained brown.

WHITE IBISES, *T. molucca*, are found throughout the country and also in Tasmania, although they tend to be more common in the north and east. In 1952 there was an influx of Straw-necked Ibises into the south-west and amongst these were numbers of White Ibises. These seem to be establishing themselves, whereas before 1952 they seldom moved lower than the Kimberleys.

They appear to be somewhat shyer birds than the preceding species, although in some localities flocks will become bold in their pursuit of insects through cultivated areas. They hunt for small aquatic creatures in swampy land.

Their habits of feeding and general behaviour are similar to those of the Straw-necked Ibises and their two to five dull white eggs are laid in a similar nest.

GLOSSY IBISES, *Plegadis falcinellus*, look very different, being smaller and entirely dark. They are not uncommon in northern Australia but become increasingly rare as their range extends southwards. They are recorded as visiting Tasmania, but only rarely—perhaps forced over Bass Strait by exceptionally dry seasons on the mainland.

As with other ibises their feeding habits make them valuable birds to farmers and pastoralists; they will even follow a plough to feed upon the insects turned up in the furrows.

Their nesting habits are somewhat different from the other ibises as they usually build in the upright fork of a small tree or in lignum bushes. The nests may be constructed of twigs, branches and leaves or entirely of leaves built up to form a hollowed platform.

The breeding season is usually from September to December, but may be delayed if the wet season is late. Three or four beautiful greenish-blue eggs are laid. These can so vary in size from clutch to clutch that sometimes it is hard to believe they belong to the same species.

Spoonbills

ROYAL SPOONBILLS, *Platalea regia*, are found throughout the continent and Tasmania except for the area around the border of Western Australia and South Australia. They have not been recorded as nesting south of the Kimberleys in Western Australia.

They inhabit marshy land, wading far out into shallow swamps in search of molluscs and other small aquatic life.

These spoonbills choose various nesting sites; some will build in trampled-down reeds, others in bushes or quite high up in trees. During the breeding season the birds grow a crest of elongated crown feathers. October to May is the nesting season, although this may vary; they lay three or four chalky-white eggs that are smeared and freckled with yellowish or reddish-brown.

YELLOW-BILLED SPOONBILLS, *P. flavipes*, are found in suitable habitats over much of Australia, but are not recorded from Tasmania, Cape York Peninsula or the Centre. In Western Australia they are distributed through the coastal areas but rarely nest south of the Kimberley area.

Except when in their breeding colonies they are wary birds. They have a habit of perching in dead trees from which there is a good view, thus making them difficult to approach.

They take similar food to the other spoonbills and, like them, feed on water insects by sweeping their plate-ended bill from side to side through the water. Spoonbills also snap up small creatures from the mud and water.

The nests are bulky structures of sticks built in a tree or near the water. Three or four chalky-white eggs are laid about September or according to conditions.

Immature

NANKEEN NIGHT-HERON 24 in.

BLACK DUCK 24 in.

ANSERIFORMES

DUCKS, GEESE AND SWANS

Shelducks

CHESTNUT-BREASTED SHELDUCKS, *Casarca tadornoides*, are typical looking shelducks found throughout southern Australia except for the Nullabor district; from the Tropic of Capricorn down through Western Australia, across South Australia to Victoria, Tasmania and southern N.S.W., although they are rare about Sydney.

They are wary birds, though not much shot at, being rank in flavour. Usually seen in small flocks, they often feed out on paddocks well away from water as well as being great frequenters of tidal flats and estuaries.

They nest in a variety of places: a hole in a tree which may be close to, or far from water, or a rabbit burrow. In Western Australia they are recorded as nesting in deep crevices between the rocks on Rottnest Island. Up to eighteen eggs have been found but it may be that such large numbers would be the work of more than one female.

The nests are made of grass and the glossy, creamy eggs are laid in a great deal of down. Breeding season is from July to December.

River Ducks

Perhaps the best known ducks in Australia are the BLACK DUCKS, *Anas superciliosa*, which are actually a greyish brown colour. Large numbers of these birds are shot each year in the duck season, but breeding programmes, bag limits and strict protection during closed season protect them as a species.

Except for desert areas they are found in most parts of the continent and Tasmania. Single birds, pairs, or flocks which may number hundreds in some localities, are seen.

Black Ducks frequent any kind of fresh-water and may sometimes be flushed from surprisingly small patches of water. They also visit the sea to forage along tidal flats and estuaries, and swim in the shallows hunting for food.

Banding has shown that these ducks make considerable journeys within the continent.

Normally they breed from July to December. The nest may be built in a variety of situations; amongst rushes or

long grass near water, in cover a distance from water, in deserted nests of other species or in the hollow limb of a tree. It appears in the latter case that the young are sometimes carried down on their parents' backs or in their beaks, or simply pushed out of the nest.

Eight to thirteen creamy or greenish eggs are laid in feathers and down.

GREY TEALS, *A. gibberifrons*, are probably as well known as the last bird. They are distributed throughout the mainland and Tasmania. Singly, in pairs or in flocks, they frequent marshes, open lakes and water courses of all kinds. They are found on salt-water flats and estuaries as well as on fresh-water.

These ducks are great wanderers—banding has shown that they travel right across the continent north to south, east to west and in the opposite directions.

They breed at any time of the year according to the local rainfall. The nests of grass, lined with down, may be concealed in clumps of herbage or built in the hollow limbs of trees. The eggs, about ten or twelve, are creamy-white.

BLUE-WINGED SHOVELLERS, *A. rhynchotis*, are found in Tasmania and in suitable localities across the continent except for the far north. They are not common in Western Australia.

Shy birds, they keep far out on open water as a rule, although they will frequent small water-holes if undisturbed. In flight the wings have a distinctive loud whistle.

The nest is built on the ground, usually in thick cover. In Tasmania it is described as 'beautifully roofed with fine grass and rushes bent down from growing plants'. I can find no record of this for other parts of Australia. August to December is the breeding season and from four to eleven glossy white eggs are laid.

PINK-EARED DUCKS, *Malacorhynchus membranaceus*, are considered to be an aberrant river duck. They inhabit Tasmania (where they are rare) and the mainland of Australia; they are normally seen in pairs or small parties on shallow lakes and swamps. In some wet seasons there are enormous increases in their numbers.

They feed by working over the surface of the water for microscopic insects and plants. These are then held back by the fringed lamellae along the sides of the bill whilst the water is strained through.

They also plunge their heads below the water in search of food. There are conflicting reports from various sources about this bird's under-water feeding habits—some say that it sifts through the bottom mud, others report that it does not.

Pink-ears lay in old coots' nests or something similar, or build in herbage near the water. Hollows in trees are also used. The six to eight creamy-white eggs are laid in a mass of down.

Pochards

WHITE-EYED DUCKS, *Aythya australis*, are the only Australian members of this tribe, and are reputed to be the fastest fliers of all our ducks. They are common in Tasmania and also

BLUE-BILLED DUCK 16 in.

MUSK DUCK ♂ 27½ in.

MUSK DUCK ♀ 22 in.

24

found throughout Australia except perhaps for the driest parts of the interior. As diving ducks, they find most of their food under water in the mud. They are normally shy and wary and frequent quiet swamps and streams.

The nests may be hollows on the ground lined with grass, in the hollows of broken branches or constructed in thick bushes growing in or near the water.

The breeding season is from September to December as a rule and the eggs, up to fourteen, are creamy-white and laid in much less down than those of most other ducks.

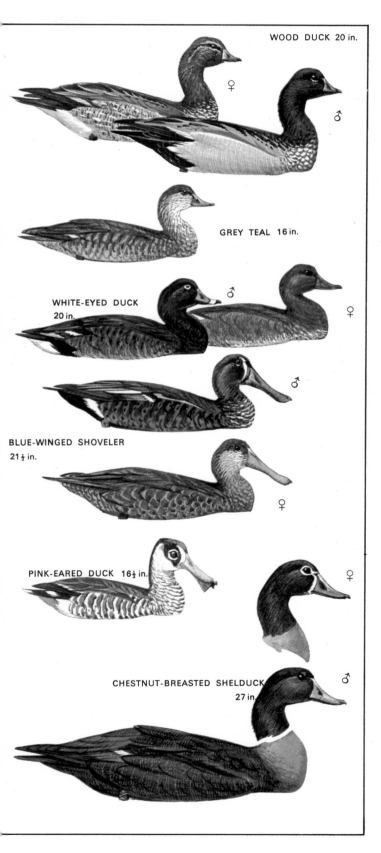

WOOD DUCK 20 in. ♀ ♂

GREY TEAL 16 in.

WHITE-EYED DUCK 20 in. ♂ ♀

♂

BLUE-WINGED SHOVELER 21½ in.

♀

PINK-EARED DUCK 16¼ in. ♀

CHESTNUT-BREASTED SHELDUCK 27 in. ♂

Perching Ducks

WOOD DUCKS, *Chenonetta jubata*, bear characteristics of both geese and ducks.

Found throughout most of Australia, and in Tasmania where it is rare, they frequent wooded waterways, perching often on trees and logs. These ducks also frequent damp grasslands where they feed on the grass and other plants.

Wood Ducks lay their six to ten glossy cream eggs in a quantity of down which is often placed in the hollow spout of a broken limb, or nests of grasses may be built in the cover of coarse herbage. The breeding season is varied and may be at almost any time, depending on local rainfall.

Stiff-tails

MUSK DUCKS, *Biziura lobata*, are fairly common birds throughout southern Australia to Point Cloates in Western Australia and north-east Queensland. It is also common in Tasmania. They are much more common in Western Australia than in the east; out of the breeding season many hundreds may be seen on lakes and estuaries in Western Australia.

They are seldom seen in flight although it appears that they do fly more than some books indicate. Most changes of locality are made at night. In spite of having their legs set so far back, which makes them clumsy out of water, they are said to walk from swamp to swamp during darkness. They are sometimes seen at sea in the winter.

They swim low in the water often with their backs more or less awash. Musk Ducks dive frequently when feeding and will dive to escape danger—even shooting—rather than take to the wing.

Young birds have been seen riding on their parents' backs, and going under when the adult bird dives, rather in the manner of grebes.

The drakes have a strong musky odour and a highly developed display, which includes the jetting of water from under their wings by snapping them shut against the body. They display to the female by swimming about her, with heads thrown back, the lobes under their bills distended, flicking their spikey tails up over their rumps. They also spin in the water in this attitude and call with a loud 'plonk' sound and a whistling cry.

The eggs are large for the size of the bird and laid in a quantity of down. The nests are usually large platforms of trampled reeds or other herbage, with the surrounding growth bent down and worked into a canopy; they may also be built in thick low bushes in or near water. There are two to six eggs with a limey coating over a greenish shell. The breeding season is from August to December.

The other stiff-tails are the BLUE-BILLED DUCKS, *Oxyura australis*. They are confined to south-western Australia, south-eastern Australia to southern Queensland and Tasmania, where they are noted as uncommon. They are shy, spending much time in thick cover, and they may be more common than it appears throughout much of their range. They are recorded as plentiful in Western Australia.

They are wary birds, usually staying well out on open water and diving to escape danger. Like the Musk Ducks they seem to do most of their flying at night, as they are seldom seen on the wing.

Blue-bills float low in the water as a rule, with their tails flat on the water or carried more or less vertically.

They dive for most of their food and stay under water for considerable periods. They have a chirruping call—quite unlike a duck.

Bulky nests, built of trampled-down reeds and sedgy growth, often have a canopy of reeds pulled over them. Often old coots' or Musk Ducks' nests are used and some nests have been recorded made of light sticks.

25

Much less down is used than in most ducks' nests and the four to six greenish eggs are large for the size of the bird. Breeding takes place from October to January.

Swans

BLACK SWANS, *Cygnus atratus*, are one of Australia's best-known birds and very common. Indeed, in some parts of the country, they flock in such overwhelming numbers in pastoral areas that they foul the water dams, compete with stock for grass, and consequently have to be reduced by shooting.

They are our only native swan although a few European WHITE SWANS, *Cygnus olor*, have been released in places and are breeding in the wild without showing any inclination to spread; nor do they appear to be increasing their numbers.

Black Swans were first seen by Vlaming in 1697 when he sailed into the estuary of what is now the Swan River in Western Australia. It is the State bird of W.A.

Frequently seen in pairs, they also fly in flocks which may number thousands. Black Swans are found all over the continent and Tasmania, wherever suitable habitats exist, except in the far north-east, although they are reported to be extending their range in that direction.

They are particularly common birds on the pastoral lands of Western Victoria where some properties might carry 20,000 birds or more. Unluckily for the farmer they are not migratory, merely moving from one feeding ground to another within a relatively small area. In 1960 it was agreed by the authorities that they had become a pest in Victoria's Western District. Many were shot, but enormous numbers still remain.

Seen through the eyes of the bird-watcher rather than the farmer, swans are romantic and beautiful birds. A flock of a thousand or so gracefully swimming on a lagoon, the elegant necks arching down as they feed, and their ruffled plumage gleaming in the sun is a grand sight. Now and then a bird will call and the sad soft trumpeting echoes over the water.

Should they be disturbed sufficiently the nearest ones will take off and as each wave of birds passes over the birds below, those in turn will take off. They run across the water, churning it white, and the air is filled with the roar of thousands of great black and white wings, their wild alarm calls and slap of pinions on the surface.

They tend to move from one feeding ground to another mainly at dusk, trumpeting to each other to keep in touch; they are also active on moonlight nights. As well as fresh-water habitats, swans are frequently seen in sea bays, estuaries and sheltered coasts. They feed in the shallows just offshore, eating aquatic vegetation, grass and small water creatures.

Swans nest now and then in isolated pairs, but normally in large scattered colonies, small sedgy islands on a lagoon being a favourite site.

The nests are constructed of whatever materials are to hand, twigs, rushes, weeds and so forth, and are usually rather bulky and lined with the bird's own down. Five or six greenish-white eggs are laid in autumn or winter, but sometimes as late as December.

BLACK SWAN 40 in.

FALCONIFORMES

BIRDS OF PREY

We are fortunate in Australia in having such a wide range of birds in this order. We have one of the largest eagles in the world, a number of dashing and beautiful falcons, shy harriers sailing over our marshes, dainty kestrels that even live in our cities, and many others besides.

All except three species of our birds of prey are protected, but this does not stop many a farmer and grazier reaching for a gun every time one floats into view. Fortunately there is a growing awareness of the good that many of these birds do in the controlling of vermin and the cleaning up of carrion. It seems unlikely that we will come to the stage of organised killing, such as takes place in some states of America where eagles are hunted from the air. One aeroplane accounted for twenty-three eagles in six hours; there is also another pilot's claim—perhaps somewhat exaggerated—of shooting down 8,000 eagles in seven years.

However, in Australia we have no cause for complacency, as a drive along country roads will show. How many times has one seen the bedraggled corpses of eagles strung along the barbed-wire fences—trophies of rifle shooting and poisoning. These dead birds are evidence of a very basic ignorance about the feeding habits of most eagles and the important ecological niche that they fill.

It is undoubtedly true that *some* Wedge-tails take lambs, but it is also true that, except for a few 'rogue' birds, they do far more good than harm by killing hundreds of rabbits every year.

The results of close checks being kept on nesting Wedge-tails suggests that many of these feed themselves and their young almost exclusively on rabbits. The balance of their diet is made up of rodents and small marsupials.

One answer to legitimate complaints by the sheepman might be to have inspections carried out by experienced field-workers and, if necessary, a licence granted to shoot a certain bird or number of birds.

A fairly recent and more insidious cause of depredation is the intake amongst birds of prey of the poisonous insecticides which are being developed and used against the advice of most biologists. Insecticides such as those based on dieldrin and heptachlor are 'accumulative'. That is to say these chemicals accumulate in the soil and water, and in the bodies of anything that lives and feeds in the contaminated area. A typical example of this is the use of an insecticide on water to kill mosquitoes. Water plankton imbibing the chemical concentrate it two hundred and fifty times. In the fish that feed on this plankton it might be concentrated five hundred times. And finally, in the birds which eat the fish—birds that will be picked up dead—the poison is concentrated eight thousand times. And this takes place even when the chemical is applied in as diluted a form as one part to fifty million parts water! Many birds of prey are particularly vulnerable in this sense, being fish and bird eaters.

The danger from these pesticides is two-fold; in the death of the bird when the concentration reaches a certain point, and in the increasing number of infertile eggs being laid.

In Scotland a survey over a wide area from 1961–63 showed the percentage of Golden Eagles rearing young was only twenty-seven per cent compared with seventy-two per cent between 1937–60. Analysis of the infertile eggs showed a significant amount of dieldrin, DDT and other chemicals.

The same thing is happening and will continue to happen in Australia as long as such poisons are used as insect, weed and rodent killers. What gives the whole problem a rather macabre, though ridiculous twist, is that the more these harmful pesticides are poured on to the earth and washed into the rivers the greater the number of insect and rodent-eating birds are killed. Thus the agriculturalist is upsetting the delicate ecological balance, a balance which controls the very pests which he is trying to reduce.

Eagles

WEDGE-TAILED EAGLES, *Aquila audax*, are about the fourth largest eagles in the world. There is a growing tendency amongst landowners, to realise the ecological niche of these eagles and their undoubted value in keeping the rabbit population down. Many are still shot and poisoned, however, and there will no doubt always be the man who takes up a gun at the sight of any bird of prey. In Tasmania the bird is protected, whereas in Western Australia there is a bounty of 50c. on its head.

They frequent open country and timber ranges alike, usually nesting in rugged tree-clad hills. They build a vast structure of branches and sticks which the birds add to year after year. Unless some mishap overtakes one of them, these eagles appear to pair for life. Fresh gum-leaves are added to the nest at laying time and the one or two eggs are laid in the winter as a rule.

PEREGRINE FALCON 15 in.

LITTLE FALCON 11½ in.

27

Some eagles *are* lamb-killers, but most of them feed on rabbits, the young of dingoes or kangaroos and carrion. They will also drive foxes and other birds of prey off their kills. In some localities where there are no trees, such as blue bush country, Wedge-tails will build in low bushes. They also build on rock ledges in the mountains, on sea cliffs or on secluded islands amongst low rocks. They are distributed throughout the continent generally, and also Tasmania.

Kites

RED-BACKED SEA EAGLES, *Haliastur indus*, or Red-backed Kites as they are now more properly being called, are northern birds found around our coasts and islands from Carnarvon in the west to the Hunter River in the east.

Their food consists chiefly of fish, crabs and other life of the seashore and mangroves. In some areas they are quite common and become bold in their search for carrion and other flotsam in harbours. Their call is a tremulous and mournful 'pee-ah-ah-h', a thin drawn-out cry that soon becomes associated in one's mind with lonely tropical beaches.

The nests are built of sticks in trees—frequently in mangroves. They may be decorated with streamers of bleached seaweed. The two eggs are a bluish-white, lightly speckled chestnut. The breeding season is from April to September in the north, and August to October on the east coast. WHISTLING KITES, *Haliastur sphenurus*, known until lately as Whistling Eagles, are true kites with typical kite-like habits.

The birds are found throughout the continent but are very rare in Tasmania. They frequent all types of country including the littoral, where they feed on all kinds of carrion deposited by the tides. In the inland they can sometimes be seen in dozens around the yards where sheep or cattle are being slaughtered. Otherwise they soar high, singly or in pairs, keeping a sharp eye on the ground for the carcass of some wild animal. Whistling Kites also take a large number of rabbits, a few small reptiles, and insects.

Their nests are flattish structures of sticks lined with leaves. They occasionally will take over the deserted nest of another species. The nests are built in the horizontal branches of tall trees or in high forks and the two or three red-spotted white eggs may be laid at almost any time of the year.

Goshawks

These are long-tailed, short-winged forest hawks and BROWN GOSHAWKS, *Accipiter fasciatus*, are typical members of the genus. Their main prey is small birds taken in mid-air, often after a dashing pursuit, twisting and turning through the trees. They also use surprise tactics—bursting over the top of a hedge or clump of scrub to pounce amongst a flock of small birds feeding on the ground: young birds are also taken out of their nests.

Goshawks often hunt in pairs, especially when the quarry is something as large as a rabbit. They harry it in turn until one of the pair manages to grip the rabbit by the skull in its enormously powerful talons. They also eat a few insects but will not touch carrion.

The female is much larger and more powerfully built than the male. Average weights being, male 10–12 oz; female 18–23 oz.

Goshawks are great marauders amongst chicken runs, and will be extraordinarily bold on occasion to secure a prize. They can also be seen now and then in large city parks.

Females have a high-pitched chattering call that might be written as 'kek-kek-kek-kek'; the males have a drawn-out plaintive 'wheet'.

Small, fairly flat nests of twigs are constructed, usually near the tops of tall trees. The females brood the eggs, only leaving the nest to be fed by their mates. Two to four eggs are laid which are whitish and speckled and smeared with red—not particularly heavy as a rule. The young birds are born with grey eyes and attain their yellow eyes at about three months. Goshawks are distributed throughout Australia and Tasmania.

GREY GOSHAWKS, *A. novae-hollandiae*, are mainly coastal and mountain area species but are also found in some inland forest areas. They are distributed across northern, eastern and south-eastern South Australia and also inhabit Tasmania.

These beautiful birds have two colour-phases: pure white (sometimes with very faint grey barring on the breast), or pearly grey on the back and white below. The two phases inter-breed but the young are hatched as one or other colour-phase, and never as a cross. The white birds occur only in Tasmania and South Australia; it was from Bruny Island near Tasmania that the first bird described to science was taken.

They are found singly or in pairs, frequenting densely timbered coastal ranges and other wooded country. They hunt in the goshawk manner, chasing small birds or ambushing them from thick cover. They will also raid chicken runs. The females can be as much as twice the weight of the males and weigh about 35 oz.

The females have been trained for falconry and found to have the same aptitude for it as the brown goshawk.

They build large stick-nests high in trees, lining them with leaves. The breeding season is from August to December and two, or rarely three, bluish-white eggs are laid.

KESTREL 12¼ in.

28

BROWN HAWK

♂ 16 in.

♀ 18 in.

BROWN GOSHAWK ♂ 18½ in.
♀ 20 in.

Immature

GREY GOSHAWK

GREY GOSHAWK
White Phase

WHISTLING EAGLE ♂ 20 in. ♀ 23 in.

RED-BACKED SEA-EAGLE 20 in.

Falcons

PEREGRINE FALCONS, *Falco peregrinus*, are widely distributed in various parts of the world. There is but one species, with slight changes in size and coloration in different localities The Peregrines are common in Australia and are found in Tasmania and throughout the mainland generally, except for Central Australia and western South Australia. Singly or in pairs they hunt over coastal cliffs, heavily timbered country and rugged mountainous terrain. These falcons are extremely fast fliers and their food consists mainly of birds taken on the wing. The Peregrines hunt by circling above their quarry and then diving or 'stooping' on it at high speed. The preyed-on bird may be struck a lethal blow on the head by the hind-claw of the falcon, or the Peregrine may 'bind' to its quarry in mid-air. Their call is a loud oft-repeated 'ka-ka-ka', or 'kee-kee-kee'.

The breeding season is from August to November and the nests are usually made on cliff-ledges, inland or by the sea. Hollow trees may also be utilised or the old nests of another species. Two or three buff eggs are laid, thickly marked with reddish-brown speckles and blotches.

LITTLE FALCONS, *F. longipennis*, are probably more common than the Peregrines and are found in Tasmania and in many areas of the mainland. It is not unusual to see these birds hunting small birds in public parks and even making forays into suburban gardens. In the bush they frequent open, lightly timbered country and mountain ranges. Their call note is a high, chattering 'chi-chi-chi'.

Their food is mainly small birds struck on the wing and often taken from below rather than being 'stooped' at from above. The old nests of other species are used and three buff-white eggs, heavily marked with reddish colours, are laid. The breeding season is September to December or later.

BROWN HAWKS, *Falco berigora*, better called BROWN FALCONS, are common in most parts of their range and may frequently be seen perched on telegraph poles or fence posts awaiting some suitable prey. They also hunt from the air, quartering open, lightly timbered country for small birds, reptiles, mice and large insects. They seldom build their own nests, but utilise the deserted one of another species. Two to four eggs are laid, which are usually covered with reddish freckles and blotches. Breeding season is June to November. Brown Falcons have two extreme colour phases with gradations between them, from dark vandyke browns with the underparts heavily marked, to light sandy browns with pale buff underparts lightly marked with brown.

KESTRELS, *F. cenchroides*, are familiar birds to many country people and may also be seen in our cities where they sometimes nest on tall buildings. They are found in Tasmania and the mainland generally, and in most places they are common. Kestrels are usually seen flying low, or hovering over cultivated land, where they do a great deal of good by capturing mice, grasshoppers and other pests. The call is a delicate, high chatter.

They nest in crevices or ledges on rock-faces or in hollow limbs of trees; sometimes the deserted nests of such birds as crows may be used. Four or five eggs are laid which are buff with varying amounts of reddish markings. Breeding season is from August to November.

WEDGE-TAILED EAGLE 38 in.

31

Ospreys

Basically there is only one OSPREY, *Pandion haliaetus*, found throughout the world, with slight variations of plumage in different localities.

Our birds are found along most of the coasts of Australia and Tasmania except the more settled parts. They also penetrate up large rivers and can be seen inland a good distance on suitable stretches of fresh-water.

They are fish eaters and catch them by diving down to the surface and snatching them in their talons: the captured fish is always carried off head first. Ospreys' feet are highly suited to catching fish; the outer toes are reversible, there are spicules on the soles of the feet and the claws are very long and curved and of equal length.

They build enormous nests, adding to them year after year, until they are a number of feet deep. Usually these great constructions are placed on rock-ledges overlooking the water, but occasionally may be in tall trees. The nests are lined with seaweed or leaves and two or three whitish eggs are laid which are heavily blotched at the larger end with reddish-purple. The breeding season is from May to September.

OSPREY 23 in.

GALLIFORMES

FOWL-LIKE BIRDS

Mound-builders

JUNGLE-FOWLS, *Megapodius freycinet*, are found across coastal northern Australia from the Kimberleys to central coastal Queensland.

Although mound-builders by definition, the nesting habits of these birds vary considerably. On Dunk Island some of the Jungle-fowls lay their eggs in individual pits on the beach. The eggs are covered with leaves and left to chance and the warming sun. On the same island some of the birds do not even dig pits but lay their eggs in suitable crevices in large flat rocks, afterwards sealing them in with leaves.

Yet another nesting variation of these birds is the utilisation of volcanic heat. On Savo, in the Solomon Islands there are two sandy areas through which volcanic steam filters. The Jungle-fowls come there in great numbers to lay their eggs. They dig shallow holes and bury the eggs where they are hatched by the steamy heat. In the more heavily shaded forest habitats, mounds are built and the eggs hatch in the heat of decaying vegetable matter.

The birds feed on seeds, young shoots, native fruits and other plant-life. They are fairly shy and if disturbed will usually depend on fleetness of foot for escape. If startled suddenly they may fly, flapping heavily off to land in the branches of some nearby tree. Their call is described as 'char-rooka' and a dawn call can also be heard which has been likened to the sounds made by a noisy typewriter.

A large number of eggs are laid in a vertical position with the larger end upwards—thus, when the chick emerges it is facing in the right direction to struggle upwards to freedom.

MALLEE-FOWLS, *Leipoa ocellata*, are the best known of the mound-builders, largely due to the excellent study of this bird by H. J. Frith, of the CSIRO. It is from Frith's studies of Mallee-fowls that I have drawn much of the material for this section.

As with the other *Megapodes* incubation mounds are built; the Mallee-fowls, however, are faced with much greater problems of temperature control than the other Australian mound-builders. As with many arid, desert-like terrains the mallee is subject to great fluctuations in temperature. Over the year this can drop to below freezing at night and above 100°F. during the day; even during the summer the temperature can drop by 30° at night.

Male birds fulfil practically all the duties of mound-building and temperature control, the hen birds only joining in at the end when all the eggs are laid. Almost every day the male birds visit the mounds, and indeed seldom stray far from them during the breeding season. Depending on whether the temperature in the mounds require raising or lowering the birds act accordingly. If fermentation is too rapid, craters are opened in the tops of the mounds to let some heat escape. Should fermentation be slowing down, more sand might be heaped up to prevent loss of heat, or alternatively, the nests may be opened on a hot day to let the sun take over.

It takes the male birds about four months of work to prepare the mounds for eggs, and after an incubation period of six to seven months, during which time the males work at temperature control, there is not much of the year left. In fact, in some cases, there is no real break between the activities of one breeding season and the next.

The actual method used by the birds to determine the temperature of the mounds has for long been a puzzle, but now it is known that the Mallee-fowls probe into the sand and vegetable matter with their open bills. Temperatures are kept astonishingly constant; one mound, in which continual temperature recordings were taken, was regulated to 92°F. with slight variations immediately being counteracted by the vigilant bird.

The chicks are as fascinating as the adult birds. Their start in life is a difficult one; having broken their way out, the chicks have to dig their way upwards to the air and light through several feet of sand; this may take anything from two to fifteen hours. Some of the birds do not reach the surface, but become exhausted and eventually suffocate.

The successful escapee bursts from the sand, resting for a moment with only its head showing, before clambering out to tumble down the outside of the mound and totter to the shelter of a nearby bush. The young birds remain in shelter resting for the first day and then at dusk start to feed and fend for themselves. They live separately from each other, and are quite unattended by their parents. Fortunately, they appear to have no predatory enemies except the introduced

BROWN QUAIL 6¼ in.

KING QUAIL 4⅛ in.

STUBBLE QUAIL 7 in.

33

fox. Field studies have shown that foxes actually catch very few of these birds, and they are well protected by the scrub and their own camouflage from birds of prey. What then keeps the population constant with so many chicks hatching every year? It seems likely that most of them must starve to death in their harsh dry environment.

The chicks of the Mallee-fowls and the other *Megapodes* are singular in having downy bodies but feathered wings, and they are able to fly within twenty-four hours or less of hatching.

Quails

The only other indigenous gallinaceous birds in this country are the quails.

The genus *Coturnix* contains but one Australian species, the STUBBLE QUAILS, *Coturnix pectoralis*. These birds are found throughout the mainland except the tropical coastal areas. They also occur in Tasmania where, although they were once common, they have, over the last ten years or so, almost disappeared. The exact causes of their decline are not known, but it is possibly a combination of modern harvesting methods and the wider use of toxic pesticides. Domestic cats which have gone wild may also be accounting for numbers of these and other ground birds.

These quails frequent open plains or any other well grassed locality, often visiting cultivated areas. Considerable flocks appear in good seasons; they are nomadic in habit, following the ripening of their seed-food.

Their common call is a loud 'two-to-weep', uttered singly, but repeated amongst the covey.

Stubble Quails lay seven or eight eggs which are buff-coloured and freckled all over with brown.

The breeding season is usually from September to January or February. The nests are hollows in the ground, lined with grass and sheltered by low bushes or overhanging tussocks: it is not uncommon for these quail to nest in standing crops.

KING QUAILS, *Excalfactoria chinensis*, are found where suit-able habitats exist throughout northern, eastern and southern Australia as far west as Adelaide.

These handsome birds are usually observed in coveys al though they have not been recorded as gathering in such numbers as the two preceding species.

Swampy lowlands are the birds' most common habitat where they hunt for seeds of grasses and various other plants they also feed on insects.

The call note is a mournful one which may be heard at intervals all through the night, and at dawn. These birds are chiefly nomadic in southern Australia, following the ripening seeds.

They build typical nests—a few grasses lining a hollow under a tussock or bush. Contrary to the usual large clutch which is typical of the group, King Quails lay only four eggs. They are pale brown and are heavily speckled with darker brown and blackish markings. The breeding season is usually from September to March.

BROWN QUAILS, *Synoicus australis*, are found across northern and down eastern Australia, to Tasmania. They are probably less common in South and Western Australia.

These quails move in small coveys or larger flocks, and inhabit a variety of localities. They may be found in low-lying grassy country but they are reported, in Tasmania in particular, to be birds of the scrub and light forest.

They are nomadic and their movements are governed by the availability of ripening seeds in different localities. Their call is a loud double whistle variously described as 'tu-whee' and 'be-quick'. They are vociferous during darkness and at daybreak. Family parties including young chicks can sometimes be seen dusting themselves on quiet tracks or roadsides. If disturbed, they scatter in all directions to crouch in cover, making it difficult for any predator to find more than one or two.

The nests are depressions under tussocks or in rushes and lined with dried grass. About ten eggs are laid and these are dull white or bluish-white and are usually freckled with light olive brown.

JUNGLE-FOWL 24 in.

MALLEE-FOWL 24 in.

GRUIFORMES

CRANES, RAILS AND ALLIED BIRDS

Cranes

BROLGAS, *Grus rubicunda*, are our only cranes and, although they are not as common as they used to be, they can still be seen in considerable numbers in certain places. Small flocks regularly visit the Western District of Victoria each winter and they also congregate on the inland grass plains of N.S.W. and Queensland. They are distributed throughout Australia except Western Australia south of Onslow, and coastal south-eastern Australia.

Like most cranes Brolgas have loud, trumpeting calls that can be heard over a mile away in open country. A trumpeting bird looks most dramatic, almost heraldic, as it arches its folded wings and droops its wingtips to the ground. The long neck is curved back and the bill points to the sky whilst the bird quivers all over with the exertion of the raucous cry. Their trachea, or windpipe, is greatly developed, being long and convoluted, and acts as a very effective trumpet. They have a variety of mellower, fluting calls which are more intimate and are used as the feeding birds communicate with each other.

In some localities Brolgas appear to be permanent residents, nesting and wintering within a few square miles. Others are nomadic, although not a great deal is known of their movements. They fly high when on the move; cranes in other countries have been reported as flying as high as two miles.

The dancing habits of the Brolgas are well known although not many people have seen them indulging in these 'quadrilles and minuets'. Any number, from a pair up to a dozen or so birds, will line up roughly opposite each other and start the dance. They prance forward on their stilt-like legs with wings half-open and shaking. Bowing and bobbing their heads, they advance and retire, gurgling and fluting softly. Now and then a bird will stop and, throwing back its head, trumpet wildly. The birds may also leap into the air a few feet and parachute back to earth on broad black and grey wings. Pieces of twig or grass are flung about and the Brolgas make attempts to catch the pieces or stab at them with their bills as they fall.

Various Aborigine tribes have incorporated these Brolga dances into their corroborees and they imitate the angular though graceful birds with great skill.

The dancing of these cranes may be used in courtship display, but they certainly indulge in it outside the breeding season. It seems then that the birds are often expressing a sense of 'playful exuberance' and a release of energy rather than anything more functional such as a sexual display.

Brolgas readily become tame and country properties often have a bird that comes to the homestead and can be fed from the hand.

Their diet in the wild is insects and small animals such as frogs, reptiles and rodents. They also eat a certain amount of vegetable matter, and occasionally will damage grain and tobacco crops.

Brolgas nest in a variety of situations. Sometimes the eggs may be laid on the bare ground; alternatively a few pieces of grass or reeds may be placed around the eggs. They also nest in wet, swampy spots, in which case the nests will be more bulky structures of reeds and other plants, and may even be floating.

Two eggs are the common clutch; sometimes one is laid, and more rarely three. They are a dull whitish colour, minutely pitted and lightly freckled reddish. The breeding season is from September to March as a rule.

Waterhens

DUSKY MOORHENS, *Gallinula tenebrosa*, are found in eastern and south-eastern Australia to southern South Australia. They also inhabit south-west Australia and the main islands of Bass Strait.

They are similar in haunts and habits to the other waterhens except that they probably swim and dive more than the others. If sufficiently disturbed they will take off in laboured flight.

In some cities they frequent park lakes, not being as shy as swamphens. Out of the breeding season moorhens do not congregate in flocks like the coot and the other waterhens.

The nests are typical of the group. Five to seven eggs are a normal clutch, but as many as twenty have been recorded when more than one female lays in a nest. The eggs are creamy-white, with spots and blotches of brown. The breeding season is from August to December.

EASTERN SWAMPHENS, *Porphyrio melanotus*, are found throughout most of the continent, wherever suitable stretches of water or marsh allow. They are also in Tasmania and on other islands. The eastern form of this bird, *melanotus*, is not found in Western Australia south of the Fortescue River. Then there is a gap before the western form, *porphyrio*, takes over in the south-west corner, from Moora to Esperance.

BROLGA 42 in.

35

DUSKY MOORHEN 15 in.

WESTERN SWAMPHEN 19 in.

EASTERN SWAMPHEN 17½ in.

COOT 14 in.

Outside the breeding season Eastern Swamphens sometimes gather in large flocks and invade gardens and crops where they do a great deal of damage. Their normal haunts are stretches of water with enough cover for them to hide and nest in, or the sedgy banks of streams and swamps.

The call is loud and strident, but hard to put into syllables. It is heard a good deal at night but the birds will cry out at any time if alarmed. They swim easily and climb trees readily, often roosting in their branches at night. Swamphens continuously flick their tails as they walk, and can run with great speed.

Their food is grass and other herbage plus fresh-water molluscs and insects.

Nests are usually built just above the water on trampled-down reeds or in a tussock. Five to seven pale, creamy-brown eggs are laid, spotted with darker brown and grey. The breeding season is from August to January.

WESTERN SWAMPHENS, *P. porphyrio*, are confined to the south-west corner of the continent. They have the interesting habit of constructing platforms similar to their nests, which they use as feeding spots. Traces of mollusc shells can usually be found on such platforms. The eastern birds may also build these platforms although I can find no record of it.

Western Swamphens are shyer birds than their relative and seldom venture from cover unless they think they are unobserved.

Nesting habits are usually similar to those of *melanotus*, but the eggs tend to vary in size and clutch number: as a rule, the smaller the clutch, the larger the eggs. As well as nesting in reeds these birds will also build nests of sticks and rushes on branches over water.

Two to five or six eggs are laid and these are a light sandy-brown with freckles and spots of browns and purple. The breeding season is from July to November or December.

COOTS, *Fulica atra*, are found throughout the continent generally and in Tasmania. They are common birds in most of their haunts although the numbers sometimes vary considerably.

They are expert swimmers and divers and have toes unique in this order of birds. Each toe is broadly lobed (rather like those of a grebe), which gives much more thrust than a waterhen's foot when the Coot is swimming and diving.

Coots swim in a distinctive manner, working their heads back and forth and jerking along rather like a clock-work toy.

They are noisy birds and have a variety of high raucous calls, often heard at night.

There appears to be a fairly regular migration between Tasmania and the mainland, as large numbers sometimes appear and then go off again and cannot be traced anywhere in Tasmania. On brackish estuaries and other large expanses of water, Coots will sometimes gather in immense, scattered flocks, mixing with the grebes, swans and other water birds that congregate out of the breeding season.

CHARADRIIFORMES

WADERS, GULLS AND ALLIED BIRDS

Painted Snipes

PAINTED SNIPES, *Rostratula benghalensis*, are found in southern Africa, Egypt and Asia Minor, and across to China, Japan and southwards to Australia.

They are polyandrous, that is to say the females will usually have two or more mates; they lay in a corresponding number of nests and leave the male birds to incubate and later raise the young. The females are larger and brighter than the male birds, which is generally the case in poly-androus species.

The trachea of the females are highly convoluted, and they are almost certainly the authors of the deep booming note of the species. They are vociferous during darkness.

These snipe are difficult to flush; when put up they fly rather weakly with trailing legs to the nearest cover and are difficult to flush a second time.

Although probably not strictly a migratory species, there is a good deal of north-south movement amongst these birds. Their food is aquatic plants and insects.

PAINTED SNIPE 9¼ in.

Oyster-Catchers

PIED OYSTER-CATCHERS, *Haematoprus ostralegus*, range along most of the coast of Australia and Tasmania. Usually in pairs or small parties, they may be seen hunting along the shore and rocks for the molluscs which make up their main diet—they also take any other small marine creatures they can catch or find. Their bills are strong and vertically flattened, and are an ideal adaptation for opening bivalves and prising limpets and other food off the rocks.

Their call is a loud, repeated whistle, with a rather mourn-ful air. Oyster-catchers are often seen in the company of other shore-birds.

Plovers and Dotterels

SPURWINGED PLOVERS, *Lobibyx novae-hollandiae*, are a familiar bird to many people, with their loud alarm cries, pugnacious habits in the breeding season and bright yellow wattles. Their distribution is eastern Australia, from the Atherton area down to Tasmania, where they are particularly common. They are also found in most of South Australia and are ex-tending their range into the south-west of the continent.

In pairs or flocks they frequent paddocks, marshes, and occasionally the beach. Spurwings are wary birds and very watchful, flying up with loud alarm cries at the slightest suspicion of danger. They are the bane of duck shooters, giving away the hunters' presence by flying and swooping overhead and calling loudly.

Their diet consists of small crustaceans, insects and herb-age. The nests are depressions in the ground or the tops of tussocks, lined with a few bents and grasses.

BANDED PLOVERS, *Zonifer tricolour*, look similar to the two spurwings in the field, but these birds have much more extensive black marking and lack the spur on their wings. Their distribution is Australia-wide, including Tasmania, although they are rare in the north of the continent. Partly nomadic, these plover appear and disappear at various times in different districts, depending on seasonal conditions and related food supply.

They are as noisy as the other two birds, swooping over an intruder with raucous calls, especially if their eggs or young are close by. They feed on seeds, plants, and insects.

BLACK-FRONTED DOTTERELS, *Charadrius melanops*, are birds of inland waterways rather than the seashore; they may,

PIN-TAILED SNIPE 10 in.

JAPANESE SNIPE 9¼ in.

however, be seen at times along the mud-flats of estuaries. They are found in suitable localities throughout Australia and Tasmania.

They are usually seen in pairs or family parties, foraging along river banks, lake and swamp margins and even in cities. They run with great rapidity, stopping and starting suddenly as they feed. If disturbed, they fly off with a plaintive 'chick-chick' note of alarm, but soon alight again.

The nests are usually situated on shingle banks or similar situations and are seldom far from water.

DOUBLE-BANDED DOTTERELS, *C. bicinctus*, are also winter migrants to Australia but from a relatively short distance. They are New Zealand breeding birds which visit us about February or March; by October most of them have departed again. These are our only land-birds known to be regular migrants between New Zealand and Australia.

In their winter dress or in intermediary moults the distinctive double bands on the chest may be missing or only slightly developed. They are common in winter in south-eastern Australia and their range extends up the coast to north-eastern Queensland and across southern Australia. Further west they become increasingly sparse until in south-west Australia records of them are quite rare.

These dotterels are usually in small flocks, and frequent the seashores, tidal mud-flats, and salt-marshes. Occasionally they penetrate inland a short distance. When disturbed they fly up on rapid wings with a piping whistle call of 'twilt-twilt'.

A few birds remain throughout the year but have not been found breeding.

HOODED DOTTERELS, *C. cucullatus*, are southern birds, being found from about Geraldton in Western Australia around our southern coasts to the south-eastern corner where they rarely travel as far up as Sydney. They are common in Tasmania, in fact Sharland considers the island to be the 'stronghold of the Hooded Dotterel'.

In the south and east, they are birds of the seashore and occasionally coastal lagoons. In Western Australia, by contrast, they are frequenters of inland salt-lakes. Usually in pairs, but sometimes in family parties, these little birds will be seen running rapidly along the beach or lakeside. On the beach they are often down on the wet sand, picking up food as each wave recedes.

Unlike most of the family, the RED-KNEED DOTTERELS, *C. cinctus*, are mainly birds of the inland. They are well distributed in most areas, but become progressively rare towards the north of the continent; they are particularly common in the south-west of Australia.

In pairs or small flocks these dotterels haunt the margins of swamps, lagoons and river-flats. They are seldom found far from water, but rarely visit salt-water habitats.

Rapid and erratic, they run along the ground stopping every so often to look about with their heads up before hurrying on once more, stabbing left and right at insects on the sand as they go.

GOLDEN PLOVERS, *Pluvialis dominica*, are migrants, arriving here during September and October after breeding in the Northern Hemisphere's summer. They are fairly common along most of our coastline, except in the west, where their relatives, the Grey Plovers are more common. They are usually seen in small flocks and frequent the beach, mud-flats of estuaries and salt-marshes. Their feeding habits and daily movements are often related to the tides. As the water comes up, covering their feeding spots, the birds move back to the coastal marshes and even grassy paddocks. As the tide recedes, the birds return to feed across the freshly exposed flats. These plovers are seldom seen in breeding plumage in this country.

GREY PLOVERS, *P. squatarola*, are very similar-looking birds in winter plumage, but may always be distinguished from the Golden Plover by the broad white bar across the upper tail.

In south-western Australia Grey Plovers are much more plentiful than the Golden Plover—the reverse of the situation in the east. The arrival and departure times of both birds are much the same.

SPUR-WINGED PLOVER 14 in.

BANDED PLOVER 10½ in.

SHARP-TAILED SANDPIPER 8½ in.

CURLEW-SANDPIPER 8½ in.

GOLDEN PLOVER 9 in.

BROAD-BILLED SANDPIPER 7 in.

SANDERLING 7½ in.

GREY PLOVER 12 in.

RED-NECKED STINT 6 in.

SANDPIPERS AND ALLIED BIRDS

CURLEWS, *Numenius madagascariensis*, are distinctive birds, their towering size and enormous down-curved bills making them unmistakable even at a considerable distance; they will usually be seen only from a distance as they are wary birds and quick to fly at a hint of danger. At low tide Curlews feed far out on the mud-flats, singly or in scattered flocks, probing into the soft mud with their long bills. Now and then their mournful 'curlew' cry will be heard as they call to each other. They are vociferous at night, calling as they feed or as they fly over in small flocks.

Curlews do not breed in this country, but arrive here about September or October. Most of them depart again during March and April to breed in the Northern Hemisphere, although a small number remain in Australia throughout the year. It may be that these are young birds not yet in breeding condition, although there is no proof of this.

Their call is well known and one of the wildest sounds to be heard over the tidal mud-flats. There is actually a good deal of variation in the sounds that these birds make. When undisturbed their cry is low and mournful, but if put up the curlews rise with a sharp 'curlee-curlee' or even a high single yelp if surprised suddenly.

JAPANESE SNIPE, *Gallinago hardwickii*, are the common snipe of Australia. As the name suggests, they are Japanese breeding birds, migrating here to escape the northern winter.

Well known as game-birds, they are the bane of many a sportsman because of their erratic flight. They are such a morsel that their esteem as game must rest on the difficulty of procurement rather than on any real contribution to the table. When flushed, snipe rocket into the air with a short sharp call—'scaap'—and rapidly zig-zag off. When out of gunshot they straighten out and fly some distance further before dropping back to cover.

Snipe tend to spend the day in the cover of some marshy spot and at dusk they 'flight'.

In ones and twos, or in 'whisps', as small parties are called, they dash up out of the sedges and vanish into the darkness, calling as they go. They feed during the night along swamp edges, river margins and other wet places. The long bill is probed into the mud in search of worms. Slightly swollen and pitted at the end, the tip of the snipe's bill is a sensitive pair of forceps. The last inch of the upper mandible can be raised and lowered enabling the snipe to pull worms from the mud even at the full depth of its probe. It is even possible for the bird to swallow its food without the bill being withdrawn from the mud.

Japanese Snipe are found throughout eastern Australia and Tasmania but have not been recorded for the west.

PIN-TAILED SNIPE, *G. megala*, breed in eastern China and Siberia and migrate here from the northern winter. Quite common in New Guinea, they are less often seen in Australia although they are occasionally recorded in north-western Australia.

PIED OYSTER-CATCHER
19½ in.

39

CURLEW 24 in.

HOODED DOTTEREL

RED-KNEED DOTTEREL 7½ in.

DOUBLE-BANDED DOTTEREL 6½ in.

SANDERLINGS, *Crocethia alba*, have an almost world-wide distribution. They nest in the Arctic and migrate as far as southern America, Africa and Australia. As the name suggests, they prefer sand to mud-flats and are more often seen on the beach than on muddy estuaries. They will also visit inland water whilst on passage. They are very energetic little birds, dashing about on a blur of short black legs in pursuit of sandhoppers, and running out after retreating waves to snatch up stranded molluscs.

The birds which visit us are in winter plumage, and in this garb are considerably lighter than other waders of the shore; in a good light Sanderlings look positively pearly white.

They do not fly readily but run along ahead of an intruder faster than a man can walk. If pressed they will take off on fluttering wings, skim low out over the sea to sweep in again to the beach behind or ahead of the intruder. As the birds run they will sometimes hold their wings up—tips to the sky —as they go.

Sanderlings arrive in Australia about September and depart again around April. They are widely distributed, but are not common in this country.

RED-NECKED STINTS, *Erolia ruficollis*, are also commonly called LITTLE STINTS in this country.

These small birds are one of the common waders of our coastlines and marshes, both salt and brackish. They usually arrive in southern Australia about August and in Tasmania in early September. They are active in their search for food, but do not speed along in the same way as the Sanderlings do. Stints feed on marine worms, aquatic insects and small crustaceans, and are usually seen foraging in mixed flocks with other waders such as Sharp-tailed Sandpipers and Curlew Sandpipers. When feeding on a marsh they will swim quite readily to cross small pools and puddles that are too deep for their short legs. Most of their food is picked off the surface of the ground or water but occasionally they can be seen stabbing into the mud at a retreating worm.

They fly swiftly in tight flocks or groups, wheeling and turning in perfect unison, flashing white or dulling grey, as they bank. The call is a triple 'Tchick-tchick-tchick', sharp and rapidly repeated. They also have a more twittering 'communication call' whilst feeding.

CURLEW SANDPIPERS, *E. ferruginea*, are also common summer visitors to our shores. As with many others of our waders these birds breed in Siberia. The bulk of the migrants reach Australia about September and depart again in our autumn.

Their relatively long, down-curved bills are distinctive and identify the birds readily if a good view is obtained, otherwise the strikingly white rumps are the most obvious field characteristic.

When put to flight the birds go up with a 'twee-twee-twee' call or a more solitary 'twer-ret'. As a flock of these sandpipers moves slowly along, feeding, they keep up a low musical twittering. At high tide the birds congregate to rest on exposed spits of sand or move back to adjacent salt-marshes. A few hours later they return, to follow the ebbing tide on to the freshly exposed feeding grounds.

Their flight is rapid and strong, but less erratic and aerobatic than that of the sanderlings or stints.

SHARP-TAILED SANDPIPERS, *E. acuminata*, are also waders that visit Australia in large numbers. They mix in flocks with other waders along most of our suitable shore-lines. These sandpipers come down from Siberia to arrive about September: they depart again in our autumn and it appears that, unlike some other of our waders, none of them stay here the whole year.

BLACK-FRONTED DOTTEREL 6 in.

These birds favour salt-marshes over beach habitats, although they are by no means a rare sight on the beach. Sometimes they are also seen inland, where numbers will visit, for a time, the margins of a fresh-water lagoon or swamp.

They feed on the usual wader diet of marine worms, aquatic insect life and the other small fry of wet places.

The Sharp-tails may be distinguished in flight from the Curlew Sandpipers by their tail pattern. While the latter birds have plain dark tails and white coverts, the Sharp-tails have dark coverts but conspicuous white margins down each side of their dark tails.

BROAD-BILLED SANDPIPERS, *Limicola falcinella*, are similar to the Sharp-tailed Sandpipers in general appearance and behaviour. They also have the same tail pattern as the Sharp-tails; they are, however, smaller and the bills are heavier and relatively longer and slightly down-curved at the tips. The whiter eyebrows and darker legs of the Broad-billed species are also noticeable in a good light.

They appear to be confined to northern and eastern Australia, as far south as Melbourne in the east, but only down to Broome in the west. They are not common anywhere within their Australian range, and their habits and habitats are similar to those of other shore-waders in this country.

Stilts and Avocets

WHITE-HEADED STILTS, *Himanotopus leucocephalus*, are black and white birds with extremely long pink legs which trail far beyond the tail when they are in flight.

They are found throughout Australia where suitable marshy places exist, but are less common in the far north and the south-west corner of the continent. They are also recorded as a rare visitor to Tasmania.

White-headed Stilts are frequenters of inland swamps, shallow lakes and marshy streams as well as similar situations by the sea. They may also be seen on the beach and tidal flats feeding in company with the hosts of other waders.

As a rule they are shy birds, not allowing the intruder any closer than a few hundred yards. They fly with rather rapid, shallow beats of their pointed black wings, giving their strange high yapping cry that sounds remarkably like that of a small dog.

BANDED STILTS, *Cladorhynchus leucocephalus*, are essentially birds of the inland salt-lakes, although from time to time there are records of them visiting estuaries and salt-marshes. They are seldom seen in fresh-water habitats.

The food of these birds is usually the brine shrimps and other small crustaceans found on the salt-lakes of the interior.

RED-NECKED AVOCET 15½ in.

BANDED STILT 13½ in.

WHITE-HEADED STILT 15 in.

41

PACIFIC GULL 25 in.

KELP GUL

PACIFIC GULL
Immature

SILVER GULL 17½ in.

SILVER GULL Immature

42

Banded Stilts are seen throughout southern Australia from Point Cloates in the west to Maryborough in Queensland; they are very infrequent visitors to Tasmania. The call is a slightly weaker version of the White-headed Stilts' yapping cry. Sharland also records a 'plaintive whistle'.

RED-NECKED AVOCETS, *Recurvirostra novae-hollandiae*, have one of the strangest bills of the bird world. They curve strongly upwards for most of their length but towards the tip there is a pronounced down-curve, giving the birds a most odd appearance. The bills are also somewhat flexible. One of the feeding techniques of these birds clearly indicates the reason for the strange shape. The Avocets wade into the water and reach downwards and outwards at such an angle as to bring the recurved bill-tip parallel with the water. As the birds wade forward, their bills are swept from side to side, on or just under the surface, to gather the minutiae of water-life that constitutes their food. They will also probe into the soft mud around the edge of a swamp or under water.

Avocets' toes are well webbed and they frequently swim across narrow arms of water. They may often be seen feeding up to their bellies in water, and no doubt frequently find themselves out of their depth.

If put up, they fly off in a rather laboured fashion with their extremely long shanks streaming straight out behind them. In flight they have a yapping note very similar to that of the two stilts: they also have a 'trumpet-like whistle' which is also usually a flight call.

Gulls

SILVER GULLS, *Larus novae-hollandiae*, are the ubiquitous 'seagulls' of popular terminology. They are common along most of our shore-lines, except some of the wilder steep-cliffed areas: neither did I find this bird along the beaches of the Northern Territory near Darwin.

In some localities they have moved inland forming colonies on areas of water a considerable distance from the sea. Inland the birds may be seen feeding in open fields.

They are useful scavengers, like most gulls, cleaning the beaches of marine offal and scraps thrown overboard by ships. Silver Gulls also feed on small fish, crustaceans and any other sea-life they can catch. They are great nest robbers, taking the eggs of other sea-birds and waders. They nest in colonies in a variety of situations: small offshore islands, shingle spits, exposed sandbars that carry some low cover and on artificial areas of water, such as salt-works and ornamental pools.

In Western Australia, there are some colonies that have two nesting seasons each year, and it may be that this is true in other localities also.

Any given spot will have its population of gulls all the year round. Some of these may be permanent residents, but the fact that some individuals travel is indicated by banding recoveries. Gulls banded in Melbourne have been recovered in Hobart, Sydney and north-western N.S.W.

PACIFIC GULLS, *L. pacificus*, are very much larger birds and correspondingly more fierce and predatory. They are southern Australian gulls, found in Tasmania and along our coasts from Point Cloates in Western Australia to north-eastern N.S.W. At the northern and western extremities of their range, they become rather rare; Victoria, Bass Strait and Tasmania are their strongholds.

These bold gulls may be seen singly, in pairs, or small groups foraging along the shore for offal on the tide-line. Like the Silver Gulls, they also follow ships and fishing boats to squabble over any jettisoned scraps. They are great preda-tors and cause a good deal of havoc amongst colonies of nesting sea-birds and waders. They take both eggs and fledglings, and, on occasion, will kill adult birds.

These gulls nest from south-western Australia to Tasmania and on islands in Bass Strait. Without being strictly colony nesters, they do tend to congregate at suitable sites. Nests are made of grasses, weed, rootlets and similar herbage. They are usually placed in the shelter of a low bush or tussock or tucked between rocks.

All gulls are a mottled brown colour in their juvenile plumage, and through successive moults, over a number of years, they gradually attain adult plumage. Pacific Gulls in particular seem to have given rise to confusion in this matter. The young, dark brown birds, are thought (quite wrongly) by many people to be a different species, and are sometimes called 'mollymawks' or 'mollyhawks'. The latter name is defended on the grounds of the bird's voracious appetite and fierce habits.

DOMINICAN GULLS or KELP GULLS, *L. dominicanus*, are New Zealand birds which have recently been extending their range into south-eastern Australia. Rather like Pacific Gulls in appearance, they are, however, slightly smaller and lack the black sub-terminal band on their tails. Their habits and life history are similar to the Pacifics.

Terns

CRESTED TERNS, *Sterna bergii*, are one of the most common terns in our southern waters. Mixing freely with the gulls they may be seen on most of our beaches, but perhaps more around the southern coasts than the northern. As the name suggests the birds are able to raise their crown feathers into a shaggy crest. They use this in displays but usually look somewhat crested and untidy about the head.

They feed by diving into the sea to catch shoal fish such as pilchards, and a flock excitedly fishing is usually a good indication of a large school of fish travelling up the coast.

Crested Terns breed in colonies, often quite large, on off-shore islands.

LESSER CRESTED TERNS, *S. bengalensis*, are a wide-ranging species, found from the Mediterranean to northern Australia. Their distribution in this country is from Point Cloates in Western Australia across to Masthead Island in Queensland, which is one of its breeding stations. They also nest on other Australian islands within their range.

Lesser Crested Terns are shyer birds, but otherwise their habits are much the same. The orange bills should serve to distinguish them from the Crested Terns which have yellow bills. In their breeding plumage the Lesser Cresteds have a black forehead, whilst the Cresteds have white ones. In the winter moult, however, the smaller birds' foreheads become extensively white.

LITTLE TERNS, *S. albifrons*, are delicate and beautiful birds with a dancing flight. They are our smallest tern and it is a marvel that such tiny birds can cross oceans, but, neverthe-less, they are found from Europe through Africa and southern Asia to Australia. Their range in this country is from Broome in north-western Australia around our northern and eastern coastline to eastern Victoria. They have not been recorded in Tasmania.

Usually seen in small flocks flying back and forth above the water, they flicker along with typical hovering flight, their heads down, watching for small fry. With a neat turn and a dive, they plummet into the water every few minutes, sending up a plume of spray. Swallowing the fish under water, they then fly straight up again without pausing on the surface.

Sandspits at the mouths of inlets and estuaries are favourite nesting sites, but they also colonise island beaches.

FAIRY TERNS, *S. nereis*, are similar birds, but slightly larger. They may be told apart chiefly by the lack of black on the tip of the Fairy Terns' yellow bills. The upper parts of these birds are paler, and there is less of a black mark in front of the eyes.

43

Their flight and fishing habits are similar to those of the Little Terns, and it is equally pleasant to watch a party of these delicate 'sea-swallows' fishing in the shallows just off shore.

Except in eastern Victoria and part of N.S.W., the normal ranges of these two small terns do not overlap. Fairy Terns are found from King Sound in Western Australia around our southern coastline to N.S.W. and are quite common in Tasmania.

Sooty Terns, *S. fuscata*, are, in general, tropical and sub-tropical birds. Their range in Australia is the coasts of western, northern and eastern Australia, as far south as Wollongong on occasion.

Sooty Terns usually nest in vast colonies and are often associated with equally extensive Noddy Tern colonies. The juxtaposition can exist harmoniously as the Sooties nest on the ground, and the noddies build in the tops of bushes.

Some local colonies have been wiped out, or nearly so, by the depredations of egg-collecting fishermen and other intruders. Sooties, however, are still a common bird.

Sooty Terns are remarkably tame and the thousands of birds hardly react to the human visitor. Adult birds will even allow themselves to be picked off the nest. On some Western Australian islands when guano collection was in progress the birds happily ignored trucks and other machinery.

All over a colony there is constant activity; birds wheeling overhead loud-voiced, calling, 'wide-awake, wide-awake', partners greeting each other at the nest, and young birds calling for food. As a background to the cacophony is the all-pervading smell of sun-baked guano. Even at night the Sooty Terns continue to call and wrangle.

After the breeding season, these thousands of birds disperse across the ocean, but just where, nobody knows for certain; their migrations have been called 'one of the great unsolved mysteries of the sea'.

Bridled Terns, *S. anaetheta*, appear black and white from a distance, with a black cap and nape and a white forehead, thus they may easily be confused with Sooty Terns. The distinguishing marks to look for are narrower white foreheads in the Bridled Terns and the extension of this white well behind the eyes, as an 'eyebrow'. The underparts are not as pure white as in the Sooties, but this is not always apparent.

Bridled Terns are found around the northern coasts of the continent; in the west they penetrate as far south as Hamelin Bay, and on the east coast down to the islands in the Bunker Group and Lady Elliot Island, Queensland.

They have the local name in the islands of 'dog terns' because of their high yapping cry which sounds rather like a puppy. They are usually seen in scattered flocks, fishing the waters in the vicinity of their breeding islands.

Quite often they nest on the same islands as the Sooties, but are noticeably shyer, flying off at the approach of an intruder.

Roseate Terns, *S. dougalli*, are an almost world-wide species, being found in northern America, Europe, Africa and Australia. Their range in this country is from just north of Fremantle in Western Australia, along our northern coasts to eastern Queensland.

They nest in this country on off-shore islands, chiefly in tropical or sub-tropical seas. Although they frequent the waters in the vicinity of their breeding grounds, they will also visit nearby salt-marshes. Their food is chiefly fish, but they presumably take other food from marshy country.

They are considered extremely graceful fliers, even amongst terns. The pale rosy hue on the underparts, which does not show in a poor light, will distinguish them from any other terns.

They breed in colonies on various islands throughout their Australian range. However, Roseate Terns also breed in the other countries which they inhabit—chiefly in tropical areas.

Gull-billed Terns, *Gelochelidon niloteca*, are also large terns with wide distribution in the world. Their heavy black bills are distinctive in the field. They frequent inland fresh-water as well as the edge of the sea.

White-winged Black Terns, *Chlidonias leucoptera*, have a wide distribution from central and southern Europe across central Asia and migrating down to Africa, the South-east Asian islands and northern Australia. In this country they occur regularly as far south as Perth and Sydney, but further south they are rare.

They are irregular visitors to our shores during the spring and summer months. Estuaries, coastal lagoons and the beach are their habitats. They do not breed in this country.

SOOTY TERN 17 in.

BRIDLED TERN 14½ in.

44

ROSEATE TERN
16 in.

LITTLE TERN
10½ in.

FAIRY TERN 10½ in.

CRESTED TERN
17 in.

GULL-BILLED TERN
17 in.

LESSER CRESTED TERN 16 in.

GED BLACK TERN 11 in.
er

WHITE-WINGED BLACK TERN 11 in.   *Winter*

45

COLUMBIFORMES

PIGEONS AND DOVES

Ground Pigeons

These pigeons and doves are mostly ground feeders, taking seeds and fruit from grasses, low bushes and vines. Some live their lives almost exclusively on the ground. Others roost and nest in trees, but none the less spend a large part of their lives on the ground.

PEACEFUL DOVES, *Geopelia placida*, are found generally throughout the country in suitable localities. These delicate little birds are often seen sunbathing, with one wing up, along the dusty borders of country roads and they also frequent farm buildings, otherwise their habitat is the open forest. They feed on the seeds of various grasses and other plants, but may quite frequently be seen perching in trees. Their call is a traditional melodious cooing, syllabised, 'doo-dee-oo'. A scanty platform of twigs suffices for their nest, usually on the horizontal fork of a tree up to twenty feet from the ground: occasionally the old nest of a mudlark is utilised.

DIAMOND DOVES, *G. cuneata*, are similar birds but may be distinguished by the white spots on their wings. They are distributed about Australia as a whole, except coastal South Australia and the south-east. They are uncommon in the south-west.

They become quite tame if in contact with humans and feed fearlessly about homesteads. In pairs or small parties they frequent permanent water-holes and rivers where they feed on the seeds and small fruit of various plants. Diamond Doves are red about the eye where the Peaceful Doves are pale green. A light structure of twigs is built low in a tree or sometimes the birds nest on the top of a stump. They have a typical 'dove-like' call, a plaintive 'whoo-whoo-whoo', with the accent on the first and last syllable.

BAR-SHOULDERED DOVES, *G. humeralis*, are found from north-western Australia, across 'the top' and down eastern Australia to N.S.W.; a few reach the Sydney area. They are also found in New Guinea. They favour mangroves when inhabiting coastal districts, but are also found in big scrub well inland.

Their call is loud and is described variously as 'hop-off, hop-off' or a penetrating 'olly-wattle'. Just as the sun is setting, they become very vociferous, almost irritatingly so at times.

Nesting is in the usual dove manner: a frail platform of twigs through which one can often see the two white eggs. The nests are usually built in a low bush or tree, in mangroves near the beach, or otherwise in thick scrub.

We have two introduced doves in this country. INDIAN TURTLE-DOVES, *Streptopelia chinensis*, have spread as far as north-eastern Queensland, N.S.W. and Victoria where they are mainly coastal, and to Tasmania. They are also found in southern South Australia and the far south-west of the continent. This widespread distribution is from various batches banded at different places from 1870 onwards. The Western Australian population started in 1898 from the Perth Zoo. In 1912 some of the doves were brought direct from India and released in Queensland. They have spread rapidly, being catholic in their habitat requirements, and are familiar birds both in the bush and in suburban gardens. On the whole they appear to be fairly harmless although bothering vegetable growers in a few districts.

Their call is a typical 'cooing'. A normal dove nest is built of sticks in a tree or bush at various heights.

The other introduced pigeons are the SENEGAL TURTLE-DOVES, *S. senegalensis*. These birds are confined to Western Australia and the original stock was released from a Perth zoo in 1898. On the whole, they have not spread very far from Perth although colonising country areas more than the Indian Turtle-dove. Isolated populations have somehow established themselves at Kalgoorlie and Esperance.

BRUSH BRONZEWING PIGEONS, *Phaps elegans*, are distributed from Fraser Island (off Queensland) down coastal eastern Australia to Tasmania and across to the Eyre Peninsula in South Australia. In Western Australia, they are confined to the south-west, as far north as the Abrolhos Islands.

These are not flocking pigeons but are usually seen in pairs or sometimes singly. They inhabit coastal scrub and heath and spend much of their time on the ground. They are able to run very fast and usually escape detection in this way rather than by flying. If disturbed suddenly a Bronzewing will take off with a clatter of wings, but usually lands again to run or into the scrub.

The call is a low, rather mournful cooing, heard frequently in the evening. These handsome pigeons are much less common than they were fifty years ago, probably due to the depredations of foxes and cats, as the birds' range coincides with the more settled areas of the country.

The nests are the usual pigeon-platforms of sticks, although somewhat saucer-shaped. They may be placed in almost any low situation: the branch of a tree, in a thick bush, on a stump or even on the ground under cover. The fledglings and sitting adults are thus an easy prey for foxes and cats.

FOREST BRONZEWINGS, *P. chalcoptera*, are rather similar birds found throughout most of Australia and Tasmania where suitable habitats permit. They may be distinguished from the foregoing species by their white foreheads and the white chins and under-eye stripes.

Forest Bronzewings are birds of the open forest and brush country. Usually in pairs, they spend most of their time on the ground. They will run off and hide if given the chance, but if flushed suddenly they rocket off with a very startling rattle of wings. They have the habit of landing in trees after a flight, to watch the intruder, and will often allow a close approach before flying off again. The wing-clapping take-off would seem to be some kind of an alarm signal, as they are quite able to rise from the ground and fly away comparatively quietly.

The call is a low 'ooom' monotonously repeated.

If dogs or cats happen to eat either of the bronzewing pigeons the effect is disastrous. The birds often feed on the seeds of a plant called Box-poison, *Gastrolobium bilobum*, which makes their entrails and bones, but not their flesh, poisonous

SENEGAL TURTLEDOVE 9in.

46

FOREST BRONZEWING PIGEON
13½ in.

BAR-SHOULDERED DOVE
12½ in.

WONGA PIGEON
15 in.

PEACEFUL DOVE
8½ in.

NG

CRESTED PIGEON
13 in.

DIAMOND DOVE
8 in.

fter eating them, dogs or cats take fits, become quite mad, iting at anyone within reach, and finally die in convulsions. he poison may affect foxes in the same way; in which case would be a kind of natural retribution for the damage the xes do to the bronzewing population.

WONGA PIGEONS, *Leucosarcia melanoleuca*, are found from stern Queensland to eastern Victoria as far as Melbourne. hese pigeons usually go about in pairs and spend much of eir time on the ground in rain-forest country and thickly mbered gullies. If flushed, the birds will jump up with ud wing-clappings, but do not fly far before dropping into tree or bush and sitting with their grey backs to the oserver. Their showy fronts being hidden, the pigeons rely their dull colour to escape notice.

Wonga Pigeons will sometimes indulge in injury feigning, practice one associates more with true ground-birds than a artially arboreal species like a dove.

There was a time, in the earlier days of settlement, when ese large plump pigeons were shot in large numbers, their esh being considered excellent eating. Now they are otected.

Their call has great carrying power, and yet seems to be ttered quite softly when one is close by. The monotonous onk-wonk-wonk' can sometimes be heard from half a mile f. It also has a kind of 'background' quality and the bird ay have been calling for some time before one becomes ware of it. The 'wonking' is repeated many times; over one ndred in succession have been recorded.

Feeding mostly on the ground, Wonga Pigeons eat the fruit of native plants and the seed of various grasses.

The nests are barely concave platforms of twigs placed in a tree up to thirty feet high.

CRESTED PIGEONS, *Ocyphaps lophotes*, are found throughout most of Australia except for the north-western, south-western and south-eastern corners of the continent.

These handsome birds with their fine crest and bronzed wings, are common pigeons and well known to most people in the country. As well as their wilder haunts they frequent man-made dams and stock paddocks close to farmsteads. Otherwise they can be seen in pairs or small flocks along timbered streams and other permanent water.

When disturbed from their feeding, these birds fly up on rapid wings that make a distinctive and unmistakable whistle. They do not go far but soon perch in nearby trees—often a small flock will all land in the one tree—to eye the intruder. Their main food is the seeds of grass and other herbaceous plants.

The nests of this species are typical pigeon-platforms of a few twigs loosely laid together. They will usually be found on leafy horizontal branches of bushes or trees at heights up to twenty feet.

47

RAINBOW LORIKEET
14 in.

RED-COLLARED LORIKEET
12 in.

PSITTACIFORMES

PARROTS AND COCKATOOS

There are about 316 species of parrots, cockatoos and allied birds in the world, of which we have roughly one-fifth in Australia.

Ever since the first explorers came to Australia, the parrot family has been a source of interest and wonder to naturalists and laymen alike. Sir Joseph Banks remarked with delight on the various species of cockatoos and parrots he saw and, on returning to England, took with him a Rainbow Lorikeet.

Lorikeets

RAINBOW LORIKEETS, *Trichoglossus molluccanus*, are fou throughout eastern Australia, from Cape York to Victor and Tasmania. These birds are usually seen in flocks, ai being to a large extent nomadic, they follow the season flowering of the eucalypts and other blossoming trees. Th are swift fliers and have a loud, sharp call-note which th utter whilst on the wing. As these beautiful birds clamb amongst the blossom-laden branches they keep up a co tinuous high-pitched chattering and screeching. The tong of these lorikeets is developed at its tip into a kind of brus enabling them to extract nectar from blossoms with gre efficiency.

There are cases of the species having become very tame even to the extent of feeding out of people's hands.

In some districts they have become a considerable pe raiding fruit crops of various kinds, and vineyards.

The nest is a hole in a tree where two white eggs are lai The breeding season is typically from September to Januar

RED-COLLARED LORIKEETS, *T. rubritorquis*, are simila looking birds distinguishable by the red collar on the na compared with the yellowish-green collar of the precedi species. They are found in north-western Australia, th Northern Territory and north-west Queensland.

They travel in flocks of various sizes, sometimes in co siderable numbers in good flowering seasons. Their voic are similar to those of Rainbow Lorikeets, as are their habit although they do not have a bad name as orchard raide —perhaps more through lack of opportunity in their wild haunts, than through lack of propensity.

The nests are holes in trees, either in the trunks or in th 'spouts' of broken branches. The nest holes are usually hig above the ground.

The breeding season is from May to December, and tw white eggs are laid.

Cockatoos

RED-TAILED BLACK COCKATOOS, *Calyptorhynchus banksii*, a found throughout western, central and northern Australia Queensland. Occasionally they come into the south-ea corner of the continent, visiting South Australia, Victor and, more rarely, Tasmania. They frequent heavi timbered country and also more open forest and banks scrub.

When not breeding, they live in flocks of up to fifty or birds. They feed on the seeds of casuarinas, banksias ar eucalypts. Like the other black cockatoos, they dig grubs or of the trunks of trees with their sharp and powerful bills.

In Central Australia Red-tailed Cockatoos are ofte associated with Aboriginal rain-making ceremonies. Th handsome scarlet and black tail feathers are worn in the ha for corroborees as well as being used to decorate variou ceremonial objects.

The nests are the usual cockatoo type, a hole high in a tre usually out of reach of any white man unless he is equippe with climbing irons and ropes. However, the Aborigine climb up to the nests and harvest the young birds, which the regard as 'good tucker'.

One white egg is laid on a few chips of wood at the botto of the nest-hole, and the breeding season is from April t August. The call of these cockatoos is a loud grating 'kree' c 'krurr' which is often uttered on the wing.

GANG-GANG COCKATOOS, *Callocephalon fimbriatum*, are more c less confined to the south-east of the continent. Their rang is from the middle of N.S.W. down the coastal forest distric to the south-east of Victoria. They are also seen on Kin Island and Tasmania at infrequent periods.

These remarkable looking cockatoos appear to have n

close relations, and are becoming quite rare even within their restricted range. Originally described in 1801, they were named Red-crowned Parrots. The strangely filamentous crest on the orange-red heads of the males is certainly a striking feature.

They are said to feed in fairly open country (in Tasmania on the fruits of introduced hawthorn and briars) during the day, retiring to roost in thickly wooded gullies as darkness falls. Most of their food is gathered in trees, where they feed on the seeds of eucalypts, acacias and other trees. They have a strange wheezy, or rasping note quite unlike that of any other forest bird, and when feeding sometimes utter a curious growling sound.

The Otway Forest is still a haunt of these interesting cockatoos in Victoria and recently I saw and heard one in a brush and tree-filled valley on the Yarra River, not many miles from Melbourne.

At any place where they are plentiful enough these birds congregate into winter flocks and move out of the forest areas. There are a number of earlier records of these birds visiting towns and feeding in the hedges and trees of botanic gardens and other cultivated spots. They are confiding birds as a rule, allowing quite a close approach—I once watched a pair feeding on a fallen tree on Mt. Buller, from only about twenty feet away.

The nests are hard to find, usually being high in a living tree. The two to four eggs are laid at the bottom of a hollow in the tree, on a few incidental chips of wood. The breeding season is from October to January.

The genus *Kakatoe* (spelt by some ornithologists *Cacatua*) contains five cockatoos. Of these the WHITE COCKATOOS, *Kakatoe galerita*, must be one of the best known Australian birds. Also called the Sulphur-crested Cockatoo, this bird is a favourite pet, many not even being caged, but left to roam at will around the owner's house and garden.

In spite of the trapping and shooting activities of the white man since his advent in this country, White Cockatoos prosper and proliferate, due in some measure to the increase of food in agricultural areas.

They are particularly fond of wheat, raiding the standing crops in great numbers, and have learned to fear and outwit man to a great extent. Above a feeding flock, a 'sentinel' bird or two may be seen sitting in a tree or on a fence-post. The watch-birds shriek a warning at the approach of danger and the feeding birds flap off to a safe distance.

A large screaming flock of White Cockatoos flying up from a crop or from a water-hole in the wilderness is an exciting spectacle of animal vigour and plenitude.

Their range is Australia and Tasmania, except for Western Australia south of the Fitzroy River and western South Australia. Outside Australia this cockatoo is found in New Guinea, the Lesser Sunda and the Solomon Islands. They nest in the hollow limbs of trees, often very high above the ground.

Gould reported that thousands of these birds nested each year in the white cliffs along the South Australian reaches of the Murray River. The nesting season extends over a large part of the year; from about August to December.

GALAHS, *K. roseicapilla*, are almost as well known as White Cockatoos. In pairs or in flocks, sometimes numbering many hundreds, they are found in open and lightly timbered country throughout most of the continent. They are regarded as being accidental to Tasmania.

They feed on the ground as a rule, on the seeds of grasses and various herbaceous plants and on bulbous roots which they dig up with their bills. They are a mixed blessing to the man on the land. Regarded as thorough pests by most farmers, they consume the seeds of many noxious plants, but also raid crops, doing a good deal of damage.

GANG-GANG COCKATOO
13½ in.

GALAH
14 in.

49

RED-TAILED BLACK COCKATOO 24 in.

A flock of Galahs is a beautiful sight, except no doubt to wheat farmer, as they wheel through the bright air, th sunlight striking, now on their silvery-grey backs and now o their flaming rose-pink fronts.

Pests or not, it is hard to imagine how anyone could i dulge in the highly unsporting 'sport' of shooting these bir at close range, as they are released from traps. Yet this is popular pastime at many country gun-clubs.

The bird was first described from a bird sent to the Par Museum in 1817. They were popular as food with the earl settlers, being the ingredient of many 'parrot pies'. They ar still eaten in some districts and I have had roasted Gala when living off the land. Dry-roasted on a stick, they ar pretty basic 'survival-food' and require some good draugh of creek-water or billy-tea to wash them down!

These handsome cockatoos are holding their own and eve thriving at present, though at times there is a bounty on thei heads. But, remembering the fate of the passenger pigeon in America which, although they literally darkened the sk in their passing millions were wiped from the face of the eart in just a few years, we should at least be circumspect in ou persecution of the 'rose-breasted cockatoo'. The threshol of numbers required to continue the race is sometimes quit high in flock animals, and should the number fall below th minimum then the animals begin to breed more slowly an die faster than they reproduce.

Galahs nest in hollows, often quite deep, in tall trees. Some times a large dead eucalypt will contain a number of nesting pairs in various hollows and broken branch 'spouts'.

Four to five eggs constitute the usual clutch and these ar laid on a bed of fresh green gum-leaves. The young bird have the adult colouring in their first feathering. The breed ing season is typically from September to November, bu may be later in various areas or in certain conditions.

The two white cockatoos known as Corellas are rather similar to each other but may be told apart mainly by the length of their bills; although one species is known as Corellas and the other as Little Corellas, they are both the same size except for the bill.

CORELLAS, *K. tenuirostris*, are found in south-western Aus tralia and north to Geraldton. They also inhabit south eastern South Australia and Victoria but not Tasmania. It also appears that scattered populations of Corellas extend into 'Little Corella Country', through Western N.S.W. and into central and north-western areas of the continent.

Once very common, in many districts they have now dis appeared or become rare. They are birds of the inland but are rarely seen far from permanent water, and are thus con sidered by bushmen as being reliable 'water-guides'.

They have been persecuted in various ways over a great deal of their territory. Continual shooting, because of their raids on crops, has depleted them and trapping has also been very heavy in the past. Added to these direct inroads has been the inevitable destruction of the grasslands that pro vided the birds with food and over much of the land remain ing they have to compete with stock.

Apart from crop-raiding, the basic diet of these cockatoos is roots, bulbous plants and tubers. These they dig up with their very developed upper mandible.

These birds are considered to be amongst the best talkers in the bird-world and consequently thousands of nests were regularly raided each year (until the species was protected) to supply the city markets with young birds. They take kindly to captivity, rapidly becoming friendly and docile.

They nest in a hole in a tree, often high off the ground. Two to four white eggs are laid and the breeding season is from August to November.

LITTLE CORELLAS, *K. sanguinea*, were once known by the translation of their Latin name and were called Blood-

CORELLA
17 in.

SULPHUR CRESTED COCKATOO 20 in.

LITTLE CORELLA
17 in.

51

stained Cockatoos, a name given to them by Gould. It was not a particularly happy choice, and Corella is no doubt a more fitting name for these handsome birds.

Their range is restricted, in the main, to the north. From north-western Australia, they spread across the Northern Territory and Central Australia to western Queensland and western N.S.W., South Australia and north-western Victoria.

The Northern Territory is one of their strongholds; the naturalist Charles Barrett writes of a boat-trip down the Daly River and the thousands of Little Corellas that flew up '. . . from trees which appeared to be covered in white blossom until the birds left their perches to fly ahead of the boat, screeching their protest . . .'

Large numbers of them are still seen in some places, in spite of persecution of various kinds, and in the north-west of Australia they are the common cockatoo. Vast flocks are met with and one such gathering near Wyndham was estimated to be between sixty and seventy thousand. They indulge in high spiralling flights mounting upwards '. . . as though climbing an aerial staircase . . .'

They are ground-feeders, eating the seeds of various plants and bulbous roots, although compared with the long-billed birds, they are much less of a digger. They also perform a useful service to the pastoralist in consuming the seeds of the 'paddy-melon', which is said to cause blindness and paralysis in horses; the 'double-gee', *Emex australis*, which causes lameness in sheep, is also eaten.

The nests are in hollows in trees growing near or even in water. They will also breed in holes in cliffs, and in treeless areas they are known to nest in cavities in the tops of tall anthills. A clutch of eggs is usually three; these are white and the breeding season is from August to October.

Cockatiels

COCKATIELS, *Leptolophus hollandicus*, are found throughout most of inland Australia in suitable habitats. They rarely visit coastal districts and are considered to be accidental to Tasmania. They prefer open country with belts of scrub and threaded by water-courses, where they may be found in the trees along the water's edge.

These handsome little parrots are nomadic, their wanderings being governed by food supply, which are the seeds of various grasses and plants.

Long familiar as a cage and aviary species, they breed freely in captivity. Apparently, the males make better pets than the females. The males will learn to talk a little, and become very attached to their owners.

Cockatiels will frequently perch in dead trees when flushed from the ground or when landing after a flight. They also have the rather odd habit of perching along a branch as often as across it.

These birds have a soft, quite pleasant, chattering note with which they call to each other while flying or busily feeding. They nest in holes in dead or living trees, often in the hollow 'spout' of a broken dead branch. Sometimes a number of these birds will be found nesting in the same trees as galahs. From four to seven white eggs are laid and the breeding season is August to December.

Aprosmictus Parrots

KING PARROTS, *Aprosmictus scapularis*, are found from Cooktown in Queensland to southern Victoria but do not cross to Tasmania. They may be seen in pairs or small flocks, and they frequent the timber and thick brush-covered ranges and valleys.

Formerly much more common than they are today, timber cutting and the clearing of land has destroyed their habitat to a great extent. Until they were protected by law,

SUPERB PARROT
16 in.

trapping also reduced their numbers. Their simple but splendid colouring made them popular as cage-birds.

The immature plumage of these birds resembles the all-green dress of the females, and the males do not assume adult dress until three years old.

When disturbed, a flock of King Parrots flies off with loud cries of 'eek-eek-eek' that rings through the forest like an alarm-signal. They also have a soft and musical whistle with which they appear to communicate with each other whilst they feed through the tree-tops. They eat the seeds of native shrubs and trees, native fruits, and in some districts they have taken to raiding maize crops.

The eggs are laid in a hollow tree, some nests being found twenty feet or so down from the entrance hole. From three to six eggs are laid (authors differ on the average number) and the breeding season is from October to December.

RED-WINGED PARROTS, *A. erythropterus*, are inhabitants of

northern Australia from the Kimberleys to eastern Australia, down through the inland areas of northern N.S.W. to north-eastern South Australia. Sometimes these birds will move further south or visit coastal districts. Indeed the bird was first collected near the coast by members of Captain Cook's expedition, but settlement has probably driven it inland.

They are not confiding birds; Gould found them naturally shy and wary and '. . . much more difficult to approach than the generality of parakeets . . .'

They are unusual in that their flight is not the typical swift and rapid progress that one associates with parrots. It has been described as slow and laboured, but it is also buoyant. All agree, however, that a flock of these richly coloured birds flying against the blue sky of the north is a very beautiful sight.

Their food is nectar, seeds, native fruits and insect larvae. Three to six white eggs are laid at the bottom of a deep hollow in a tree, often far below the entrance: the breeding season is from September to December.

Long-tails

SUPERB PARROTS, *Polytelis swainsoni*, are well named with their bright emerald-green plumage set off with crimson and golden-yellow.

They are found from about the region of the Murray River, along the border of N.S.W. and Victoria and extending northwards to the upper reaches of the Castlereagh and Lachlan Rivers. Occasionally birds are reported as far east as the Sydney area.

These parrots have long been favourites as pets, which has done them no good as a species, heavy trapping reducing their numbers almost from the time that they were discovered. Nowadays they are hardly ever seen, being confined to the park-like, tree-dotted plains of middle-eastern N.S.W.

As cage birds they will learn to talk, but are great fliers and are 'happier' in aviaries, where they will sometimes breed. The following account of the male bird's display is by the Marquis of Tavistock, a great authority on aviculture; the display of wild birds would probably be much the same.

'Sometimes he will fly in a very slow and laboured fashion around the hen, bowing as he alights, with contracting pupils and uttering a great variety of calls. When very excited he will puff his head feathers, draw his body plumage tight, partly spread his wings and race to and fro round the hen in a series of rapid hops, "scrooging" at the top of his voice. If the object of these intentions is favourably impressed she crouches motionless with puffed head feathers and partly spread wings.'

The strange thing is that this display takes place months before the birds are in full breeding condition, and is not repeated later in the year.

These parrots feed on grass seeds and other plants and the nectar of flowering eucalypts. The nest is a hole in a tree, high above the ground.

Rosellas

Rosellas constitute our largest genus if we include the Blue-cheeked Rosella which appears to be a form of the Pale-headed. Amongst them are some of our best known parrots and some of our most decorative.

The name rosella is said to be derived from the fact that rosellas, or 'rosehill parrots', were first seen and named in the Rose Hill district of Sydney.

CRIMSON ROSELLAS, *Platycercus elegans*, are one of the best known of the group and great favourites with bird-fanciers and breeders. The breeders usually refer to this bird as Pennant's Parakeet, and indeed seem to have their own names for all rosellas, all of which terminate in parakeet.

They become quite tame in such places as national reserves, coming to picnics to share in the bread and pieces of fruit.

The Crimson Rosella was first given the name 'Beautiful Lory' by Latham in 1781. He was describing it from a very good specimen owned by Sir Joseph Banks.

These rosellas are not particularly destructive but they did learn early to take advantage of the settlers' corn fields. They have remained common even in places settled by man, and may often be seen in city parks and gardens. In the bush they frequent heavily timbered ranges and valleys and make bright flashes of colour in the deep fern-tree gullies.

The females are not as large as the males and are of a less brilliant colour, although having much the same disposition of colour. Young birds are green and do not attain adult plumage until the third year.

They nest in a hole in a tree which may be either dead or living. Five to eight white eggs are laid and the breeding season is from October to January.

RINGNECK PARROT
13 in.

53

GREEN ROSELLAS, *P. caledonicus*, being named after the island of New Caledonia, have been named in error, for they are confined to Tasmania and the islands of Bass Strait.

They are regarded as very common and it is pleasant to come upon a handsome parrot that does not seem to have suffered as a species at the hand of man.

They are something of a nuisance to orchardists and farmers at times, but remain abundant in spite of persecution. Green Rosellas do not confine themselves to agricultural areas, however, and may be found on the thickly wooded mountain slopes, in the brush-filled gullies and out in more open, park-like country; practically anywhere, in short, where they can find food.

They feed on a variety of things. Gould records that '. . . the flowers of the *eucalypti* with insects and their larvae constitute a considerable portion of its food . . .' Sharland says that this rosella prefers the high rainfall areas, as a rule, '. . . although there is scarcely a district in which it does not appear from time to time'. There appears to be a good deal of colour variation in Green Rosellas; it seems that birds which live in heavy rainfall areas in the mountains are duller than the birds in the drier country areas.

The call is 'kussick, kussick' and the bird may be heard in thick forests far more often than it is seen. When perched, or on the ground, they have a series of fluting or bell-like notes which are most pleasant.

The size of the flocks increases in winter, and they forage along the country roadsides in the hawthorn, briar and bushes for berries and seeds.

The nest is a hole in a tree and four to five white eggs are laid. The breeding season is from about November to December.

ADELAIDE ROSELLAS, *P. adelaidae*, are confined to the Flinders Ranges and Mount Lofty areas in South Australia. Apparently they are more common about Mount Lofty where they may be seen in pairs or small flocks. Their life and feeding habits are similar to those of most other rosellas, and they are sometimes a nuisance to orchardists.

Five to seven white eggs are laid in a hole in a tree and the breeding season is from September to December.

PALE-HEADED ROSELLAS, *P. adscitus*, are found from northern and eastern Queensland to northern N.S.W.; they have been recorded as rare visitors as far south as Sydney.

These subtly coloured and very beautiful parrots seem to be maintaining their numbers in spite of being fairly local in distribution.

They are often seen in company with Eastern Rosellas and it seems that they interbreed. Pale-headed Rosellas with red colouring on the head are probably the result of this cross. They are birds of the open forest and are usually seen in pairs or small flocks.

The nest is a hole in a tree or short stump and often the egg-chamber is several feet before the entrance hole. Attention is often drawn to the nesting tree of these and other rosellas by the very loud noises made by the nestlings.

From three to five or six eggs are laid and the breeding season is from September to December typically, but may be at almost any time after good rains.

There appears to be a race or variation of the Pale-headed Rosellas inhabiting Cape York Peninsula, starting more or less where the Pale-headeds leave off. These have been called the BLUE-CHEEKED ROSELLAS, *P. adscitus amathusia*. Whether this is a cline—with one type merging into the other—or whether there is a clear distinction between the two types, is uncertain.

In any event the habits of the Blue-cheeked birds appear to be similar to those of the Pale-headed Rosellas.

NORTHERN ROSELLAS, *P. venustus*, are found in the Kimberley area in north-western Australia and the northern

54

CRIMSON ROSELLA
13½ in.

EASTERN ROSELLA
12½ in.

GREEN ROSELLA
14 in.

parts of the Northern Territory.

This bird is known as the 'Smutty' amongst bird-trappers, in sharp contrast to the very poetic name 'Moondark' given to this rosella by the Port Essington natives.

They frequent grassy meadowland and the fringes of swamps where they feed on the seed of grasses and other plants. Sometimes in pairs, but more commonly in flocks of twenty or so the birds move across the ground feeding busily.

The call of these parrots is a frequently uttered double 'trin-se, trin-se'. They fly low in a rapid zig-zag and seldom further than from tree to tree.

Nesting is in the usual hole in a tree; the breeding season is from August to October and two or three white eggs are laid.

YELLOW ROSELLAS, *P. flaveolus*, are found along the river systems of the Lachlan, Murrumbidgee and lower Darling in N.S.W., and along the Murray River to South Australia; they are rarely seen in southern Queensland.

In pairs or small parties they frequent the timber along water-courses, feeding out in the nearby open country. They are usually seen on the ground foraging for grass seeds and similar food. If disturbed they fly off to the nearest timber uttering their pleasant whistling calls whilst on the wing. There is considerable variation in plumage colour amongst these rosellas but they are usually quite recognisable.

They nest in a hole in a tree, laying four or five white eggs, and the breeding season is about December or January.

EASTERN ROSELLAS, *P. eximius*, are probably the rosellas known to more people than any other. It is also one of the most beautiful, familiarity perhaps making it less exciting to bird-watchers.

As Charles Barrett says in his book *Parrots of Australia*, the Eastern Rosellas early became popular '. . . for puddings and pies, and for ships to take to England'. Those sent to England and Europe to the breeders and fanciers quickly became extremely popular and even before the turn of the century these birds had been '. . . so frequently bred on the Continent and in England that it might almost be looked upon as a European bird'.

They feed both in trees and upon the ground, searching for berries and fruit of various kinds and the seeds of grasses and other plants. Eastern Rosellas are sometimes guilty of raiding orchards and other cultivated crops.

Cross-breeding in the wild with Crimson Rosellas is not unknown, and in north-eastern N.S.W. they interbreed quite frequently with Pale-headed Rosellas.

Nests have been found in holes in fence-posts but usually the more normal site, a hole in a tree, is used. From four to nine eggs may be laid, and the breeding season is from September to January.

BLUE-CHEEKED ROSELLA 13 in.

WESTERN ROSELLA 11¼ in.

ROSELLA
nature

NORTHERN ROSELLA 12¼ in.

ADELAIDE ROSELLA 13 in.

55

COCKATIEL 12 in.

BUDGERYGAH
7¼ in.

WESTERN ROSELLAS, *P. icterotis*, are confined to south-western Australia. Their distribution extends up to Moora in the north and in the east to the Wongan Hills, Merridin and the Dundas district.

Their habits are much the same as the other rosellas. A good deal of their time is spent on the ground searching for grass seeds and similar food, but they also do some damage in orchards. Because of its depredations it was declared 'vermin' in 1921, although being less destructive than some other parrots. The call note is syllabised as 'chink-chink'.

The nesting site is the usual hole in a tree; from three to seven eggs are laid. The breeding season is from August to December.

Ringneck Parrots

RINGNECK PARROTS, *Barnardius barnardi*, are typical parrots of the mallee country. They are found in the interior of southern Queensland, western N.S.W., north-western Victoria and eastern South Australia to the York Peninsula.

They move about in pairs or small flocks and frequent scrub, open forest and the timber along creeks and rivers.

These handsome parrots spend a great deal of their time on the ground, seeking out seeding-grasses and other plants, but also feed in trees on the flower buds of various eucalypts, chattering as they move through the foliage.

Due to the clearance of large areas of mallee and other scrub to plough the ground for wheat, the Ringnecks are gone from many of their old haunts.

The nest is a hole in a tree, and four or five white eggs are laid. The breeding season is from July to December.

Psephotus Parrots

RED-BACKED PARROTS, *Psephotus haematonotus*, feed in flocks, which out of the breeding season may be quite large. The rank grasses along the borders of country roads are a favoured spot, and they may often be put up as one drives along.

When resting between feeding times, or early in the morning whilst waiting for the weak winter sun to warm them, they have the habit of sitting in rows shoulder to shoulder along the dead bough of a gum tree. Their delicate yellowish-green plumage and the few spots of red where a bird has turned its back make a handsome picture against the silver-grey dead wood and the pale blue sky.

The range of these parrots is from south-western Queensland to Victoria, southern and north-eastern South Australia. In Victoria they sometimes visit coastal districts.

The birds' call notes have a pleasant whistling, sibilant quality, 'almost approaching to a song, which is poured forth both while perched on the branches of the trees and while flying over the plains'.

A hole in a tree is chosen for a nesting site and this may be at almost any height. The breeding season is from September to December, and five to seven white eggs are laid.

Neophema or Grass parrots

BLUE-WINGED PARROTS, *Neophema chrysostoma*, are found from western N.S.W. and Victoria to southern South Australia, King Island and Tasmania.

In Tasmania the birds tend to be summer visitors, arriving in September and departing again in February or March. However, a few birds have been observed remaining throughout the year.

In pairs or small flocks these charming parrots frequent grassy country and sparsely wooded terrain.

They are inconspicuous amongst the long grass in which they feed and, although they communicate with soft twittering notes, these are so subdued that one might easily pass them by.

Blue-wings are often quite fearless; threading their way through the grass they will permit a close approach before flying up with soft cries. They will settle again a short distance off or fly into a thick tree.

Oddly enough, these parrots show a great deal more timidity when in captivity. The Duke of Bedford writes in his book *Parrots and Parrot-like Birds*, '. . . the Blue-wing has the inveterate habit of killing itself by flying against the roof of its cage or aviary when suddenly frightened . . .'

When displaying, the male bird draws himself up to his full height, the wings are lowered to display the blue on the wing and food is brought up from the crop. All the time he utters a call described as 'scroop-few'.

The food of these parrots appears to be obtained entirely on the ground, being the seeds of grasses and herbaceous plants.

Nesting is in a hole in a tree or stump, at the bottom of which seven or eight eggs are laid without any nesting material. The breeding season is from October to January.

ELEGANT PARROTS, *N. elegans*, range from southern N.S.W. to western Victoria and South Australia north to the Flinders Range area. There is a south-western Australian population from Esperance in the east to Moora in the north.

They are somewhat similar in habits and appearance to the foregoing species, frequenting open types of country where there is a plentiful supply of seeding grasses. Seemingly unlikely spots such as salty marsh-country attract these parrots if the rank herbage which grows in such places is seeding.

Elegant Parrots are nomadic but not strictly migratory, as their movements are governed by the seasonal ripening of grasses.

Unlike Blue-winged Parrots they are usually very shy. When flushed they go up in a zig-zag flight; if not seriously disturbed they may alight again, but more usually they mount into the sky and fly off at a considerable height. There is a 'pretty warbling call-note' which the birds utter whilst flying. In captivity the grass-parrots have a name for being delicate, but the Elegant Parrots are perhaps the most hardy of the group. Even in English winters they have survived in outdoor aviaries without artificial heat.

ORANGE-BREASTED PARROTS, *N. chrysogaster*, are distributed along the coastal areas of south-eastern South Australia, part of Victoria, Tasmania and more rarely in southern N.S.W. As with the other grass-parrots, one usually comes across these birds in pairs or in small flocks.

They are swift runners, as are most of the grass-parrots. Most of their time is spent on or near the ground seeking out the seeding heads of grasses and various herbaceous plants. Swampy coastal areas as well as the more likely plains-country are favoured habitats.

They often become very fat from whatever seeds they feed upon, even to the point of being difficult to skin; one earlier collector mentions that they 'were replete with fat, which had to be mopped up in the form of oil during skinning'.

Orange-breasted Parrots are very rare in captivity—they are not even mentioned in the Duke of Bedford's book on parrots—and it appears that no one has successfully bred and reared them in an aviary.

They nest in a hollow limb or in the hollow of a tree; sometimes a hollow log on the ground may be utilised.

SCARLET-CHESTED PARROTS, *N. splendida*, are distributed from western N.S.W. through northern South Australia to the coastal areas of the Great Australian Bight.

In Western Australia there are scattered populations where they are considered to be inland birds although there appear to be no records of them nesting in that State.

RED-BACKED PARROT 11 in.

These beautiful parrots were first described in the *Proceedings of the Zoological Society*, London, in 1840, by Gould. There was only a single Western Australian specimen available, although in 1845 several fine specimens were forwarded to Gould by the unfortunate Johnson Drummond, who was murdered by a native in his party whilst on a collecting trip for Gould.

Even in Gould's day this parrot was '. . . of a very shy disposition and nowhere very numerous'.

The next published account of the parrot is in Campbell's *Appendix to the Nests and Eggs of Australian Birds*, 1901, describing how a female and two eggs were taken from a nest in a mallee-tree. During the next five or six decades there were no additional records of the existence of this bird, and it was considered by many ornithologists to be extinct.

This was not so, however, and although it is rare, scattered populations inhabit the dry inland areas where patches of scrub occur to give it shelter. Often they are found far from water. An account by somebody searching for these elusive parrots in 1936 describes their home-ground as 'spinifex-covered sandhills with stunted mallee gullies'.

The account goes on to say, 'this country in which they are found is waterless and I was puzzled to know how they obtained their drink, until one hot day . . . I saw one of them move its beak along the leaves and thereupon examined this bush and found that it had a very sappy round leaf . . . and on pressing it between my fingers a small drop of quite palatable juice was obtained from a leaf'.

These parrots are now frequently bred in aviaries, where they require care but they are not the most delicate of the grass-parrots.

In the wild these parrots follow a nesting procedure similar to that of the other Neopthema parrots. However, the nesting hole is usually lower and they select a ragged-edged hollow and do not chew around the edge of the entrance like other parrots, thus there are no indications to show that the hollow might contain a nest.

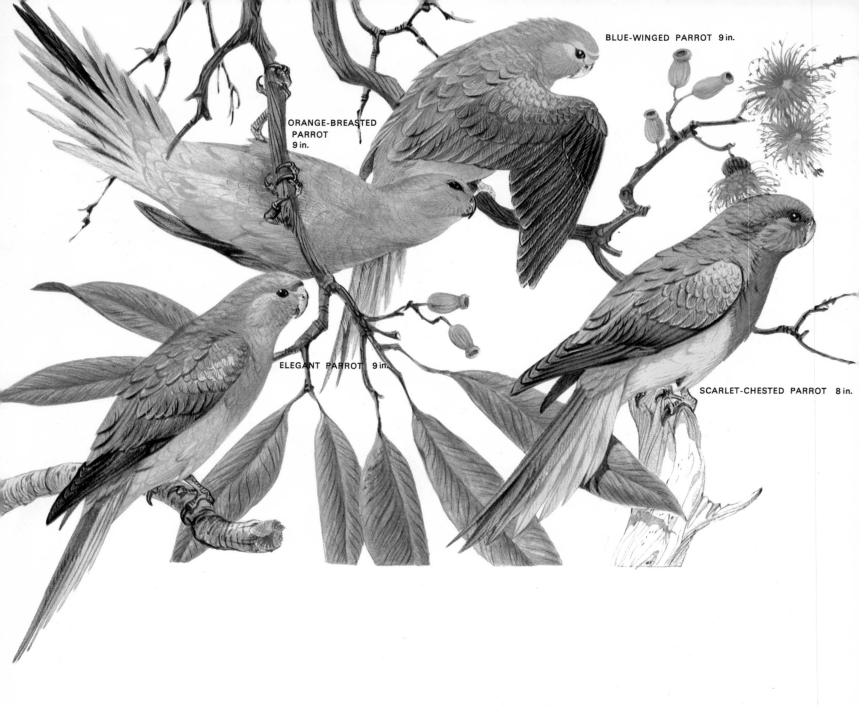

ORANGE-BREASTED PARROT 9 in.

BLUE-WINGED PARROT 9 in.

ELEGANT PARROT 9 in.

SCARLET-CHESTED PARROT 8 in.

Budgerygahs

BUDGERYGAHS, *Melopsittacus undulatus*, are no doubt one of Australia's best known birds, especially in the various colours that have been aviary-bred. In the wild state these delicate little parrots are greenish, mottled with darker greens, black and browns.

Their distribution is inland Australia generally. At irregular intervals they appear in various coastal districts, perhaps because of bad drought conditions inland.

The typical habitat of Budgerygahs is open country scattered with trees and areas of scrub. They are a nomadic species, with a tendency to move south in late winter and early spring. They were first described in 1840 from a specimen that was probably collected from the Parramatta district. They were seen in great abundance by Captain Sturt during his journey into N.S.W., and Gould writes that 'this gentleman informed me that on the extensive plains bordering the Murrumbidgee he met with this lovely species in immense flocks, feeding upon the seeds and berries of the low stunted bushes . . .'

The name of the bird is Aboriginal and means 'good bird' or 'good food'. A popular, anglicised version of the spelling is Budgerigar. There are also a number of 'Aboriginal' ways of spelling the name, such as: Betcherrygah and Boodgereegar.

Sometimes very large flocks have been seen in the interior

and the birds are fortunately still quite common. They may be very tame if intent upon drinking at a water-hole or while feeding. Most of the time the birds keep up a constant chatter which can become quite monotonous if one is camped nearby.

They nest in colonies, many being found in the one tree where every suitable hollow will have its pair of birds. Some years, quite inexplicably, a flock will not appear at their usual breeding spot, but may return again the following year. They also may not appear as passing flocks, in a locality where most years they are common. These population movements are probably dependent on food supply. In good years it is quite possible that they breed twice, and perhaps in a bad year some Budgerygahs do not nest at all.

Gould introduced the species into England and within a few years they were being bred as readily as canaries. Many colour variations have since been developed, and a vast literature has grown up on the subject of their care and breeding.

In the wild they nest in a hole in a tree, and from four to eight white eggs are laid; the breeding season is usually from October to December.

The Budgerygah is a species that suffers very badly during a long drought when hundreds may be found dying around the dehydrating water-holes.

RED-WINGED PARROT
13½ in.

KING PARROT 16 in.

CUCULIFORMES

CUCKOOS AND ALLIED BIRDS

The cuckoo family is well represented in Australia with fourteen of the one hundred and twenty-seven species in the world. Not all cuckoos parasitise other birds, but all except one of our species do have the family characteristic of laying their eggs in the nests of other birds.

A number of eggs are laid by the hen cuckoo at about two-day intervals. Each one is deposited in a different nest, but only in the nests of one species, and usually one whose eggs most resemble her own.

The female cuckoo will usually have the selected nests under observation as they are being built, and when the victim has laid an egg or two the cuckoo flies to the nest, removes one of the clutch, lays her own egg in its place and flies off with the stolen egg.

It was believed that, in the case of domed nests, the female laid her egg on the ground and then deposited it with her bill through the small entrance to the nest. Observation suggests that, in fact, the cuckoo props herself with her wings and tail spread for support, against the nest entrance, and ejects her egg into the nest.

PALLID CUCKOO 12 in.

A female Shining Bronze Cuckoo, which usually lays in the domed nests of such birds as wrens, forces her way into the nest, sticking her head through the far wall. After laying her egg, she flies off through the hole she has made. The owners of the nest return and unconcernedly repair their damaged nest.

On hatching, the well-known procedure develops where the young cuckoo ejects the other young birds or any remaining eggs by wriggling beneath them and hoisting them over the edge on its shoulders.

If by chance two cuckoos' eggs are laid in the same nest and they hatch out together, the two blind and naked chicks struggle against each other for some time without either bird being able to toss the other over the edge of the nest. After three days or so the instinct to clear the nest of competition dies and the two cuckoos live amicably together.

Cuckoos

Perhaps our most 'typical' cuckoos are the two species in the genus *Cuculus*. PALLID CUCKOOS, *Cuculus pallidus*, one of the most common Australian cuckoos, are found throughout Australia and Tasmania where suitable habitats occur.

They are migratory birds, appearing in spring in southern Australia and moving northwards again in autumn. A few birds have been recorded as remaining in the south throughout the year.

These cuckoos are very vociferous when they first come south and the loud whistling call—a run of ascending notes with a rather plaintive sound—is familiar to many people. It keeps up this call for hours at a time on hot spring mornings, and such local names as 'Scale-bird' and 'Brainfever-bird' are some indication of the persistence of the birds' calls.

Pallid Cuckoos eat insects of various kinds, and fulfil a useful function in eating large numbers of hairy caterpillars which few other birds will touch.

Foster-parents for the young of these cuckoos are very diverse, more than eighty species being recorded. They do, 59

NARROW-BILLED BRONZE-CUCKOO 6 in.

GOLDEN BRONZE-CUCKOO
6 in.

SHINING BRONZE-CUCKOO
6 in.

however, usually choose open, cup-shaped nests. Many species of honeyeater are parasitised, as well as some robins and flycatchers, wood-swallows and many others.

The eggs of Pallid Cuckoos are pale pinkish flesh-colour, some quite plain, and others with a few darker spots. The breeding season is from September to January.

It is only the male birds that have the characteristic ascending whistle, the call of the females is a hoarse 'kheer' sound.

FANTAILED CUCKOO
10 in.

FANTAILED CUCKOOS, *Cacomantis pyrrhophanus*, are fairly common through most of their range, and are found from Cape York down eastern Australia across to the Eyre Peninsula. They are common in Tasmania and there is a population in south-western Australia.

These cuckoos are mainly birds of the forests and scrub country although they may be met with in gardens and in open park-like habitats.

Their call is a descending trill; a drowsy, summery sound with a plaintive quality that is quite unmistakable.

Fantailed Cuckoos are largely migratory, or at least nomadic, moving northwards after each breeding season. The south-western Australian birds do not migrate outside their range but merely undertake seasonal movements within it. A few birds in various parts of the country also remain in the same vicinity throughout the year.

Fantailed Cuckoos have the typical cuckoo flight, direct and rather sparrowhawk-like. When the birds land, the tails are elevated, almost as if to maintain balance.

As well as the descending trill, there is said (by Sharland) to be another call that resembles the call of the European cuckoo '. . . more closely than do any of our cuckoos' calls . . . the listener can with a little imagination hear the drawn out double note that suggests the call of the English bird' They can quite often be heard trilling during darkness in the spring.

A large number of foster-parents is known; about fifty have been noted. These are usually birds that are considerably smaller and that build domed nests. More rarely, they will lay in the open nests of such birds as silvereyes.

The breeding season is from August to December, and the egg is a dull white with small spots of purplish-brown, sometimes forming a vague zone at the larger end.

NARROW-BILLED BRONZE CUCKOOS, *Chalcites basalis*, are found throughout most of Australia, except Cape York Peninsula, and in Tasmania, the Malay Archipelago and the Aru Islands.

This is a cuckoo of the open forest, heathlands and, sometimes, country gardens. In the main it is a migratory bird, although some remain in their haunts throughout the year. The bulk arrive in early spring and depart about March. Their exact migration routes and destinations are not yet known.

They may often be seen perched on high dead twigs at the tops of bushes. This is often the singing post from which the handsome little birds utter their call; a high-pitched rather mournful whistle, piping down the scale. During the breeding season the birds often call at night. Insects and caterpillars are the birds' staple diet.

There are about sixty-five species of foster-parents recorded. Both domed and open nests are chosen, but domed nests near the ground seem to be preferred. The egg is pinkish with small red spots; the breeding season is from July to December.

SHINING BRONZE CUCKOOS, *C. lucidus*, are only birds of passage in Australia. They are a common breeding species in New Zealand but have not been recorded as nesting in Australia.

The bulk of these cuckoos make the 2,000-mile journey to their wintering grounds in the Solomon Islands over the open Pacific Ocean. A few birds, however, reach our eastern coastline and follow it on their way north.

This ocean-spanning journey is a considerable flight to be undertaken twice a year by a bird only about six inches long. More remarkable is the fact that the young 'birds of the year' follow some time after their parents. Instinctively they find

BARN OWL 14 in.

TASMANIAN MASKED OWL 14¼ in.

BOOBOOK OWL 16 in.

GRASS OWL 14 in.

MASKED OWL 14 in.

their way north over the trackless ocean to the relatively small area of the Solomons.

GOLDEN BRONZE CUCKOOS, *C. plagosus*, are common birds found throughout a large part of Australia where suitable habitats occur.

Their range is eastern and southern Australia, from Cape York to south-eastern South Australia. Separated by the dry centre, there is a population of these cuckoos in south and mid-western Australia. They are also found in Tasmania. Outside Australia they range to New Guinea, the Lesser Sunda Islands and the Bismarck Archipelago.

Golden Bronze Cuckoos are migrants to the southern parts of our continent, arriving to breed in the spring and departing again before the winter.

In Western Australia, the earliest call recorded is May 4th, the birds leave for the north in February. In N.S.W. a few birds have been recorded as remaining the whole year.

They are useful birds, being great insect eaters and destroying large numbers of injurious caterpillars.

The call note is vigorous and has been syllabised as a repeated 'pee-pee-pee' ending with a drawn-out 'pee-er'. The bird usually calls from a dead twig at the top of a bush or tree.

The Western Australian population of these cuckoos migrate to such places as the Lesser Sunda Islands, whilst the eastern population appear to go to New Guinea.

About sixty-five species have been recorded as foster-parents, mostly birds that build domed nests. Yellow-tailed Thornbills are popular hosts, and Fairy Wrens, Spotted Scrub Wrens and the Brown Thornbills are also recorded as common hosts in Western Australia; no doubt this holds true in the eastern States.

The eggs are pale greenish-olive or bronzy-brown colour. If an egg is rubbed with a wet finger, the colouring comes off, revealing a pale blue shell. The breeding season is from August to December.

STRIGIFORMES

OWLS

Barn Owls

BARN OWLS, *Tyto alba*, are the 'type-birds' of this group and are found in only slightly varying forms in many countries of the world. They are the owls which are usually most closely associated with man, often nesting, as the name suggests, in farm buildings and other sites where their rodent food might be abundant.

Some owls are somewhat or entirely diurnal, but the Barn Owls are strictly birds of darkness. They are very local in their habits, using the same spots to hide by day, and returning year after year to the same nesting site. Presumably they also mate for life.

Experiments have shown that Barn Owls appear to hunt more by ear than sight. Captive Barn Owls, in a totally blacked-out room, were watched with infra-red lamps. Mice on the floor were ignored whilst stationary, but as soon

61

OWLET NIGHTJAR 8½ in.

BOOBOOK OWLS, *Ninox boobook*, are named after their cry of 'boo-book' or 'more-port'. They are also known by many country people as the 'Mopoke'. Distribution is throughout most of Australia where suitably wooded habitats allow.

They are night hunters, and during the day, rest and sleep in the hollow of a tree, a rock crevice, or deep in thick foliage. They are often common in towns, where they may be seen hawking at the insects attracted to street lamps, or heard in parks and large gardens. Apart from insects, their food is small rodents and birds. As well as the well-known call, the bird has a cry which rather resembles the mewing of a cat.

The largest of our owls are the Powerful Owls, *N. strenua*. They are found from south-eastern Queensland to eastern and southern Victoria, their normal habitat being the big scrub and brush-filled gullies of mountain country. I have seen one, however, in the light scrub only a mile or two back from the coast at Mornington, Victoria.

They are large, heavy-looking birds with rather small heads in proportion to their bodies. Like other owls, they appear short-necked, although in fact, all owls have rather long necks under their bulky feathering. Their necks are also very pliant; having their eyes in front of their head gives the owls the advantage of binocular vision, but they have to turn their heads to look at anything that is to one side or behind them. An owl is able to swivel its head completely round and stare down its own back.

POWERFUL OWL
24 in.

as they stirred, rustling the leaves scattered on the floor, the owls pounced with unerring accuracy.

The Australian representative of the Barn Owl is found throughout the continent and Tasmania, wherever habitats allow. It usually inhabits forest land or lightly timbered cultivated country.

Barn Owls have a number of calls; an odd assortment of clucking and snoring sounds and a long-drawn-out, unearthly scream.

As well as rodents, they feed on bats, insects and reptiles; they also take small birds. One of these owls will sometimes fly along an ivy-covered wall, or similar site, brushing the foliage with its wings to flush the sleeping sparrows and other small-fry. If a bird is unwise enough to blunder out, it is soon snatched up in the owl's powerful talons.

The nest site is in a hollow of a tree trunk or limb; alternatively, they will nest in farm buildings, church-towers and other large isolated structures.

MASKED OWLS, *T. novae-hollandiae*, are more heavily-built birds and are darker: the facial disc is a creamy-brown compared with the almost white face of the Barn Owls.

They are found in forest country generally, throughout the continent. They appear to be strictly nocturnal, hiding and sleeping during the day in hollow trees or in thick dark foliage.

The call is a screeching cry, similar to, but more powerful than, the Barn Owl's. They feed on small mammals and reptiles and, like all the *Tyto* group, are considered to be beneficial to man in their depredations amongst rodents.

Tasmanian Masked Owls, *T. castanops*, are very much darker and more orange all over; this is particularly noticeable on the breast. The facial disc is darker, being a deep coffee-brown, whilst in the mainland species, it is quite a pale buffish-white.

A variety of rasping, hissing notes may be uttered and the birds also have a loud screaming cry, used when hunting. Their food is small mammals and birds.

GRASS OWLS, *T. longimembris*, are rare birds, occurring from the Northern Territory down the eastern states to Victoria.

It is this ability and habit that has given rise to the old story that, if one walks around an owl sitting on a stump, it will continue turning its head to keep one in sight, until it wrings its own neck.

The call of the Powerful Owls is a rich, deep 'who-whoo'. They also have a number of murmuring and bleating calls. The wild 'murdered-woman' shrieks hitherto attributed to these birds are now considered to be made by Barking Owls.

Powerful Owls catch possums and gliders, which constitute their main diet. In some localities, they also take a number of rabbits and a few small birds.

CAPRIMULGIFORMES

Nightjars and Allied Birds

SPOTTED NIGHTJARS, *Eurostopodus guttatus*, are birds of the inland parts of the continent generally and Cape York Peninsula. The Great Dividing Range separates these birds from the White-throated Nightjars throughout most of their range. The Aru Islands and New Ireland also have their populations of Spotted Nightjars.

By day they are usually seen singly—if they are seen at all —nesting amongst fallen leaves, sticks and other debris. They are extremely well camouflaged and one can walk within inches of a bird without seeing it. If in imminent danger of being trodden upon, the nightjar springs up on silent wings. It presents a beautiful sight as the chestnut, grey and mottled umbers of the plumage are displayed for a moment at close range before the bird takes off.

At dusk they begin hunting and sometimes a number may be seen at once, dashing back and forth against the darkening sky in pursuit of moths, beetles and other flying insects.

The call is most odd; a number of cawing sounds followed by a gobbling, bubbling cry which diminishes in volume.

No nest is built; the single cryptically marked egg is laid on the ground.

Frogmouths

Frogmouths are a strange-looking group of birds with sad, wild eyes and beautifully mottled plumage. Of the four species in this country, the most common are TAWNY FROG-MOUTHS, *Podargus Strigoides*. They are found throughout most of Australia, where suitable habitats permit, and in Tasmania. They are frequently called the 'Mopoke' but in fact its call is

SPOTTED NIGHTJAR 12 in.

LAUGHING KOOKABURRA 17½ in

othing like this. It is the Boobook Owl's call which resembles
'mopoke' or 'boo-book'. The cry of the Tawny Frogmouth is
an oft-repeated 'oom' which carries a great distance.

There is great variation in their plumage. The most common
colour is a basic mottled grey, with some birds being a
light pearly colour and other specimens grading to a dark
slate-grey. The size is also very inconsistent, some frogmouths being as much as half the size of others. The prey of
the frogmouths is the crawling, wriggling host found on the
floor of the open forest: beetles, larvae, crickets and other
insects. They also will eat mice and other small mammals.

During the day Tawny Frogmouths are difficult to find as
they spend their time perched upright on stumps or amongst
the larger branches of trees. Their mottled plumage and un-
bird-like silhouettes bear a remarkable resemblance to mossy,
broken branch-stumps. The nests are loose platforms of
sticks placed in trees. They have saucer-shaped depressions
which are usually lined with green leaves. If surprised at
their nests the frogmouths display at the intruder, fluffing out
their feathers to make themselves appear much larger, and
snapping menacingly with their heavy bills.

Owlet-nightjars

OWLET-NIGHTJARS, *Aegotheles cristata*, inhabit most parts of
Australia where suitable wooded habitats permit, and are
common in Tasmania.

These elfin little birds, with their large heads and attenu-
ated bodies appear to be distantly related to frogmouths.
During the day they hide in hollow trees and stumps but are
often curious enough to come and peer out of their roosting-
hole if the tree is tapped.

At dusk they emerge to hunt for insects.

The nest is a hole in a tree or stump. At the bottom of this
hole the eggs are sometimes laid on the wood-dust but more
frequently a nest of leaves is made.

APODIFORMES

SWIFTS

In Australia we have three common species of swifts. The
larger swifts are extremely fast and powerful fliers, some
species being credited with speeds up to 200 mph. Most of
their lives are spent on the wing, some birds even staying out
all night. Whether they are able to 'cat-nap' whilst actually
in the air is not known.

Pictures of swifts on high-speed film have shown that they
are able to beat each of their wings at slightly different speeds,
thus facilitating the rapid turns characteristic of their flight.

All swifts have very small and weak feet and legs, and are
never seen perching in trees or on the ground. If brought to
earth by some mischance, swifts are only able to take off
again if there is some prominence or cliff edge to which they
can struggle; otherwise the unfortunate birds cannot raise
themselves high enough off the ground to spread and use
their very long wings.

When the birds do land, they cling vertically to a cliff face
or building, hooking their small sharp claws into a crevice or
over a ledge. In some species all four toes point forward to
make a more efficient hook. Most also have short, stiff tails
which support them as they cling.

Swifts tend to be migratory. As their food consists entirely
of insects caught on the wing, the birds must leave their
nesting grounds at the end of each summer to visit warmer
parts. Like swallows, they often return to exactly the same
nesting spots year after year.

In spite of being rather similar in appearance and habits to
swallows, they are not related. The two groups of birds are,

AZURE KINGFISHER 8 in.

indeed, a good example of convergent evolution: unrelated
species that have developed similar physical appearances
because of similar habits. One of the main outward differ-
ences between swifts and swallows is that the latter perch and
'sing' and are thus fairly typical passerine birds.

Being delicately boned birds, the fossil records of swifts are
scarce. A few fragmentary remains found in France were in
Oligocene deposits, showing that the family was clearly
differentiated 40 million years ago. The nearest relatives of
the swifts—and they are sometimes classified as apodiformes
—are the hummingbirds. It seems likely that millions of
years ago they shared common ancestors. The eggs of the
two families and the construction of the wing bones certainly
seem to relate the birds more nearly to each other than to any
other birds.

Swifts

FORK-TAILED SWIFTS, *Apus pacificus*, are usually seen high in
the air and sometimes will mount up out of sight in circles
and dashing zig-zags.

Their forked tails are not particularly apparent, quite
often appearing pointed in comparison to the squarish tails
of the Spine-tailed Swifts. But as the birds wheel and bank
the tails are sometimes spread and the forked shape becomes
obvious.

They are migratory birds and their numbers appear to
fluctuate from year to year in various districts. They breed
in Asia and arrive here in our spring, departing again towards
the end of summer. Their appearance is often associated with
stormy and humid weather. It may be that the swifts are
present in clear dry weather but are flying unnoticed at considerable altitudes. On stormy days they fly low, presumably
because the high-flying insects are forced lower in such conditions. All their food is obtained on the wing and the birds
never perch in trees nor land upon the ground.

During migration they usually travel in flocks, sometimes
mixed with numbers of Spine-tailed Swifts. They are
normally in flocks at other times of the year also, although
pairs and even solitary birds may be seen occasionally.

The nest is placed against the rocky wall of a cave or cliff
over-hang, glued into place with the birds' saliva. They do
not nest in Australia.

SPINE-TAILED SWIFTS, *Hirundapus caudacutus*, are slightly
larger birds and very fast fliers. They are found throughout
most of Australia and in Tasmania, and are, in fact, the
more common species in the Eastern States.

In Western Australia the Fork-tailed is the common swift,
there being very few acceptable records of the spine-tailed
bird in that State.

Spine-tails breed in eastern Asia and migrate to our
continent to escape the northern winter. They arrive in the
late spring, beginning to drift northwards once more towards
the end of summer.

Except in humid, thundery weather they fly high—often
out of sight of the naked eye—in pursuit of insects. They are
not uncommon throughout their Australian range, but vary
in numbers from year to year in a given locality.

65

SACRED KINGFISHER
8 in.

FOREST KINGFISHER
7 in.

♂

FOREST KINGFISHER
♀

Like other swifts they never intentionally land on the ground, nor can they perch in trees. They cling with their diminutive feet in an upright position to a rock-face or the bark of a tree; they are also recorded as roosting in thick foliage.

The nests of these birds are similar to those of other typical swifts. They are a conglomeration of wind-blown material, such as feathers and light grass, which the birds catch up in their bills as they fly. This is gummed together in a saucer-shape and stuck to the nest site with the birds' saliva. They nest in colonies, usually in a cave or under a rocky overhang; sometimes large hollow trees are utilised. Two or three dull white eggs are laid in the northern spring; the bird does not breed in this country.

CORACIIFORMES

KINGFISHERS AND ALLIED BIRDS

The early Greeks believed that kingfishers nested on the open sea, thus they called them *Halkyons* (*hals*, sea and *kyon*, conceiving). Being favoured by the gods, the sea was calmed for them for the two weeks or so preceding the winter solstice, allowing the little birds a peaceful nesting period. *Halkyon* became *Halcyon* in Latin, and periods of quiet and calm have been called 'halcyon days' ever since.

Actually, by no stretch of the imagination could any of the kingfishers be called sea-birds, although some species are associated with mangrove swamps and other habitats of the littoral.

There are eighty-four species in the world, which ar broadly divided into two sub-families: the *Alcedinidae*, c fishing kingfishers, and the *Daceloninae*. The latter are know as forest kingfishers and are often found far from water, wher they prey on insects, small reptiles and small mammal rather than fish.

We have representatives of both sub-families in Australi with ten species covering a great range of size, colour an habits.

The largest of our kingfishers and one of the best know Australian birds is the Laughing Kookaburra. Early settler and visitors to our shores, their ears attuned to the melodie of thrush and nightingale, were appalled by the wild laughin cry of this giant kingfisher. But the 'jackass', or 'jack' as it familiarly called, has become a general favourite and is ofte tamed to the point where the birds will come pecking at th window for their daily handout.

Kingfishers

AZURE KINGFISHERS, *Alcyone azurea*, are widely distribute from the Kimberley area in the north-west, east and south t south-eastern Australia and Tasmania, in which State i is considered to be uncommon, being confined mainly to th north and west of Tasmania. North of Australia the rang of this bird extends to New Guinea and the Molucca Island

Either singly or in pairs they may be seen along fresh-wate or brackish streams. Typically kingfishers in their hunting they perch on a dead branch over the water awaiting thei prey, frequently bobbing their heads as they sit. As well a small fish, they take yabbies, small frogs, water-beetles an crabs. Crustaceans are dashed against the birds' perch t dismember them before being swallowed. Dives into th water may be made from a few inches, or up to thirty feet o so. When disturbed from their perch the birds fly off with shrill cry. They dash off over the water and prefer to follov the twists and curves of the river rather than cut across th land.

66

A nesting tunnel about two feet long is dug into the river-bank. At the end of this is a rounded chamber six inches or so in diameter. A clutch of five or six eggs, rounded and glossy white, is laid. A nesting hole appears to be used by the same pair of birds in consecutive years and two broods are often raised each season.

No nesting material is used, and the young birds soon foul the nest with regurgitated fish debris and their own excreta. No nest-cleaning is carried out by the adult birds.

The breeding season is from July or August until January in most parts, but in the north can be as late as April.

In the genus *Halcyon* we have four kingfishers that tend to inhabit dry scrub and woodland areas as much as creeks and rivers.

SACRED KINGFISHERS, *H. sanctus*, are fairly common birds that may be seen in all States including Tasmania. Basically they are insect eaters and may frequently be found far from water. Occasionally, however, a pair of birds may take up residence on or near a creek and will fish as well as capture insects, small reptiles and frogs.

They are migrant kingfishers, reaching the southern limits of their travels in August and September and departing northwards again in March. A few birds have been recorded as remaining all the year. Outside Australia their range extends to New Zealand and, in the north, to New Guinea and many other South-east Asian islands.

Their note is a loud clear 'kee-kee-kee', which may sometimes be heard at night, especially if the bird is disturbed. They are pugnacious, and will defend their nest with harsh grating cries and fluttering attacks upon an intruder.

They hunt in the usual kingfisher manner except that they seldom fish. A number of favourite perches will be used, from which the bird darts out to capture a passing insect or dives down to pick up some small animal from the ground.

The nest may be found in a variety of sites. In Western Australia the birds commonly use a hollow branch 'spout' or any other suitable hole in a tree. In the east, a river bank, tree-stump or termite's nest is frequently used. The birds excavate a tunnel into the hard soil of a termite's nest by pecking and drilling with their sharp bills. The nest cavity is hollowed out and the termites seal off the passages encroached upon by the kingfisher's digging. Four to six spherical white eggs are laid and the breeding season is from October to January.

FOREST KINGFISHERS, *H. macleayi*, are found from north-western Australia across the top of the continent and down the eastern States as far south as the Port Stephens district in N.S.W.

In the northern parts of their range they are year-round residents, but the southern population moves north in March and returns again in about September.

Their habits and habitats are similar to those of Sacred Kingfishers and like them they favour dry country as much as or more than water-courses.

They have a loud 'kingfisher' call, a rather harsh 'tsee' uttered many times throughout the day. Their food is insects, crustaceans, small fish and lizards.

The nest hollow is excavated in a termite's nest or a tree, often at a considerable height from the ground. Four to six white eggs are laid and the breeding season is from October to December.

LAUGHING KOOKABURRAS, *Dacelo gigas*, are the largest kingfishers in the world and one of the best-known of Australian birds. The name kookaburra is Aboriginal and has been selected from a large number of similarly onomatopoeic names such as kowburra, akkaburra, arkooburra, googooburra, gurgaga, gingarga and a host of others.

Kookaburras range from inland Cape York and down through eastern Australia and southern Australia to the Eyre

DOLLAR-BIRD 12 in.

BEE-EATER 10 in.

67

Peninsula and Kangaroo Island. They were introduced into Western Australia in 1898 and are now firmly established in the south-west corner. In 1905 they were introduced into Tasmania where they are thriving in the north but only slowly extending southwards. Because of their depredations amongst small birds they are not protected in Tasmania.

The wild laughing cry of these birds was not looked upon kindly by the early settlers and explorers who, almost unanimously, described it as unpleasant in one way or another. Typically, it was described as 'apalling as the ravings of a madman . . . It strikes upon the ear with a wild clash . . . and ends in a prolonged sardonic chuckle. Kookaburras are most vociferous at dawn and sunset and are often the first birds to be heard just before first light.

In pairs, singly, or sometimes in small groups, they favour open forest country. Kookaburras are common birds and have taken readily to man-made parks and gardens, often becoming tame and accepting offers of food. In the bush they are catholic in their diet, eating practically any kind of animal food. Large insects are taken, as well as fish, crabs and other crustaceans, small reptiles and birds. Their prowess as snake killers is well known, if somewhat exaggerated at times. Snakes up to thirty inches or so will be attacked, sometimes by a number of birds in co-operation.

Kookaburras are inveterate nest-raiders; they take many nestlings and are persecuted in return by small birds. Such species as wagtails and honeyeaters are very pugnacious towards them. I have watched Bell-miners pestering one of these kingfishers for an hour at a time. Flying at the larger bird, the honeyeaters continually buffet their target, striking it with their wings, beaks and feet until tiring of the activity. The kookaburra usually sits through it all, apparently unconcerned, or flies off a few yards, only to be set upon by other birds upon whose territory it has encroached.

The nest of a kookaburra is usually in a hollow, fairly high in a large tree. Sometimes a chamber is hollowed out of a termite's nest in a tree or, more rarely, a tunnel is bored into a bank of earth.

From two to four eggs are laid, these are roundish and pure white. The breeding season is from September to December.

Bee-eaters

Also included in the *Coraciiformes* are two Australian birds that are not kingfishers. The first of these, the BEE-EATERS, *Merops ornatus*, commonly called Rainbow-birds, are found throughout most parts of Australia where habitats permit. They migrate southwards from the islands to the north of Australia. The birds reach the southern limits of their range about September and October and move northwards again in February and March.

Bee-eaters frequent open park-like country and cultivated areas. They have a great fondness for bees and many are shot by apiarists. However, they also do a great deal of good by taking 'harmful' insects including blow-flies, dragon- and robber-flies, the latter two of which are predators of bees.

Bee-eaters have a high churring call note, often uttered on the wing as they dart and glide gracefully in pursuit of insects. They spend a good part of their time perched on fence-posts or exposed branches, from which they sally forth after their prey.

The nest is a tunnel excavated by the birds in the flat ground or in a bank. Often three feet long or so, this requires considerable effort by the two birds. They burrow by loosening the soil with their bills, and then, resting on their 'shoulders' shooting the earth back with their feet, sending showers out of the entrance hole.

At the end of the nest tunnel a hollow is made in which the five to seven glossy white eggs are laid. This nest hollow and

FORK-TAILED SWIFT 7 in.

SPINE-TAILED SWIFT

the entrance tunnel become littered with the remains of insects fed to the nestlings.

The breeding season is from October to February.

Dollar-birds

ROLLERS, *Eurystomus orientalis*, or Dollar-birds as they are equally well known in this country, are fairly common in northern and eastern Australia. In South Australia and Tasmania they are considered wanderers or accidental visitors, reports of them being rare.

They breed in Australia and are migrants and birds of passage northwards through New Guinea to the Moluccas, Celebes and the Bismarck Archipelago. Rollers also reach Lord Howe Island and New Zealand.

At the end of September and during October they spread to the southern limits of their range in Australia, departing again in February and March.

Like other species in this order, they spend much of their time perched on a bare branch, usually a high one, from which they make wheeling flights in pursuit of passing insects.

Rollers are active at dusk and appear to be able to see well enough to hunt in the half-dark.

At sunset and dusk the bird is particularly vociferous, giving out its very harsh 'kak-kak-kak', usually when in flight.

Nesting takes place in a hole high in a tree. Three to five white round eggs are laid and the breeding season is from October to December.

The name Dollar-bird derives from the conspicuous white spot on each wing. Roller is a name which refers to the bird's remarkable display flights, during which it rolls over as it flies and even somersaults in mid-air.

PASSERIFORMES

PERCHING BIRDS

The remainder of the birds in this book belong in the one order, the Passeriformes. This is by far the largest and most complex order of birds in the world and contains over half the living species.

Although an extremely diverse order, containing such widely differing species as the birds of paradise and the honey-eaters, there are a number of characteristics which inalienably link them all together.

The primary common feature is the perching foot, from which the group derives the name passeriforme or passerine. Passerines have four toes, three pointing forward and one directed backwards, none being webbed. It is a foot admirably suited and developed for perching—able to curl around a branch and grip tightly. The tendons of the leg are so arranged that as the bird relaxes—squatting lower—the toes are pulled into a tighter grip. So even while sleeping a passerine bird is safe upon its perch.

All species in the order hatch naked, or nearly so, helpless, and with their eyes closed. They are reared in the nest and do not leave it until the feathering is well developed; on leaving the nest they are fed for some time by their parents.

Passeriformes are found on all the major land masses and most islands throughout the world, being absent only from Antarctica.

PITTIDAE

Pittas

These are largely terrestrial birds and when disturbed scurry off into the densest parts of the undergrowth. If they are put into the air, pittas fly direct and fast on rapidly beating wings. Pittas have no 'song' but call with loud double or triple whistles. Although they spend the daylight hours on the ground hunting for food, at night they roost in trees, like many ground-frequenting species.

BUFF-BREASTED PITTAS, *Pitta versicolor*, are found down coastal eastern Australia from Cape York to central N.S.W. They are birds of the dense forest and big scrub areas, spending most of their time on the ground where they hunt for snails and insects. A bird will often have a favourite anvil-stone upon which it breaks open snail-shells. Small berries and other native fruits are also included in this bird's diet.

They are inquisitive and can be attracted to within a short distance by a whistled imitation of their loud call, which has been described as 'walk-to-work' or 'want-to-watch'. A single mournful note is also uttered, sometimes during the night.

The nest is a large loosely-built affair of dead twigs and moss; it is domed, with a circular entrance in one side. The nest site is usually on the ground between the sheltering buttress-roots of a large tree.

An odd habit of the pittas is their construction of a 'door-mat' of moist animal dung on the platform entrance to the nest, which is gradually carried into the nest chamber on the birds' feet.

MENURIDAE

Lyrebirds

The lyrebirds have been made familiar by their depiction on crests and emblems of various kinds throughout the country, although the tail is usually represented in a position never assumed by the bird.

Their fine voice is almost equally famous, and justly so, for the birds have a variety of rich notes of their own and are superb mimics. By the time lyrebirds are a few years old they will have the notes of most of the local birds in their repertoire. Even the unbirdlike kookaburra's chuckle will be heard from time to time. Sounds such as the whine of a circular saw, trucks changing gear, the barking of dogs and other sounds are incorporated into the lyrebirds' 'songs'.

There are two species, although it is surprising how many people, especially in Victoria, are unaware of the fact. The range of both starts in coastal Queensland but only SUPERB LYREBIRDS, *Menura superba* or *M. novae-hollandiae*, extend into Victoria. The other birds, the PRINCE ALBERT LYREBIRDS, *M. alberti*, are found only as far south as the Richmond River area in north-east N.S.W.

Superb Lyrebirds have a rather more handsome tail, and display to a much greater extent than the northern birds; the Superbs also construct display arenas, whereas the other species do not, indulging in lesser displays in any open spot on the forest floor. In the matter of voice, however, the Prince Alberts are almost as accomplished as their relatives, having a rich song of their own and being great mimics.

Both species are unusual in that they nest in the winter. During the summer months the lyrebirds are not particularly vociferous. They spend their days quietly hunting for food amongst the debris on the forest floor. Their feet are very large and the claws long and curved, making efficient raking instruments.

During autumn the male Superb Lyrebirds become more and more animated, and they begin to sing a great deal through the day—where before they tended to sing only early in the morning and at dusk. Part of this autumn activity is the building or renovating of the display mounds. Each male bird might have up to a dozen or so in his territory. These are prepared by clearing out a circular patch in the bracken or other underbrush. By dint of much trampling, biting and scratching, a space from four to six feet across is reduced to bare earth and a mound perhaps nine inches high is scraped up in the centre. Although quite a number of these mounds are prepared within each bird's territory, he

BUFF-BREASTED PITTA 8¼ in

PRINCE ALBERT LYREBIRD 27 in.

♂

PRINCE ALBERT LYREBIRD

♀

SUPERB LYREBIRD 27 in.

♀

♂

will have two or three favourites which are used more frequently than the rest. Some mounds even become time-honoured display spots that may be used for a decade or more by different generations of birds.

In the height of the breeding season from May to September the lyrebird might display a number of times each day.

After scratching at the mound for a moment or two and strutting about upon it he gives out a strange churring sound —the prelude—and then he bursts into song. The long tail is sometimes thrown forward over the bird's body, becoming a shimmering veil of silver filaments that rapidly vibrate as the rich and varied song comes pouring forth. This must surely be one of the most powerful and melodious bird voices in the world. Not content with his own voice the lyrebird soon launches into mimicry, mixing into his own song that of practically every species that would be found in the locality.

Sometimes the female might visit her displaying mate, but not for long. She steps up on to the mound and he comes forward to cover her with his shining tail which now vibrates more rapidly than ever. The song pours out, loud and clear and perhaps they touch bills momentarily before she turns and springs off into the undergrowth leaving the male to display alone.

As well as the song and tail-shimmering display, the lyre-bird also occasionally 'dances', stepping forwards, sideways, and backwards in a regular movement. With his body swaying rhythmically from side to side the bird emits a 'clonk clonk' sound, now and then jumping from one foot to another. The whole performance—the magnificent tail, beautiful voice, and the ceremonial dance make up one of the most fascinating sights in the bird world.

Superb Lyrebirds are found in the hills of coastal eastern Australia, from the Dandenong Ranges near Melbourne to the Stanthorpe area in Queensland. They frequent thickly timbered gullies and hill-slopes and, except for a few birds that come into frequent contact with people in national parks, they are secretive and wary.

Although such terrestrial birds, spending most of their time raking over the debris of the forest floor in search of food, at night they retire to the top of a tall tree to roost. Apparently not powerful fliers, the birds ascend in short flapping jumps from branch to branch. In the morning they fly down to earth in a long impressive glide.

Prince Albert Lyrebirds are similar except that they are slightly smaller, are more rufous in colouring and have a less spectacular tail. They have become rather rare throughout much of their range due to the clearing of their rain-forest habitats. One of their strongholds is the McPherson Range in Queensland.

ALAUDIDAE

Larks

BUSHLARKS, *Mirafra javanica*, are found in suitable habitats from the Carnarvon District in Western Australia through northern and eastern Australia to eastern South Australia.

In open grassy country these birds may be quite common, and are seen in pairs or flocks of various sizes. Large numbers sometimes travel and feed together outside the breeding season.

A singing bird flutters high up into the air, hanging now and then on rapidly beating wings, while it pours out a rich song which is similar to that of the British Skylark.

In the field they may be confused with Australian pipits and introduced Skylarks, but they have much heavier, almost finch-like bills. On the ground they run and walk rapidly, but not as quickly as the pipits, nor do they wag their tails up and down as the pipits do. The diet of Bushlarks is grass-seeds and insects.

They mimic the songs of other birds to some extent and may often be heard on moonlit nights. The nest is usually beneath the shelter of a tussock or boulder and is a domed grass ball with an entrance in one side.

SKYLARKS, *Alauda arvensis*, are found in southern South Australia, Victoria, Tasmania and southern N.S.W. Early in the 1850s these famed singers were introduced into Victoria from Britain. Skylarks have thrived in this country and may be heard in the spring and summer in most open grassy habitats. They appear to be less common in N.S.W. than elsewhere.

The song, so extolled by the poets, is similar to that of the Bushlarks. Skylarks might, in fact, easily be confused in the field with them, but are rather more heavily built birds.

SKYLARK 7 in.

PIPIT 7 in.

BUSHLARK .5 in.

WHITE-BACKED SWALLOW 5½ in.

♂

WELCOME SWALLOW 6½ in.

FAIRY MARTIN 4½ in.

TREE MARTIN 5 in.

HIRUNDINIDAE

Swallows

WELCOME SWALLOWS, *Hirundo neoxena*, are our best-known swallows and general favourites, their common name indicating the pleasure with which their return is noted each spring. They are distributed throughout most of Australia and Tasmania except for the far north of the continent.

On the whole they are migratory, but on a sunny day in winter a few will sometimes appear where there were none before, so presumably some stay south all the winter.

These swallows have delicate twittering songs and often a number of them will sing at once as they sit along a fence or telegraph wire. They feed on flying insects.

The nest is a cup of mud pellets strengthened with odd pieces of grass and straw. The eggs are laid in a deep lining which is usually feathers, but may have a mixture of hair and grass through it.

WHITE-BACKED SWALLOWS, *Cheramoeca leucosterna*, are largely birds of the interior, extending to the coast in only a few places. Usually in small communities they frequent open country in the vicinity of a creek or river. They are nomadic as a rule, their movements being governed, no doubt, by water conditions and the consequent insect population.

They take shelter during cold windy weather and a number of birds may often be found nesting in the one nesting burrow.

This nest burrow is up to three feet long and is dug into the bank of a creek or in a similar situation. At the end is a nesting chamber lined with leaves and grass.

Martins

FAIRY MARTINS, *Hylochelidon ariel*, are common birds throughout most of Australia except the driest parts, but is rare in Tasmania.

In flocks of various sizes, these pretty little birds may be seen in the vicinity of creeks and rivers, where they fly back and forth in pursuit of insects. They often favour a locality where there is a bridge for them to build under. Nomadic on the whole, they will sometimes remain in the locality if the weather remains mild and insects abound. The nest is an interesting bottle-shaped structure of mud pellets. Dozens may be built adjoining each other so that the collection of nests appears as a number of short-tunnelled entrances to a great irregular mass of mud pellets. The nesting site may be under some projection on a building, beneath an overhanging river bank or under a bridge.

TREE MARTINS, *H. nigricans*, are found throughout most of Australia and Tasmania except in the very dry parts; they also become less common further north except when on migration. Outside Australia, they are also found in Timor, New Guinea, the Moluccas and the Aru Islands.

Tree Martins migrate to southern Australia from these northern islands, arriving in flocks about August, and departing towards the end of March. Some birds will remain in the south throughout a mild winter.

The nest is usually built in a hollow tree or in a rock crevice or cave. Sometimes the birds utilise buildings, but not as frequently as their relatives the Fairy Martins. A suitable hollow is lined with grass and leaves and a large entrance hole may be partly sealed off with mud. They usually nest in proximity to other Tree Martins but occasional pairs nest alone.

CAMPEPHAGIDAE

Cuckoo-shrikes

BLACK-FACED CUCKOO-SHRIKES, *Coracina novae-hollandiae*, are perhaps the most familiar of this genus. They may often be seen in suburbs where large trees are plentiful. They also have a soft churring call, usually uttered in flight.

The flight is buoyant and undulating, and when the birds land they shuffle their wings a few times as though arranging them comfortably.

Out of the breeding season they may be seen in small flocks, and are partly nomadic, perhaps even migratory, in some districts. Their diet consists of insects, grubs and various berries.

They are faithful to a favoured breeding spot, some birds even returning to build in the very tree-fork previously used.

The nest is a slight, saucer-shaped platform of twigs and spider-webs, placed on the horizontal fork of a branch. It is usually about twenty to forty feet high, but may be as low as four feet.

LITTLE CUCKOO-SHRIKES, *C. robusta*, are found from eastern Queensland down to Victoria and south-eastern South Australia.

These are typical cuckoo-shrikes and may be seen in pairs or small parties outside the breeding season. They have the buoyant flight of the family and call 'kiseek-kiseek' as they fly. They appear to be nomadic, following the seasonal increases in insects and their larvae. Although they feed mainly in the foliage of trees, they also catch insects on the wing.

PAPUAN CUCKOO-SHRIKES, *C. papuensis*, are birds of the north, as their name suggests. Outside Australia they are found in the Molucca Islands, Papuan Islands and New Guinea. Their Australian range is restricted to north-eastern Queensland from the Cape York Peninsula to the Cooktown district.

They are similar to the other cuckoo-shrikes in their habits, calling wheezily in flight and being mainly arboreal in their feeding. Their diet consists mainly of insects and their larvae. Open forest country and coastal mangroves are the typical habitats of this cuckoo-shrike. The nest and eggs closely resemble those of the White-breasted Cuckoo-shrikes.

GASCOYNE CUCKOO-SHRIKES, *C. gascoynensis*, are found in the vicinity of the Gascoyne River in mid-western Australia. These birds are now known to be but a paler northern race of the Black-faced Cuckoo-shrikes and not a full species. The bird figured in the illustration is an immature specimen of the pale type. It was one of these that was described as a separate species. Neither the nest nor the eggs of the northern form have been described although they will probably prove to be similar to those of the Black-faced Cuckoo-shrikes.

GROUND CUCKOO-SHRIKES, *Pteropodocys maxima*, are somewhat aberrant members of the family and are placed in a different genus. They are far more terrestrial than their relatives, although the other cuckoo-shrikes do forage on the ground occasionally. They have fairly long tails and are rather stout-legged birds. When they are on the ground they walk and run rather than hop.

They are distributed generally throughout the interior of Australia becoming less common in the north. They seldom visit coastal areas except in the west. These cuckoo-shrikes are often seen in small flocks or family parties and they frequent sparsely timbered countryside.

LITTLE CUCKOO-SHRIKE
10½ in.

Immature

PAPUAN
CUCKOO-SHRIKE
11 in.

GASCOYNE CUCKOO-SHRIKE 13 in.

BLACK-FACED
CUCKOO-SHRIKE
13 in.

GROUND CUCKOO-SHRIKE 13 in.

73

WHITE-WINGED TRILLER 6¼ in.

♀

WHITE-WINGED TRILLER ♂

♂

VARIED TRILLER 7 in.

♀

the males are responsible for much of the nest building and incubating.

The nest is a typical 'cuckoo-shrike' platform of light twigs, rootlets and grasses, bound and matted together with cobwebs. It is built into the horizontal fork of a branch at any height from a few feet to thirty or so.

VARIED TRILLERS, *L. leucomela*, are found in the coastal areas of the Northern Territory, eastern Queensland and down as far as north-eastern N.S.W. Unlike the previous bird they are not migratory, but they do appear to be nomadic in degrees depending on local conditions and insect populations. Also, they are less vociferous than the White-winged Trillers, their chief call being a soft insect-like 'karr-rr'.

They feed on insects and their larvae, and various native fruits, which they hunt for on the ground and through the foliage. The edges of jungles and scrub are the typical habitats of these trillers.

The nest is a small saucer-shaped platform of rootlets and grass, bound together with spider-webs, and it is usually built into the horizontal fork of a branch only a few feet from the ground.

DICRURIDAE

Drongos

The sole representatives of this family in Australia are the SPANGLED DRONGOS, *Chibea bracteata*, found from north-western Australia to northern Queensland and southwards to eastern Victoria. Drongos are considered to be accidental wanderers in Tasmania. Outside Australia they also occur in New Guinea.

These handsome, glossy birds are frequenters of both the jungle and the more open forest country. They tend to be migratory, coming down from the north in October and departing again in March. On the whole they are a northern species, but a few spread down as far as south-eastern N.S.W., and more rarely into the east Gippsland forest country of Victoria. In the north a few birds remain with us all the year. Drongos will usually be seen perched on some exposed vantage point from which they make sallies in pursuit of insects. Launching out, they fly strongly, twisting and banking after a flying beetle or large butterfly. The prey is

Their call notes have been described as a high-pitched 'chee-er, chee-er', and 'kee-lik, kee-lik'. The alarm call is a loud 'queel'. They frequently call whilst on the wing.

Ground Cuckoo-shrikes are not common, but where they do occur they tend to gather together, sometimes even nesting in proximity. They carry their communal existence to the stage where a number of adult birds will be found indiscriminately feeding the young birds of two or more nests that are built close to each other.

Trillers

WHITE-WINGED TRILLERS, *Lalage sueurii*, are found throughout the continent generally, but are considered to be very rare visitors to Tasmania. These birds migrate to Australia from New Guinea and Timor, reaching the southern limits of their journey about September and departing again in February.

On the wing they often whistle their call of 'joey-joey' as they fly buoyantly amongst the scattered timber.

In some years these birds are noticeably common but are inexplicably scarce during others. Their diet is insects and caterpillars for which they hunt amongst foliage and on the ground. Although such conspicuous black and white birds,

74

SPANGLED DRONGO

12 in.

RAVEN   20 in.

LITTLE CROW   18½ in.

brought back to the perch and devoured there. Small birds are sometimes attacked and they also supplement their diet with berries and other fruits.

They are very noisy, their scolding chattering notes being uttered both while perched and in flight. Some birds are also quite able mimics. The nest is an open shallow saucer, composed of vine tendrils, rootlets and plant stems. It is usually built into the forked branch of a bushy tree at heights of up to fifty feet or so.

CORVIDAE

Crows and Ravens

Amongst this family are some of the birds best known by the general public. They are regarded with mixed feelings, probably with the scales weighted against them in general. Crows and Ravens have usually been associated in literature with the sinister or the mysterious and many farming people regard them with disfavour.

In most countries Crows have thrived in spite of (perhaps in some cases, because of) man and his activities. They are omnivorous feeders and show great sagacity in avoiding danger and traps. Most people in the country feel that a Crow or a Raven can tell the difference between a man with a gun and one without; they are even said to be able to distinguish between a gun and a stick.

The *Corvidae* are considered by many ornithologists to have highly developed brains and for this reason they are often placed high on the evolutionary scale. Much of the evidence supporting 'intelligence' is rather anthropomorphic, although the family does show considerable learning and adaptive ability. They also appear to 'play', like the Ravens of Gibraltar. I have an eye-witness account of these birds disporting themselves on a flight of steps. A number of them would spend considerable time hopping up one of the long flights of steps on the Rock, giving a 'caw' at each jump.

Upon reaching the top each bird would turn and launch itself into space to glide down to the bottom and start its next ascent. It would be difficult to explain such unproductive behaviour except in terms of recreation.

Most of the *Corvidae* will become quite tame, especially if reared from nestlings, and with patience they can be taught a few words.

CROWS, *Corvus cecilae*, are found throughout northern Australia and south as far as northern South Australia, as well as Western Australia and, occasionally, Victoria. In the latter State it extends further south but not into the south-west corner which is the domain of the raven. These birds are found in most types of country where they are likely to be able to find food. Mountain ranges and tree-bordered waterways are probably their favourite haunts. Crows are also common on some beaches. They are omnivorous feeders, taking carrion of all kinds, insects, small animals, young birds and eggs, and fruit including cultivated varieties.

Crows are persecuted a good deal by pastoralists, but apparently with little effect on their numbers. They are accused of killing lambs, but rarely do so. Their activities in clearing up carrion must contribute significantly to the control of blow-flies. Crows may be distinguished from ravens by the snow-white bases to the body feathers. The call is a varying number of short 'ka-ka-ka' sounds.

The nest is a solid construction of sticks and twigs with a deep cup. It is lined with grass, horse hair or wool. It is usually high in the forked branches of a tree but in treeless country may be on a telegraph pole or on the platform of a windmill pump.

RAVENS, *C. coronoides*, are distributed from the Rockhampton district in Queensland down through south-eastern Australia on the Eyre Peninsula. These birds are also found in the south-west corner of the continent and are common in Tasmania.

In the country, Ravens are wary birds and difficult to approach, although in the suburbs they often take little

WHITE-WINGED CHOUGH 16 in.

MUDLARK 10½ in.

nough notice of humans. They are birds of the open country on the whole, 'flighting' at dusk, back to some nearby wooded area to roost. Ravens have a variety of coarse cawing notes that are a familiar sound in most parts of the bush.

Omnivorous by necessity, they seem to prefer a flesh diet when it is obtainable. They are great scavengers and even visit beaches in search of tide-line offal.

Large numbers of insects are consumed by these birds but they are still most unpopular with farmers and graziers because of their depredations amongst lambing ewes. They are also considerable robbers of birds' nests, taking both young and eggs.

Ravens are rather larger than Crows and have strongly lanceolate feathering under the throat. They may also be identified (in the hand) by the dusky bases of the body feathers compared with the snow-white of the Crow.

GRALLINIDAE

Mudlarks

MUDLARKS or MAGPIE LARKS, *Grallina cyanoleuca*, are probably the best-known birds of this family. They are found throughout most of Australia where there is fresh water and are common in most towns and cities. They are a useful species, as they feed on many harmful insects, and eat fresh-water snails which harbour the fluke parasite that causes damage to the liver of sheep and cattle.

Their loud calls are also well known and they are one of the few species to sing in duet. Two birds will perch in the branches of a tree, one calling 'tee-o-wit' and the other immediately answering 'tee-tee'. It is a high, somewhat raucous sound and difficult to describe. As they call in perfect time they vigorously open and shut their wings in synchronisation. The 'tee-o-wit' call is also uttered as the birds fly. Mudlarks pair for life and will nest in the same place in successive years, even repairing their old nest or building on the same bough.

Their flight may be erratic and lapwinged, especially when they are excited, or direct with a full flapping motion of the wings. In the spring, mudlarks indulge in wild aerial antics. Two or three birds will chase each other at great speed in and out of the tree-tops with amazing agility. Now and then they will tower up into the air, twisting and turning and almost tumbling about in space, before plunging back to tree-top level. They call as they go, and one bird might perch for a moment to give full voice, until almost knocked off the branch by a power-diving companion.

The nest is a mud bowl built onto a fairly stout branch or limb, and usually near or overhanging water. It is reinforced with grass and lined with grass or occasionally, feathers. Very frequently a wagtail will build its nest on a lower branch of the same tree or one nearby.

Choughs

WHITE-WINGED CHOUGHS, *Corcorax melanorhamphus*, inhabit the inland areas of central Queensland, N.S.W., Victoria and South Australia. In some places in N.S.W. its range extends to the coast.

These rather mysterious birds are usually seen feeding in small parties on the ground. When approached, they fly up into nearby trees with strange grating cries and mournful whistles. They are very restless and hop heavily from branch to branch elevating and spreading their tails and staring down out of deeep red eyes. As they fly, the large white area in the wing is very noticeable. If one of a party of these birds is shot or wounded in some way its fellows do not fly off, but hop around the fallen bird calling in a dismal hooting manner.

WHITE-BACKED MAGPIE 18 in.

Choughs feed on insects and their larvae which they sometimes dig deeply for in the ground, and they also take seeds and berries. They have also been known to raid the nests of other birds for the young fledglings.

The nest is a rather large bowl-shaped mud or cow-dung construction which is reinforced with grass. It is usually lined with dry grass, bark-fibre or pieces of wool and built on a sturdy branch at heights from twenty to sixty feet. A number of birds will co-operate in the building of a nest which will then be laid in by two or more hen birds. The young will also be raised by a group of adults. A pair of choughs, however, will quite frequently nest on their own.

CRACTICIDAE

Magpies

Australian 'magpies' are not related to the birds of that name in Europe but to a genus peculiar to Australia, and known, more strictly, as piping crow-shrikes. However, it is extremely unlikely that their more popular name will ever be changed.

WHITE-BACKED MAGPIES, *Gymnorhina hypoleuca*, are our most common and are found from south-eastern N.S.W. down to Victoria and southern South Australia; they are also common in Tasmania but are rarely seen in Queensland.

They have adapted quite readily to living in closely cultivated country and have also moved into towns and cities. They visit suburban gardens and city parks quite freely and often nest in such places. During the nesting season these birds become very pugnacious and territory-conscious. They will drive off most birds and attack cats, dogs and humans with a great show of ferocity. Diving low at an intruder the birds

77

GREY BUTCHER-BIRD
11½in.

will strike with their wings or bill, and it is a quite unnerving experience to be the recipient of these attentions.

The voice of the magpies is justly famed, and the bird is considered by many people to be one of our best songsters. Alfred Russel Wallace, a great naturalist and traveller, felt that no European bird was a more gifted songster. The rich medley of warbling notes certainly has a wild and splendid sound, especially when heard on a fine spring morning or on moonlight nights.

Magpies have some strange nesting habits, especially in country where there are few trees. They build on telegraph poles to such an extent in some areas that the authorities have been obliged to put up nesting-baskets for them. Odd materials such as old lengths of cloth and large pieces of paper are often used. Some nests found have had varying amounts of wire in them, or have even been entirely of wire.

Butcher-birds

GREY BUTCHER-BIRDS, *Cracticus torquatus*, are found from the Gulf of Carpentaria to south-eastern Australia and across to South Australia: they extend north to Alice Springs and the Ashburton River and out to the coast in mid-western Australia. They are also common in Tasmania, where they move into suburban and city gardens in the autumn.

Considered by many to be among our best songsters, the birds have a series of rolicking warbling notes and loud whistles. Their song is at its richest in autumn.

They have the shrike-like habit of making a 'larder' where they hang small lizards, insects, mice and birds. Their prey is impaled on a thorn or other sharp spike, and such spikes are also used by the birds to help tear up their food. Butcher-birds also wedge their prey into a forked branch for the same purpose.

They are bold birds, and will even kill caged birds and drag them out through the wires of the cage. Their boldness also makes them tameable, and they can often be trained to feed from the hand.

A cup-shaped nest, rather untidily constructed, is built in the fork of a branch, from a few feet up to sixty feet off the ground. The nest is neatly lined with rootlets and fine grass and three, four, or more rarely five, eggs are laid. These may be grey-green, grey-blue, olive or light brown, marked with dull reddish-brown. The females do most (perhaps all) of the incubating, and are sometimes fed at the nest by their mates.

PTILONORHYNCHIDAE

Bower-birds

Bower-birds are remarkable architects, constructing bower which the male bird decorates and in which he courts th female bird; the males also appear to 'play' in these bower quite apart from any courtship displaying. No other birds i the world go to such trouble or build such elaborate structure that are not used for nesting. Some of the bowers are so larg that it seems impossible that they could be built by one sma bird; indeed, early explorers imagined that they must b the play houses of native children.

The most 'practical' use to which the bowers are put is t attract the female birds, since the males display there mating often takes place within the bowers and this is usuall the last that the male birds have to do with domesticity The females go off alone, build the nest and rear the youn It may be that there is polygamy amongst bower-birds bu this has yet to be proved.

Bower-birds can be divided into three groups according t the complexity of their bowers. Some build fairly simpl platforms, another group builds around the central suppor of a small tree and the third group builds a walled avenue c sticks and sometimes paints the walls with a mixture of saliv and various natural substances.

SATIN BOWER-BIRDS, *Ptilonorhynchus violaceus*, inhabit easter Australia from the Atherton Tableland to the Otway Rang in Victoria. Living in pairs during the breeding season, the gather into small flocks during the autumn and winter These groups are largely made up of females and youn males, who are less shy than the fully mature, deep blu males. There is some evidence to suggest that the female attain the blue plumage when they grow old. (A. H. Chis holm: *Bird Wonders of Australia*.)

Satin Bower-birds are not uncommon in the coastal brus country throughout their range. Their call is a vigorou 'cheroo' or 'whee-ooo' and a number of curious churrin sounds. They are also habitual mimics, adding to thei repertoire as they grow older.

In the autumn and winter, when in flocks, they sometime raid orchards, doing considerable damage amongst sof fruits. Their natural diet is wild fruit of various kind supplemented with insects.

The bower is a platform of fine sticks and twigs, about

ot long, from which rise two walls fifteen to eighteen inches igh. These walls are arched inwards and sometimes meet verhead making a graceful vault. Whilst the bower is in se, throughout the spring and summer, decorations are onstantly being added and perishable additions such as lowers are renewed. Satin Bower-birds are attracted by nything blue, which is interesting when one considers that he male is a deep blue and both sexes have china-blue eyes.

The following are objects found in a Satin Bower-bird's ower, listed by Alec Chisholm:

Eight bluebags, 10 pieces of blue matchboxes, 1 blue cigarette packet, 1 blue envelope, 1 piece of blue string, 34 pieces of blue glass, 17 blue feathers, 1 blue marble, 1 ticket with blue printing, 4 blue chocolate papers, a blue invitation card, 8 yellowish wood-shavings, a piece of yellow-green onion peel, 8 snail-shells, 1 cocoon, 6 cicada cases, numbers of blue and yellowish-green flowers and a very large quantity of yellowish-green leaves.

f such oddments are not available to a bird living away from uman habitation, such things as flowers will be used, large umbers being strewn about the bower and constantly re- ewed as they wither.

There is one interesting case of a Satin Bower-bird turning redator. An aviculturalist found that a number of his lue-coloured finches were disappearing; he eventually dis- overed that a Satin Bower-bird in the same aviary was illing them and taking them off to decorate its bower.

The deep satiny-blue plumage of the males is not assumed or some time (probably a number of years) and during this ime their colouring is similar to the green of the females: ut at all ages, the juvenile males' green bills distinguish hem from females, which have horn-coloured bills.

The young, green males construct rudimentary bowers and umbers of young birds will gather at these; sometimes as many as ten or fifteen may be seen. A sketchy bower, often just a few sticks laid together, may sometimes be found in an open spot. It may be that this is made by a female or perhaps a young male. But there is nothing communal about the full-scale, decorated bower of an old male bird. It is jealously guarded and displayed in by the builder alone.

In the spring the display dance reaches its height. The bird stalks into the bower, rearranges a few ornaments per- haps, and then begins to dance. With a churring sound deep in its throat, the bird steps along the platform; now with wings drooping to the ground, now raised until they arch above his shining blue back. With feathers puffed out all over his body, the bird then minces on tiptoe all about his stage, and all the time keeping up the churring note as a strange accompaniment to the weird dance.

In addition the Satin Bower-bird paints the sticks of the arbour. Bringing a bundle of small pieces of fibrous bark to the edge of the bower, the bird picks one up in its bill, drawing it right into its mandibles. The 'paint' appears to be vegetable juices or charcoal mixed with saliva, and the wad of soft bark is half paint brush and half cork, to retain the painting mixture in the bird's bill. Each stick along the wall of the bower will be carefully and slowly coated with the mixture.

The nest of the Satin Bower-bird, built and attended upon entirely by the female, is an open, rather shallow cup of small twigs lined with soft dry leaves. It is usually built into the fork of a tree or in a clump of mistletoe at a height of ten to fifty feet. Two, or sometimes three, eggs are laid that are a dark cream colour, spotted with brown and slate-grey. The breeding season is from October to December.

SPOTTED BOWER-BIRDS, *Chlamydera maculata*, inhabit the interior of Queensland and range down through inland N.S.W. to north-western Victoria and the upper Murray River in South Australia. In some districts in Queensland they are also found near the coast where suitable habitats occur.

In pairs or small flocks these are birds of scrub and open forest country. Spotted Bower-birds will often settle for a time near homesteads, becoming a nuisance in the garden and orchard.

They are remarkable mimics; such things as the twanging of wire fences, the scream of a rabbit and creaking branches are all faithfully rendered, and dogs barking, the croak of frogs, rattling gravel and the whistling wings of crested pigeons are all on the list of mimicry.

There is a report of a bird imitating thunder so well that it deceived a person, and another bird rendering the sound of three people all talking at once.

Their bower is usually built beneath the low branches of a tree or shrub. It is an avenue or longish platform with the walls constructed of dried grass, or, rarely, sticks. Sometimes the tops of the walls droop over making an archway.

If they show a preference for any colour it is white; bones and pebbles being commonly brought to the arbour. An in- teresting fact is that, should any green berries brought in turn ripe and become red, they are always taken away. Almost anything that the birds can pick up will be brought back to the bower, and they even steal things from houses and cars. One bower in N.S.W. had 320 bones and another contained approximately 2,500 snail shells, all of which indicates con- siderable labour on the part of the bird.

Spotted Bower-birds appear to use their bowers throughout most of the year, and not just for spring-time displaying. In some cases, congregations of these birds have been reported at one arbour.

Although it is not uncommon to find bowers, their nests are harder to find. They are saucers of small sticks, lined with smaller twigs or sometimes with dry grass, and built at heights up to about thirty feet in bushy trees.

SPOTTED BOWER-BIRD

12in.

79

PARADISE RIFLE-BIRD 11½in.

The two eggs are greenish-yellow, covered with lines of umber and blackish-brown over grey markings. They are beautiful with the tracery of lines forming interesting patterns. The breeding season is usually from October to December.

There is an interesting account of the display of a Spotted Bower-bird in *Birds of Western Australia* (Serventy and Whittell) which is freely drawn on here.

The male bird fluffs out his feathers, displaying his beautiful pink mantle to great advantage. With harsh cries he advances into the middle of the playground, making a vigorous attack upon some decorative object lying nearby. He advances and retreats, hops from side to side and jumps into the air, and then with much apparent ferocity rushes at his female who stands close by. She will respond with a short harsh cry at times, but on the whole, appears to regard her mate's demonstrations as hardly worthy of notice.

This display may last for an hour or more and while it progresses, other bower-birds will squat about in the branches overhead; occasionally one of them might utter a harsh cry almost as though applauding or encouraging.

Eventually the displaying male hops up into the tree and the flock flies off together.

The mantle on the hind-neck mentioned above is a rose or lilac-pink colour and is assumed by adult males and eventually by elderly female birds. This strange pink colour is very rare in the bird world, although this pink 'cape' is present in all the *Chlamydera*.

PARADISAEIDAE

Birds of Paradise

The stronghold of the Bird of Paradise family is, of course, New Guinea and the neighbouring islands. They have not been closely studied on the whole, and some species are known only by a few museum specimens that have been collected, without any accompanying data, by native hunters.

The knowledge of the existence of these birds, however, dates back to before the sixteenth century. Skins were brought into the Orient by Chinese traders and voyagers, and the first seen in Europe were sent to the King of Spain in Magellan's ship *Victoria* in 1522.

It did not seem credible that such unbelievably beautif[u] creatures could possibly live on the earth, and the Spaniar[d] decided that they must be visitors from paradise—and Bir[d] of Paradise they have been ever since.

The bulk of skins coming into Europe in the early day[s] were prepared by natives, who removed the legs for ease [o] skinning. Thus, all kinds of fanciful and charming tal[e] arose about birds that never alighted. They were said t[o] live entirely on the wing, and to fly continually towards th[e] sun. Females laid their aerial eggs in holes on the ma[le] bird's back.

In the latter half of the nineteenth century the demand f[o] the skins for trimming women's hats and other garments w[a] extensive. During the last two decades of the centur[y] approximately 50,000 skins a year were being taken out [of] New Guinea. This means that the horrifying total of som[e] thing like one million of these beautiful birds were killed— probably rather more, as the export of them was not banne[d] in New Guinea until the 1920s.

The four species that we have in Australia are not among[st] the most gorgeous. PARADISE RIFLE-BIRDS, *Ptiloris paradise[u]* have the widest range of any of the group in this country an[d] are found from the Mackay district in Queensland down [a] far as the Hunter River in N.S.W.

These handsome birds frequent the forest and big brus[h] country of the coast and coastal ranges. The males hav[e] full, bird of paradise style of display, spreading their wing[s] throwing back their heads and turning this way and that t[o] show off the gleaming metallic hues. They have a speci[al] display perch as a rule, on the edge of a forest or overlookin[g] a gorge or valley.

The diet of Paradise Rifle-birds is native fruits and insect[s] The insects they gather by probing into crevices in trees [o] lifting the bark. Their call is a loud resounding doubl[e] screech.

In captivity these birds have been known to kill mice an[d] small birds and eat only the brains; whether they have [a] similar habit in the wild state is not known.

A shallow bowl-shaped nest is built of dead leaves and vin[e] tendrils. This is lined with finer stems and twigs and drape[d] with cast-off snake skins in the same manner as the Quee[n] Victoria bird's nest. It is hidden in the thicket of a mass [of] vines or other deep foliage near the top of a tall tree deep i[n]

he forest. Two reddish-cream eggs are laid, beautifully
arked with longitudinal streaks and spots of chestnut,
urple-red and grey. The breeding season is from October
 December.

CLIMACTERIDAE

Australian Treecreepers

he treecreepers of Australia do not appear to be closely
elated to the birds called creepers and treecreepers in other
arts of the world. The Northern Hemisphere birds really
o creep over the boles and limbs of trees, using their stiff,
ointed tail feathers as props to aid them in clinging on.
ur birds move swiftly and vigorously over the branches,
ripping with their long toes and standing up, with their
odies held well away from the bark.

Unlike sittellas, which work in every direction, treecreepers
art near the bottom of a tree and spiral upwards and per-
aps out along a limb. They then fly down to the bole of the
ext tree and begin another spiralling climb. They may also
e distinguished from sittellas by their noticeably curved bills
nd their tendency to remain in pairs, rather than flocks,
uring the non-breeding season.

The treecreepers are often known as 'woodpeckers' in the
ush, but are quite unrelated; we do not have any wood-
eckers in this country.

White-throated Treecreepers, *Climacteris leucophaea*, are
idely distributed and one of the more common of the groups.
hey are found from south-eastern Queensland down
rough central and coastal N.S.W. to Victoria; they also
xtend into south-eastern South Australia but are rare in
asmania where they have never been recorded as a
reeding species.

They are very vigorous birds, moving rapidly up the trunks
nd branches of trees in well-timbered country—sometimes
 quite dense forest. Unlike some other treecreepers they
re strictly arboreal and climb upwards in the manner
pical of the family.

These birds are usually seen in pairs and attention may be
rawn to them by their rich, very liquid bubbling notes,
eard in the spring and summer. They also have a shrill
ngle note which may be uttered quickly a number of times.

The nest is built in the hollow of a tree-trunk or in a
ollow branch, usually rather high up. The nesting hole is
ned with bark-fibres, wool and other soft material. Three
hite eggs are laid, which are sparsely marked with reddish
nd purplish-brown spots. The breeding season is from
ugust to December.

Little Treecreepers, *C. minor*, have a restricted range,
eing found only in north-eastern Queensland. They move
 pairs and inhabit the upland rain-forests. They are
milar in habits to the White-throated Treecreepers, hunting
r insects on the bark of tree-trunks and branches.

The nest is built in some hollow part of a tree, the cavity
eing lined with green moss and soft bark-fibres. Two
eamy-white eggs with small spots of reddish-brown and
le lilac are laid. The breeding season is from October to
ecember.

Red-browed Treecreepers, *C. erythrops*, are found in well-
mbered country in the coastal and mountain districts.
heir range extends from south-eastern Queensland to
ictoria.

These active little birds are usually seen in pairs and are
milar in habits to the White-throated Treecreepers, except
at they may frequent the lower parts of the trees. They
pidly work their way over tree-trunks and branches in a
pical treecreeper manner, always working upwards, and
ten in a spiral movement.

WHITE-THROATED TREECREEPER 6¼in.

LITTLE TREECREEPER 5in.

WHITE-BROWED TREECREEPER 5¼in.

RED-BROWED TREECREEPER 6in.

81

BLACK-CAPPED
SITELLA
4¼in.

STRIATED SITELLA
4¼in.

ORANGE-WINGED SITELLA
4¼in.

SITTIDAE

Sittellas

ORANGE-WINGED SITTELLAS, *Neositta chrysoptera*, are four from the extreme south-east of Queensland, through N.S.V to Victoria excepting the far western portion.

In pairs in the breeding season, or in small flocks at oth times of the year, these birds frequent open forest and oth well-timbered country.

They are very active little birds and run in all direction over the trunks and branches of trees, with a preference pe haps for the higher limbs and branches. They seem equal at home creeping along the undersides of the branches or eve working head-downwards as they probe into crevices beneath the strips of bark. Insects and grubs form the diet these birds.

Whilst feeding, and as they fly from tree to tree, they ke up an almost constant twittering. In flight the orange-ta patch on the wings is very noticeable.

The nest is a neatly built cup of plant-fibres, soft bark ar spider-webs. On the outside the nest is 'shingled' with ove lapping strips of bark, which usually closely resembles t adjoining live bark. The usual site is the upright fork of branch at any height from about five to fifty or sixty fe above the ground.

BLACK-CAPPED SITTELLAS, *N. pileata*, are found from t Pilbara district in Western Australia, through southern ar Central Australia to Alice Springs, and further eastwards western N.S.W. and western Victoria. They are probab the commonest and most widespread of the group.

Similar in habits to the Orange-winged Sittellas, they cree quickly but rather mousily over the branches to the trun In pairs whilst nesting, or in small flocks at other times, the frequent all kinds of timbered country.

Apparently quite unaffected by any discomfort, the readily hang upside-down or head-downwards in their searc for insects on and under the bark. The plain underparts ar black cap (a whole black head in the female) should serve distinguish them from the preceding species; they also hav an orange wing-patch. As they feed and move from tree tree a constant conversational twittering is kept up. In som areas they have been known to visit the suburbs in the winter flocks.

The nest is a beautifully decorated and well disguised ope cup. It is built of bark-fibres and other fine materia matted together with spider-web. Overlapping shingles bark, often neatly cut into regular shapes, are attached to t outside of the nest, making it most inconspicuous.

STRIATED SITTELLAS, *N. striata*, are confined to nort eastern Queensland, from Cape York to Inkerman.

In pairs, or in small flocks, both in and out of the breedin season, these birds are found in timbered country throughou their range. They have the reputation for being the mo active of the sittellas as they hunt for spiders, insects ar grubs in the bark of trees.

Striated Sittellas are similar in their habits to the oth *Neosittas*, working rapidly about the branches, probing in crevices and under bark with their sharp bills. They wo erratically in all directions and frequently progress hea downwards.

The nest is similar to those of their relatives: a small ne cup of bark-fibres and other soft materials. This is careful camouflaged with small shingles of bark.

As the small flocks of these sittellas feed and move throug the timber they continuously call in twittering notes, and they fly, a whitish wing-patch is noticeable.

Their call has been described as 'a rapid high-pitched hissing chatter'. Nesting takes place in the hollow of a tree, usually up to about forty feet from the ground. The nest is a felt of bark-fibres lined with fur. Two pinkish-white eggs are laid which have small spots of reddish-brown and dull purple. The breeding season is from August to January.

WHITE-BROWED TREECREEPERS, *C. affinis*, are widely distributed from central Western Australia, through central Australia to south-western Queensland, western N.S.W., north-western Victoria and inland South Australia.

Usually seen in pairs, these birds frequent timber and scrub-covered terrain, including mulga country. They may be seen searching tree-trunks and branches for insects in the typical treecreeper manner, or hunting for their food amongst fallen timber.

They are very quiet birds but the call notes are said to resemble those of the White-throated Treecreepers.

The nest is a felt of fur, grasses, soft bark and plant-down or any other soft material, placed usually at heights up to about thirty feet, in a hollow branch 'spout' or tree-trunk. Three pinkish-white eggs spotted with pinkish-red and purplish-red are laid. The breeding season is usually from September to December, but birds have been found breeding as late as May.

TIMALIIDAE

Babblers

GREY-CROWNED BABBLERS, *Pomatostomus temporalis*, are widely distributed, common and well-known birds. Their familiarity to country people is marked by the list of unofficial names such as Apostle-bird, Chatterer, Cackler, Catbird, Codlin-moth-eater, Arco, Happy Family Bird and Hopper.

Their range is from Cape York down through eastern and south-eastern Australia to eastern South Australia.

They are usually seen in small flocks of up to a dozen or so, moving through scrubland, open forest or belts of timber in farming country. They suit their name well, as they are very noisy and active birds. They spend a good deal of their time feeding on the ground where they forage for insects, and no doubt are beneficial to man.

With their wide variety of weird cackling notes and playful gymnastic habits, babblers are entertaining creatures, and are well thought of by most people in the bush. Many of the calls are difficult to describe but the loud 'arco' or 'ya-ho' is unmistakable once heard.

A large, untidy, dome-shaped nest is constructed of sticks and twigs. The entrance is a loose spout or tunnel leading into the well-lined nest chamber. Bark-fibres, wool, grass or any other soft materials may be used for lining the nest. Old nests are sometimes used in subsequent seasons, being repaired and added to, so that they may become surprisingly large for such relatively small birds. Usually babblers will nest close together (although I have found solitary nests), and sometimes even in the same tree.

The nest is built into the upright forks of a tree, usually only about twenty feet or so from the ground.

Grey-crowned Babblers are not a wandering species, and a flock will frequent one small patch of scrub or line of timber for a number of years, both in and out of the breeding season.

RED-BREASTED BABBLERS, *P. rubeculus*, appear to be but a central-western Australian form of the Grey-crowns rather than a full species. They are considerably redder on the underparts than *temporalis* but are similar in habits and life history.

The nest is a typical untidy, babbler construction of sticks, with an entrance spout, and lined with various soft materials. In the west the birds have sometimes been observed to change the lining of their nests after heavy rain, the loose roof of sticks affording little protection. It may be that the same thing takes place with other species of babblers.

WHITE-BROWED BABBLERS, *P. superciliosus*, are widely distributed throughout the inland areas of south-western Australia, central Australia, South Australia, southern Queensland, western N.S.W. and central and western Victoria.

They are gregarious birds and live in small flocks or family parties as a rule. Their chief habitats are scrub, open forest and belts of timber left standing on farmland.

Their harsh, animated chattering is a well-known sound in many country districts, and like the other babblers, they are usually a welcome species. Much of the time these birds may be seen foraging on the ground, where they destroy many injurious insects.

The nest is a bulky, untidy structure of twigs and small

GREY-CROWNED BABBLER
11in.

♀

♂

WHITE-BROWED BABBLER 8in.

HALL'S BABBLER 11in.

CHESTNUT-CROWNED BABBLER
8¼in.

RED-BREASTED BABBLER 9¼in.

83

SPOTTED QUAIL-THRUSH 10½in.

♀

♂

branches, with an entrance spout of longer twigs. The nest-chamber is lined with soft materials such as wool, bark-fibres or grass. Nests are built into the upright forks of trees, at heights from ten or twelve feet up to about twenty feet.

CHESTNUT-CROWNED BABBLERS, *P. ruficeps*, are birds of the interior, found from southern Queensland to western N.S.W., north-western Victoria and eastern South Australia. They are similar in habits and ecology to the other babblers, but are considered to be shyer.

In May 1963 a British Museum field party discovered a new species, WHITE-THROATED BABBLERS, *Pomatostomus halli*, or HALL'S BABBLERS, in honour of H. W. Hall, who financed the expedition.

The birds were discovered and the type specimens collected near Langlo Crossing in south-western Queensland; the extent of their range has not yet been entirely established although Sydney Museum ornithologists have recently discovered more about their distribution.

They generally resemble the White-browed Babblers but are broadly white on the throat and dark brown on the rest of the underparts. Their general habits will no doubt prove to be much the same as the other babblers.

Quail-thrushes

SPOTTED QUAIL-THRUSHES, *Cinclosoma punctatum*, extend from south-eastern Queensland down the eastern States to Tasmania, and westwards to the vicinity of Adelaide.

Almost always in pairs, they inhabit forest country and spend almost all their time upon the ground, preferring to run and hide rather than fly. Should one be put up, it flies off with a startling whirr of wings. After a short distance the bird will land, sometimes in a branch, to look around. More frequently it will dive back into thick cover and run off.

It is said that a pair of birds communicate with each other by means of a low whistle; should they become separated each whistles until reunited.

The food of these quail-thrushes is seeds and insects of various kinds.

84

COLLURICINCLA
[PACHYCEPHALIDAE]

Shrike-thrushes

No doubt the best known of our native shrike-thrushes a⟩ the GREY THRUSHES, *Colluricincla harmonica*, which are di⟩ tributed throughout much of eastern and south-eastern Au⟩ tralia, from Cape York to the Spencer Gulf in South Au⟩ tralia. They are also found on Kangaroo Island an⟩ Tasmania.

The Grey Thrushes were one of the first Australian singin⟩ birds (passerines) to be recorded and figured. In White⟩ *Journal of a Voyage to New South Wales*, published in 179⟩ there is an account and an interesting plate of the 'Po⟩ Jackson Thrush'.

These birds are found in a variety of habitats, and the⟩ seem as much at home in heavily timbered wet country as i⟩ the drier mallee and she-oke areas.

They are highly esteemed and famous for their beautif⟩ notes. Grey Thrushes come into full song in the spring an⟩ summer months, although there are records of the bir⟩ being quite vociferous at other times. In the early sprin⟩ the development of their song can be traced from a tentativ⟩ piping, which grows with the advancing season into a variet⟩ of rich whistling calls.

They are somewhat unusual in that they sometimes sin⟩ whilst feeding or searching on the ground for insect foo⟩ They will also call loudly immediately after a gunsho⟩ a habit they share with Rufous Whistlers.

Grey Thrushes become quite confiding if living nea⟩ humans, and will nest in close proximity to buildings, a⟩ though in the bush they are not a bold species.

They are, to a large degree, quite useful birds, consumin⟩ many insects; they are also particularly fond of spider⟩ Another habit, less endearing and less well known, is the⟩ nest robbing. Grey Thrushes quite frequently take the egg⟩ of other birds, and they will eat nestlings.

The nest is a rather bulky cup of bark, roots, grass an⟩ dead leaves which may be found in a variety of sites; th⟩ hollow of a broken-off limb, the top of a stump, in the up⟩ right fork of a tree, or sometimes hidden in herbage on th⟩ ground. Around dwelling places they will nest und⟩ verandahs or in any other suitable nook. Hollows in creek⟩ banks also provide nesting sites and even the disused home ⟨ a mudlark may be used.

BROWN THRUSHES, *C. brunnea*, are found in northern Au⟩ tralia from Roebuck Bay in the west to the Leichhardt Rive⟩ district in Queensland. They are said to be similar in habi⟩ to Grey Thrushes, but I have found few published observation⟩ of this bird. Brown Thrushes usually frequent forest countr⟩ and are seldom found in the type of dry, small-scrub are⟩ which the Grey Thrushes sometimes frequent.

LITTLE THRUSHES, *C. parvula*, are confined to north⟩ western Australia, from the Admiralty Gulf to Arnhe⟩ Land. They inhabit brush thickets and sometimes man⟩ groves, and favour the dense growth along creeks and rivers⟩ They are generally seen on or near the ground where the⟩ procure most of their food. Their diet is principally *col⟩ optera* but includes other insects of various kinds.

This species has a fine thrush-like song, very clear, lou⟩ and melodious. A great colour variation is noticeable i⟩ specimens of these birds from various localities.

SANDSTONE THRUSHES, *C. woodwardi*, are found in th⟩ north-west of the continent and Northern Territory, fron⟩ Napier Broom Bay to McArthur River. They haunt ope⟩ sandstone terrain and other rocky country. Little has bee⟩ observed of their habits; they are extremely shy and difficul⟩ to approach. All the observer sees as a rule is a glimpse o⟩

wo of the birds as they fly or hop from rock to rock. They
vill be exposed for a mere moment on some promontory
before diving into the shelter of a crevice or overhanging
rock. They may also be seen climbing vertical rock-faces in
he manner of a treecreeper.

They have strong and melodious voices typical of shrike-
hrushes. Their strong and melodious calls ring and echo
hrough the sandstone gorges in a most dramatic and stirring
manner. The food of this species is insects and other small
ry, all obtained upon the ground and from rock-faces.

RUFOUS THRUSHES, *C. megarhyncha*, are fairly well dis-
ributed in eastern Australia from Cape York to the Hastings
River district in N.S.W.; they also occur in New Guinea.

Gould was familiar with Rufous Thrushes, finding them
'tolerably common' in the thick brushes skirting the lower
Clarence and Richmond Rivers where, no doubt, they are
still as plentiful. They prefer to remain in thick growth, and
are seldom seen in more open country.

Like their relatives, Rufous Thrushes have a rich variety of
notes. One of their chief calls has been described as 'tu-whee,
wot-wot', and they also give more sustained songs at times,
and occasionally mimic other birds.

STRIPE-BREASTED THRUSHES, *C. boweri*, are found in the
highlands of north-eastern Queensland. Their chief haunts
are in the Ballenden Ker Range. They are true mountain
birds, being found in heavy rain-forests and never in any of
the low river-scrub areas.

They are not particularly shy, and are reported to fly
down readily to pick up an insect from near a person's feet.
Very little has been recorded of their habits, however. Their
song is loud and rich in the typical shrike-thrush manner;
they feed on insects.

GROUND-THRUSHES are considered by some authorities to
be *Turdus*, but by others are given the name *Oreocincla
lunulata*. They are found from northern and north-eastern
Queensland to Victoria and westwards as far as Adelaide.
They also inhabit Kangaroo Island, Tasmania, and some of
the Bass Strait islands.

They appear to be a resident species on the whole, although some birds may be more nomadic outside the breeding season. They tend to be found in the coastal districts and
the seaward-facing ranges, but in a few places they have
penetrated west of the Great Dividing Range and also into
some dry forests of central Victoria.

RUFOUS SHRIKE-THRUSH 7½ in

STRIPE-BREASTED SHRIKE-THRUSH
8½ in

GREY SHRIKE-THRUSH 9½ in.

LITTLE SHRIKE-THRUSH 7½ in

SANDSTONE SHRIKE-THRUSH
8½ in

BROWN SHRIKE-THRUSH
8½ in

GROUND-THRUSH 10½ in.

85

BLACKBIRD 10in.

♀

♂

SONG THRUSH 8¼in.

They may be seen hopping quietly about in the under-brush turning over leaves as they go, and stopping with head cocked as they watch or listen for insects. Worms, snails, grubs and anything of a similar nature are also eaten.

Ground-thrushes are retiring, but are not particularly shy birds. If disturbed they will often freeze, allowing one to walk past within a few feet, suggesting that they rely on their protective colouring to escape notice.

A single high-pitched whistle will occasionally be heard from them, and even more rarely, one might hear them sing a glorious blackbird-like song. Dawn and dusk are the times when their very beautiful voices are most likely to be heard.

TURDIDAE

Thrushes and Blackbirds

Song Thrushes, *Turdus philomelos*, were introduced into Victoria in about the middle of the last century. They were also introduced into Queensland and N.S.W. but have not notably thrived anywhere except around Melbourne. They are useful birds about the gardens, taking many snails and other pests, and contribute a fine rich voice to suburban bird song.

A bowl-shaped nest of grass, rootlets, straw and similar materials is lined with mud and built into the forked branch of a thick bush or low tree.

Blackbirds, *T. merula*, are found from central eastern N.S.W. down through Victoria to Tasmania and South Australia. Introduced in the 1860s they have thrived much more than thrushes. They have become very common in parks and gardens and have spread to many country areas. In some localities, particularly in Tasmania, the birds have become a considerable pest in soft-fruit orchards.

The nest is similar to, but larger than that of the thrush.

SYLVIIDAE

Old World Warblers

Brown Songlarks, *Cinclorhamphus cruralis*, may be found in most parts of Australia where suitable open grassy habitats permit. Grass plains and cultivated paddocks are their haunts. They are absent from Tasmania and, no doubt due to lack of suitable country, from Cape York.

They are a migratory species, moving north and south within the continent, and also perhaps, tending to move to more coastal plains in the breeding season. Brown Song larks usually put in an appearance in south-eastern Australia during September, and depart again for the plains o the interior about February. In the south-west they are considerably earlier, arriving in June and July, nesting through August and onwards and departing again by December and January.

They spend a good deal of time on the ground foraging for seeds and insects; males will also frequently be seen perched on some vantage point such as a fence-post, stump or dead tree, from which they will sing.

They indulge in song-flights, soaring upwards with their legs hanging down, often gliding, and giving vent to their curious, creaking song. This has been rendered as 'witchy-weedle' and 'whittacker-whittacker' and likened to the sound of a wheel turning on a rusty axle. The singing bird descends on fluttering wings with a more chuckling song. When perched, these songlarks will sometimes elevate their tails to an almost vertical position.

In the breeding season the male birds assume a very much darker plumage (quite black on the throat and breast) than during the remainder of the year. The males are consider-ably larger than the females, being up to three inches longer. The difference in size between the sexes in these birds and the Rufous Songlarks is unique amongst Australian passerine birds. The species also appears to be polygamous (Cayley).

Rufous Songlarks, *C. mathewsi*, are found throughout most parts of Australia where suitable, open grassy country allows. They are absent from such places as the heavily forested Cape York and the extreme south-west corner of the continent; neither are they found in Tasmania nor the forested mountains of eastern Australia.

They are somewhat similar in their habits to the Brown Songlarks except that they are found in more heavily timbered country. They are migrants to the southern part of the continent, arriving during August, September and October, and departing between December and February in different localities.

BROWN SONGLARK 9in.

RUFOUS SONGLARK

GOLDEN-HEADED FANTAIL-WARBLERS, or TAILOR-BIRDS, *Cisticola exilis*, are common birds throughout much of their range, and are one of the few species that have benefited from man's activities, rather than the reverse.

They are found throughout northern, eastern, and south-eastern Australia. The species also occurs sparingly on some Bass Strait islands and in the north of Tasmania. The species is largely coastal, but in a few suitable areas penetrates to the sub-interior.

Tailor-birds frequent swampy areas, standing crops and, more rarely, open, grassy paddocks. They are vociferous in the spring and summer, and draw attention to themselves with their persistent singing and lively flights, just above the herbage.

The male song is a buzzing 'zwitt-zwitt-zwitt', followed by two or three sharper notes. They sing on the wing a great deal but also from a perch. Their rapid, low and rather erratic flight ends with a sudden dive into cover. They are not shy birds, however, and will perch and sing within a few yards of one.

The nest of this species is built in low vegetation, often near the edge of water but not necessarily so. It is a very attractive domed nest with an entrance near the top. Constructed of fine grasses, it is bound together into a purse shape with spider-webbing; frequently, leaves are stitched on to the outside.

Tailor-birds go into an eclipse plumage. The golden crowns of the males become striped like the females, and both sexes grow noticeably longer tails. The singing displays cease, and the birds tend to congregate in loose flocks, to feed in crops and other concealing vegetation. The diet of the birds is moths, grubs, grasshoppers and various other small insects.

Our REED-WARBLERS, *Acrocephalus australis*, are closely related to the common species of reed-warblers in Europe and are in the same genus.

They are found throughout Australia and Tasmania, wherever suitable aquatic habitats prevail. Usually in pairs, these birds frequent reed-beds and sometimes other tall growth in and around fresh-water. They are fairly shy, and more frequently heard than seen.

They are one of our night singers, and their rich voices were mistaken for those of nightingales by early visitors to our shores. The vigorous song can be rendered 'twitchee-twitchee-twitchee, quarty-quarty-quarty'.

Reed-warblers are at least partial migrants within the continent. They depart from southern Australia in March

REED WARBLER
6¼ in.

Winter

TAILOR-BIRD
3¼ in.

Summer

LITTLE MARSHBIRD
5 in.

TAWNY MARSHBIRD
7¼ in.

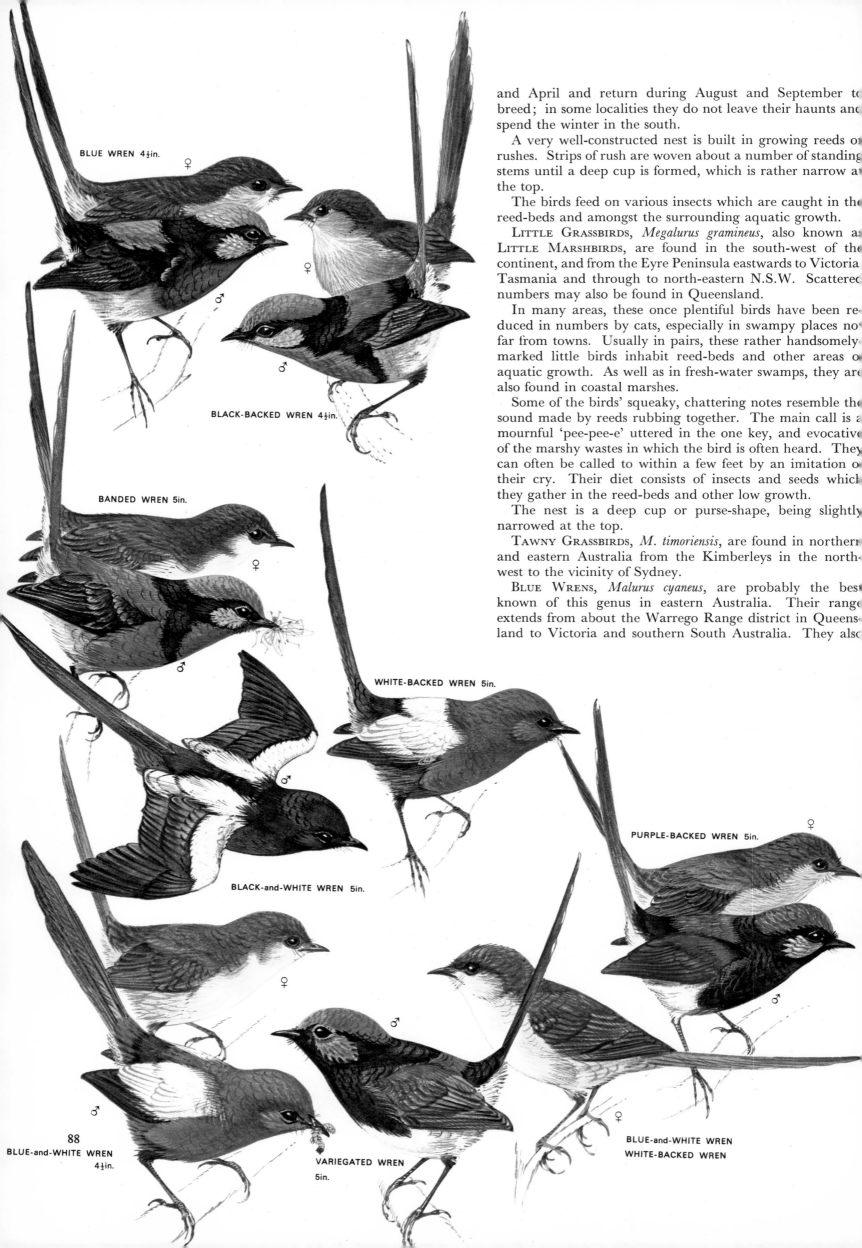

BLUE WREN 4½in. ♀

BLACK-BACKED WREN 4½in. ♂

BANDED WREN 5in. ♀

WHITE-BACKED WREN 5in.

BLACK-and-WHITE WREN 5in.

PURPLE-BACKED WREN 5in. ♀

BLUE-and-WHITE WREN 4½in. ♂

VARIEGATED WREN 5in.

BLUE-and-WHITE WREN
WHITE-BACKED WREN

and April and return during August and September to breed; in some localities they do not leave their haunts and spend the winter in the south.

A very well-constructed nest is built in growing reeds or rushes. Strips of rush are woven about a number of standing stems until a deep cup is formed, which is rather narrow at the top.

The birds feed on various insects which are caught in the reed-beds and amongst the surrounding aquatic growth.

LITTLE GRASSBIRDS, *Megalurus gramineus*, also known as LITTLE MARSHBIRDS, are found in the south-west of the continent, and from the Eyre Peninsula eastwards to Victoria, Tasmania and through to north-eastern N.S.W. Scattered numbers may also be found in Queensland.

In many areas, these once plentiful birds have been reduced in numbers by cats, especially in swampy places not far from towns. Usually in pairs, these rather handsomely-marked little birds inhabit reed-beds and other areas of aquatic growth. As well as in fresh-water swamps, they are also found in coastal marshes.

Some of the birds' squeaky, chattering notes resemble the sound made by reeds rubbing together. The main call is a mournful 'pee-pee-e' uttered in the one key, and evocative of the marshy wastes in which the bird is often heard. They can often be called to within a few feet by an imitation of their cry. Their diet consists of insects and seeds which they gather in the reed-beds and other low growth.

The nest is a deep cup or purse-shape, being slightly narrowed at the top.

TAWNY GRASSBIRDS, *M. timoriensis*, are found in northern and eastern Australia from the Kimberleys in the north-west to the vicinity of Sydney.

BLUE WRENS, *Malurus cyaneus*, are probably the best known of this genus in eastern Australia. Their range extends from about the Warrego Range district in Queensland to Victoria and southern South Australia. They also

88

inhabit Kangaroo Island and are the only members of the genus to have reached Tasmania, where they are quite common.

In pairs or in family parties, these lively and brilliantly-coloured birds are found in a variety of habitats. Light scrub, thickets along roads and hedges, and the bush lining the edges of streams and pools are favourite haunts. They are common on farmland and often live in gardens, especially in country districts. The birds are restless little creatures, seldom still as they hop and flit about the undergrowth in search of insects.

The song is a rapid reel of high lisping notes. The birds sing frequently in the spring and summer, and will quite often be heard at night. They also have a thin, harsh, scolding call when disturbed.

In the winter, family parties, comprising a number of broods, live together. After the breeding season the males lose their bright colours and moult into a brown eclipse plumage. They may then be distinguished by their black bills and by their tails, which remain blue.

A dome-shaped nest is built, with a side entrance. It is composed of bark-fibres, grass and cobwebs, and thickly lined with feathers, wool or similar materials. It is usually very well hidden in thick growth near the ground.

BLACK-BACKED WRENS, *M. melanotus*, occur from central-western Queensland, south to north-western Victoria and westwards to the Flinders Ranges in South Australia.

As a rule they inhabit more open country than the preceding species. Low scrub, such as mallee and mulga on the plains, are favourite haunts, and they are also found on the scrubby slopes of low hills. They may be seen in pairs during the breeding season, and in family parties throughout the remainder of the year. The high-pitched but rather musical song is similar to that of Blue Wrens.

A dome-shaped nest with an entrance near the top is made near the ground in a dense bush.

BANDED WRENS, *M. splendens*, are confined to Western Australia, and are most common in the extreme south-western corner from Geraldton to Esperance, although scattered colonies are recorded as far north as Shark Bay and the upper reaches of the Ashburton River and inland to Wiluna.

These birds are usually in small gatherings, even during the breeding season.

A rather untidy, oval nest is constructed of dry grass, with an entrance at one side. It is lined with feathers and hidden in a bush or creeper at a height from ground-level up to about four feet.

BLACK-AND-WHITE WRENS, *M. leucopterus*, are confined to Dirk Hartog Island and Barrow Island, both off the coast of Western Australia.

The origins of these two colonies, which are about three hundred and fifty miles apart, have been the subject of great conjecture. Did these birds evolve independently out of Blue-and-white Wrens isolated on the two islands, or are the two populations survivors of a form which has since disappeared on the mainland? The second theory is perhaps more probable.

BLUE-AND-WHITE WRENS, *M. cyanotus*, are distributed through most of the drier, more inland parts of the continent, from northern Queensland down to north-western Victoria and further south to the vicinity of Adelaide in South Australia. They are also found in the Northern Territory and in Western Australia from the Pilbara district down to Perth.

Their characteristic habitats are dry areas such as lightly covered sand-plains, *Casuarina* scrub on the low hillsides and the samphire-flats around salt-lakes and estuaries.

A typical domed wren's nest is built of dried grasses with

WHITE-THROATED WARBLER 4in.

FAIRY WARBLER 4in.

BROWN WARBLER 3½in.

♀

♂

BLACK-THROATED WARBLER 4in.

NORTHERN WARBLER 4in.

BUFF-BREASTED WARBLER 4in.

WHITE-TAILED WARBLER 4in.

an entrance to one side near the top. It is well lined with plant-down, wool or other soft material. The usual site is in a low bush only a foot or two from the ground.

WHITE-BACKED WRENS, *M. leuconotus*, are now considered to be only a geographical variant of Blue-and-white Wrens, with the white on the wings joining across the lower back. Their general habits, nests and eggs are similar to those of *cyanotus*.

VARIEGATED WRENS, *M. lamberti*, are birds of the coastal districts of southern Queensland and N.S.W., to approximately two hundred miles south of Sydney.

In pairs or small family parties they are found in all kinds of undergrowth, heathlands, and the low scrub along the borders of bigger brush. They are considered to be shyer than some of the other wrens with a call similar to that of the Blue Wrens, but not quite so vigorous.

A domed nest is built of dead grass and plant-down, and this is usually well concealed near the ground in a low bush or tangled growth.

PURPLE-BACKED WRENS, *M. assimilis*, are considered by many ornithologists to be a form or perhaps a sub-species of Variegated Wrens. Their distribution is from eastern Australia, west of the Dividing Range, northwards to the Gulf of Carpentaria and south to north-western Victoria; through central and South Australia they spread to Western Australia, except in the extreme south.

In the main, they appear to have the same habits as their close relatives, *lamberti*. They are a silent and retiring species, but do have a song consisting of a few brief chattering notes.

WHITE-THROATED WARBLERS, *Gerygone olivacea*, are distributed generally through northern and eastern Australia, from Derby in Western Australia to north-eastern Victoria. More rarely, they have been recorded in southern Victoria and south-eastern South Australia.

In the spring they have a most pleasing song. It is a descending scale of notes, considered by many people to be one of the sweetest of Australian bird songs. The popular names of 'Bush Canaries' and 'Native Canaries' attest to the opinions of country people about their voices.

White-throated Warblers are migrants within the continent. They move down into south-eastern Australia early in the spring. Scrub and open forests are the favoured habitats, where the birds may be seen hunting insects amongst the outer twigs and foliage. As the autumn progresses they move northwards again to escape the dearth of insects in the south.

A rather neat, elongated, pear-shaped nest is built. The entrance hole, to one side and near the top, is hooded over with nest material. The nest is constructed of bark-shreds bound together with spider-webbing and a tail hangs from the underside. Usually it is attached to the thin twigs of a gum sapling or a larger tree, at heights from a foot up to fifty feet from the ground. It is interesting that the birds often build in a tree infested with ants.

BROWN WARBLERS, *G. richmondi*, are found from south-eastern Queensland down to eastern Victoria. These rather insignificant little brown birds are usually seen in pairs. They inhabit dense scrub during the summer and as the cooler months come on they move into more open forest.

Brown Warblers are very active amongst the outer foliage of the trees and shrubs, where they hunt for all kinds of insects. This species does not have as full and sweet a song as White-throated Warblers. The call note sounds like 'citron-cit, citron-cit' repeated a number of times.

A domed nest is built of grass and pieces of lichen bound together with spider-webbing, and decorated on the outside with more flakes of lichen. Near the top is a spout-like entrance, and depending from the bottom of the nest is a tail of nesting material. It may be built at almost any height,

and is usually attached to thin twigs or a thorny vine in the forest.

FAIRY WARBLERS, *G. flavida*, are confined to eastern Queensland from about the Herbert River district to Bundaberg. They are pretty birds, with olive-green backs and yellow underparts. They are the most brightly coloured of the group except for the Black-throated Warblers.

Fairy Warblers have a pleasant song, reminiscent of the white-throated birds, but less 'wistful'. Like the other warblers they spend most of their time out amongst the outer foliage procuring a diet of insects. Their favoured habitats appear to be scrub and trees bordering creeks.

A roughly globular nest is built with a side entrance near the top. This is protected by a noticeably larger hood than the other warblers construct. The nest is made of fine strips of bark bound together with spider-webbing. It is usually attached to thin horizontal twigs at a height from about five feet upwards. Often they will build in a tree that contains a colony of wasps.

NORTHERN WARBLERS, *G. mouki*, appear to be restricted to the Cairns district in Queensland. Closely related to the Brown Warblers, they may come to be considered but a form of these birds. They are similar in habits to the Brown Warblers, spending most of their time in the outer twigs and foliage of dense scrub.

Domed nests are built, with side entrances. The birds often build over water, suspending their nests from thin twigs near the end of branches.

BUFF-BREASTED WARBLERS, *G. levigaster*, are another northern species, found from Derby in Western Australia across to Cape York Peninsula.

These insignificant-looking, brownish birds, have much the same habits as the other *Gerygone* warblers. Most of their time is spent actively hunting about the outer foliage and twigs in open forest and scrub-country. Their call is a delicate twittering, the fuller 'warbler-song' not having been noted.

A domed nest, with a hooded side entrance, is built of grass stalks and similar material. It is usually suspended amongst the fine twigs near the end of a branch. A tree containing a communal nest of wasps is often chosen, presumably for protection.

BLACK-THROATED WARBLERS, *G. palpebrosa*, are found in northern Queensland from Cape York down to the Cardwell area; outside Australia they inhabit New Guinea and the Aru Islands.

These warblers are the most striking of the genus, and are the only ones with any kind of bold colouring. Usually in pairs, they frequent heavy, tropical scrub and forest areas. Typically warbler in their habits, they spend much of their time in the outer foliage hunting for insects.

The young birds are rather unusual in that they have four peculiar head-plumes. If they are disturbed, the young birds raise their plumes and quiver them vigorously—which no doubt looks threatening to any but a human intruder.

A neat and compact, pear-shaped nest is built, which has a hooded entrance to one side near the top; there is also a tail-piece hanging below the nest. The materials used are palm-fibres and bark-shreds, bound together with cobweb. Lichen is often used in the nest and also to decorate the outside. The nest is suspended from thin twigs or a vine, and is frequently built close to the nest of aggressive wasps—presumably for protection. Indeed, these warblers are sometimes called the 'Hornet-nest birds'.

WESTERN WARBLERS, *G. fusca*, also lately called WHITE-TAILED WARBLERS, are widespread, being found throughout most parts of the interior and sub-interior and in the more southern parts of South Australia and Victoria. They are occasionally reported on the coastal side of the Great

TAILED THORNBILL 4¼in.

YELLOW-TAILED THORNBILL 4in.

TRIATED THORNBILL 3½in.

TASMANIAN THORNBILL 4in.

LITTLE THORNBILL 3½in.

BUFF-BREASTED SCRUB-WREN
4¼in.

WHITE-BROWED SCRUB-WREN
4½in.

LARGE-BILLED SCRUB-WREN 4½in.

Dividing Range, but are more commonly found spreading to the coast in Western Australia.

These active little birds frequent the outer foliage and branches, where they hunt for insects. Like most of the warblers, their habit of feeding high in the trees makes them difficult to observe. They are, in fact, often better known by their song than their appearance. The notes have a melancholy air, and a sweetness reminiscent of brown warblers. The birds never seem to give a finishing flourish to their song, but dawdle pensively on with its melody. In some areas the song is heard only at certain times of the year, which suggests that perhaps the birds are somewhat nomadic.

Their nest is an oval or pear-shaped structure of fine bark and grass, matted and woven together with cobweb. There is a hooded side entrance and usually a tail hanging below the nest. It is well lined with feathers. The nest is usually suspended in the outer twigs of a leafy branch at a height from a few feet up to perhaps twenty feet from the ground.

LITTLE THORNBILLS, *Acanthiza nana*, are found throughout many parts of eastern and south-eastern Australia, from the Dawson River in Queensland down to south-eastern South Australia, where they range north to the Flinders Ranges.

In pairs or small scattered flocks and parties these lively little birds may be seen hunting for insects in the outer foliage. They seem especially fond of wattles and *casuarinas*.

Little Thornbills call frequently to each other as they pass through the tree-tops, and the first indication of their presence is often the 'tiz-tiz-tiz' call.

A very small, domed nest is built of bark-fibres and grass, often decorated with moss. The entrance hole is near the top and the egg cavity is lined with feathers or fur. The usual site is amongst the outer, leafy twigs of a tree, sometimes quite high off the ground.

STRIATED THORNBILLS, *A. lineata*, are eastern birds, found from central inland Queensland to south-eastern South Australia; they also inhabit Kangaroo Island.

These birds mostly frequent the outer canopy of fairly high trees, and are rarely found in the underbrush. They are very active, moving so quickly that even at close range it is difficult to observe them well. They can become quite bold, hopping into camps in the bush in search of crumbs of food. I have even seen them hopping along the logs of a smoking campfire. They keep up a busy twittering call as they go.

The pear-shaped nest is made of bark and grass matted together with spider-webs. It has a hooded entrance and is

91

lined with feathers, fur or other soft material. It is usually built into the twiggy branch of a tree at various heights up to fifty feet or so.

TASMANIAN THORNBILLS, *A. ewingi*, are confined to Tasmania, King Island and the Furneaux Group of islands in Bass Strait. They are similar in many respects to Brown Thornbills and their ranges overlap. However, the Tasmanian species prefer thick cover and forest country, whereas Brown Thornbills may be found both in forests and more open terrain.

The song of both birds is also quite similar, and it is strange perhaps that, with so much in common, they have remained differentiated as species.

Tasmanian Thornbills build a rather neater and more compact nest than their relatives, and the round entrance hole is protected by a hood. The domed nest is built of bark-fibres, and is often draped with moss; some nests are covered to the extent that they resemble neat, green balls of moss. They are usually suspended from a few small twigs in a bush or tree at heights up to about fifteen feet.

YELLOW-TAILED THORNBILLS, *A. chrysorrhoa*, are one of the best known of the eastern *Acanthizas*. They range through Australia generally, south of the Tropic of Capricorn, and extend north in Queensland to the Gulf of Carpentaria.

In most parts of their range they are common, and they have taken well to living in farming areas. Their more natural habitat is open forest and all kinds of lightly covered country. They frequently visit orchards and gardens, where they no doubt clear up a large number of insects harmful to agriculture.

The nesting habits of these well-known birds are of particular interest. An untidy, domed nest is built, with an entrance hole low down on one side. On top of this nest, however, a second cup-shaped nest is constructed. As the eggs are laid in the bottom chamber, the cup on top has been the subject of much debate.

It was thought that the male bird might sleep in it, but there is no evidence to support this. Another theory is that it might be to delude the bronze cuckoos, which parasitise this species, to lay their eggs in it. There is no evidence to support this theory either; on the contrary, the cuckoos continue to lay their eggs in the 'proper' place.

The most likely explanation seems to be that it is the result of nest-building impulses remaining after the domed nest is completed.

BROWN WEEBILL
3¼in.

BUFF-TAILED THORNBILLS, *A. reguloides*, are found from southern Queensland to Victoria and south-eastern South Australia. In pairs or flocks these small birds frequent scrubland, lightly timbered hills, and open forests generally.

They are both terrestrial and arboreal, hunting with restless energetic movements for insects. Like most of the thornbills they have a jerky flight, giving an impression of stopping and starting in mid-air.

The domed nest of this species is composed of grass and soft bark, bound together with cobwebs. It is well lined with fur, feathers or other soft material. A variety of nesting sites are recorded: behind a slab of loose bark on a tree, in a shallow hole in a tree-trunk, or in a low bush; nests have even been found on the ground under tussocks of thick grass.

WHITE-BROWED SCRUB-WRENS, *Sericornis frontalis*, are perhaps among the best known of their group. They range from southern Queensland to Victoria and south-eastern South Australia, and are also present in the Kent Group in Bass Strait.

Scrub-wrens look much the same as each other, although some are identifiable by their locality. But where the ranges of different scrub-wrens overlap, the birds can be difficult to identify with certainty. They are active birds but have a deliberation in their movements which some small birds, such as the thornbills, lack.

White-brows are inhabitants of thick underbrush and although retiring in their wilder habitats, soon become quite bold when living near human habitation. Their food is insects, grubs and small worms mostly picked up on the ground, but the birds also feed in low bushes.

Their call is a sharp whistle and they also have a vigorous scolding note. This is a harsh 'wizzit-wizzit-wizzit', and is a rather fierce little call, heard up to a dozen times or so in succession.

A domed nest with a side entrance is built of bark-fibres, leaves and grass, usually on or near the ground in thick cover.

BUFF-BREASTED SCRUB-WRENS, *S. laevigaster*, are distributed from north-eastern Queensland to north-eastern N.S.W. They frequent the thick brush and wet scrub country found within their range. In pairs or small parties, they may be seen industriously working over the ground, pecking here and there as they go. Their insect and grub diet is also procured in the underbrush.

The domed nest of this species is chiefly made up of dead ferns, with a few other plant pieces added. It is lined with feathers and is well hidden in low, thick cover.

SPECKLED WARBLER
5 in.

LARGE-BILLED SCRUB-WRENS, *S. magnirostris*, are an eastern Australian species, found from the Cooktown area in Queensland to the vicinity of Melbourne. In the main, they are a species of the coastal scrub and contiguous areas. Their habits are much the same as the other members of the genus; they hunt assiduously on the ground, flicking over dead leaves and other debris in search of spiders, insects and minute grubs. Some of their food is also procured amongst the foliage and twigs of the undergrowth.

Their simple sharp calls are reminiscent of the White-browed Scrub-wrens, but not quite so vigorous.

A relatively large, oval nest is built of dead leaves, moss and grass, and lined with feathers. The usual nesting site is in the drooping twigs of a low branch or in a clump of vines.

The birds known outside Australia as wren-warblers are far better known here as the fairy wrens. The group contains a number of the best-known and favourite Australian birds.

BROWN WEEBILLS, *S. brevirostris*, are found from central Queensland down to Victoria, South Australia and south-western Australia, where they extend northwards to about the mid-western areas.

In pairs or small parties, these small birds spend their time hunting for insects in the outer foliage. They will be seen in both low saplings and tall trees. Brown Weebills are continuously active, swinging and clinging amongst the leaves and thinnest twigs. Sometimes they hover about the outside of the leaf canopy picking insects off the foliage.

Their chief call is a brisk chattering, uttered frequently. There is also a distinctive song which has been syllabised 'winnie wieldt' and 'pee-pee, p'wee-weep'.

These birds build a small, globular or purse-shaped nest, with a hooded entrance to one side near the top. A cup nest is made first, and the hood is built on afterwards. Fine grasses and spiders' cocoons are bound with cobwebbing and the nest is usually suspended in thin leafy twigs. Nesting heights may be anything from two or three feet up to thirty or so.

SPECKLED WARBLERS, *Chthonicola sagittata*, range from central-eastern Queensland down to Victoria and eastern South Australia. Dry, open forest country, with light under-brush, and also more park-like country with well-spaced timber, are their chief habitats.

Much of the time these birds will be seen upon the ground hopping about in search of insects, grubs and seeds. However, they will quite readily perch in bushes and trees. In their feeding, Speckled Warblers will sometimes be found associating with other terrestrial feeders, such as thornbills, finches and Whitefaces. Outside the nesting season they tend to gather in small parties.

The most frequently heard call of the species is a 'charring' chatter, but there is also a sweet, though slight, song. If alarmed, Speckled Warblers will fly up to a low branch to scold the intruder with subdued harsh notes interspersed with mimicry.

A nest of dead grass and bark is constructed which closely resembles its immediate surroundings of natural debris. Inside, the nest is more neatly finished off with bark-fibres and grass and then lined with feathers or fur.

MUSCICAPIDAE

Old World Flycatchers

BROWN FLYCATCHERS, *Microeca leucophaea*, are well known and much loved little birds. They are found in many parts of Australia where the habitat permits. They are absent from deserts and the denser jungles in the far north, and absent also from the south-west corner of the continent.

Brown Flycatchers, or Jacky Winters as they are frequently

LEMON-BREASTED FLYCATCHER 5 in.

BROWN FLYCATCHER 5 in.

called, appear to be quite undisturbed by the spread of farms and homesteads in country areas, and have taken quite readily to nesting in gardens.

They are fearless birds, and will dart and hover around one's head or feet to snatch insects out of the air or small fry disturbed on the ground.

They have a sweet, rather lisping song, in addition to their well-known call of 'jacky-jacky-jacky' or 'peter-peter-peter'.

Their nest is a delightfully neat and small structure, about two inches across, made of grass, horse-hair and scraps of lichen bound and matted together with spider-webs. As a rule it is built snugly into the horizontal fork of a branch at almost any height from a foot or so up to seventy feet from the ground.

LEMON-BREASTED FLYCATCHERS, *M. flavigaster*, are northern birds found in northern Australia from the Kimberleys to northern Queensland as far south as the latitude of Mackay, but probably not on the coast.

Unlike the Brown Flycatchers, they are largely arboreal. They are very lively little birds, dashing out from their perch on a branch or fence-post, to capture a passing insect or flicking momentarily down to earth to pick up some tit-bit. They have a bright, twittering song which is extremely varied. The early morning song is particularly fine. There are reports of mimicry of other species' songs by these birds.

Their nest is even smaller than that of the foregoing bird, being only about one-and-a-half inches across by half-an-inch deep. Constructed of bark-fibre and grass, it is bound and matted together with spider-webs, and built neatly into the horizontal fork of a branch. A dead branch is often chosen and the nest may be at almost any height.

DUSKY ROBIN
6¼in.

SCARLET ROBIN
5in.

♂

♀

♀

HOODED ROBIN 6¼in.

♂

RED-CAPPED ROBIN 5in.

♂

♀

94

Dusky Robins, *Petroica vittata*, are confined to Tasmania and various islands in Bass Strait. They frequent lightly timbered country and farming land. They are friendly little birds and may often be found in the vicinity of homesteads. Patches of land newly cleared of cover are favoured spots where they apparently find ample supplies of insects. They are ground feeders, and will quickly appear where wood is being chopped or the ground dug up, boldly picking up grubs and the like.

Their note is a low and somewhat melancholy 'choo-wee choo-wee-er'. They are not as common as they once were, probably due to the depredations of cats.

Their nest is a cup of bark, rootlets and grasses, and is rather untidily built. Tree cavities, in the end of a log or on the branch of a small tree, are common nesting sites.

Hooded Robins, *P. cucullata*, are very handsome black and white birds found in most parts of Australia except for tropical north-eastern Queensland and Tasmania.

The males are showy birds but they can easily be overlooked, being quiet and unobtrusive in their habits. Hooded Robins are not vociferous, but when they do call, their 'yapping' notes are quite distinctive. The birds call during darkness and immediately before and after dawn. During the day they are usually silent.

A cup-shaped nest is built of rootlets, soft bark, or grasses, or a combination of such materials. It is lined with hair or plant-down, and the whole is matted together with cobwebs. The nest may be built into the fork of a tree or a hole in a stump or tree-trunk. It is usually within ten feet of the ground, but may be as high as twenty feet.

Scarlet Robins, *Petroica multicolor*, are widely distributed in eastern Australia and there is also a population in the south-west corner of the continent. They may be seen in many parts of N.S.W., Victoria and south-eastern South Australia, as well as Kangaroo Island, Tasmania, Norfolk Island and some other Pacific Islands.

Scarlet Robins are usually seen in pairs, frequenting scrub, open woodland, and orchards and gardens in settled areas, depending on the time of year. They are fairly quiet birds and spend most of their time in low growth, from which they frequently dart down to pick up insects and other small fry from the ground. They often perch sideways on a vertical trunk, in the same manner as the yellow robins. Their call note is a slight trill, the song a more sustained trilling.

A beautiful nest is built of dry grass, fibrous bark and mosses. The thick walls are bound and matted together with cobwebs and there is a lining of hair, feathers or wool. It is built into a forked tree-branch, or in the hollow of a trunk or on an old stump, at a height usually not more than about fifteen feet.

As part of their courtship display the males feed the females; they take no part in building the nest, but may share in the incubation. The young are fed by both birds.

Red-capped Robins, *P. goodenovii*, are found in many parts of the interior of Australia, extending to the coast in only a few districts, although they are reported to be coastal birds in winter in mid-western Australia.

They are usually seen in pairs, and they like scrub country and open forest as a habitat. These robins feed on the ground a good deal, but also pursue flying insects. They dart out from their perch in a flycatcher manner, or flutter up from the ground to snap at some low-flying insect.

The call note is a gentle tapping or ticking sound, not unlike a clock ticking, and the territorial song has been described as 'tick-it-terr-rri-ri-ri', and has a rather lisping quality.

A very decorative nest is built; cup-shaped and made of green moss and lichen strengthened with a few fibrous pieces of bark. Spider-webbing is frequently used to bind the whole together. The lining is soft material such as rabbit fur or hair. The nest is built into the fork of a branch, often quite near the ground, but sometimes as much as forty feet above the ground.

SOUTHERN YELLOW ROBINS, *Eopsaltria australis*, are common and well-known birds throughout much of their range. They extend from the south-east corner of South Australia through Victoria to N.S.W. but are absent from Tasmania.

They are trustful birds, at times appearing quite unafraid of man. They will often suddenly appear out of the scrub to perch on a nearby branch and regard one quietly out of their large black eyes. They frequently perch sideways against a trunk, and also have the habit of flicking their wings or tail while perched.

Their call note is a loud double 'choo-choo', almost thrush-like in its intensity. Their other call is a monotonous and very plaintive piping; a 'tu-tu-tu-tu' sound repeated many times. They are among the first to call at dawn and the last to call as night falls. They also pipe out of sight in the thickets when disturbed.

Their diet consists of insects of various kinds, many of which are picked up from the ground.

A cup-shaped nest is built, neatly made of bark-strips, a few grasses and sometimes pieces of paper or rag. The nest is bound with matted cobwebs. Sometimes the outside of the nest may be decorated, and camouflaged with pieces of

NORTHERN YELLOW ROBIN 6 in.

5 in.
SOUTHERN YELLOW ROBIN

lichen. It is usually built into an upright fork but may be on a horizontal branch at heights from a foot to about twenty feet from the ground.

NORTHERN YELLOW ROBINS, *E. chrysorrhoa*, are found from the latitude of Cooktown in Queensland to about the Hunter River in N.S.W. They are closely related to the southern yellow robins, which they resemble in both habits and voice.

The northern birds may be distinguished by their brighter yellow, almost golden rumps, which show up brightly in the dense forests which these robins inhabit. They are known to frequent the forests of the coastal belt, and may also occur in similar habitats further inland.

BLACK-FACED FLYCATCHERS, *Monarcha melanopsis*, are found all the way down eastern Australia from Cape York to the vicinity of Melbourne. They are migrants to the southern part of Australia, arriving to breed in the spring and returning northwards in February and March to escape the colder weather and consequent lack of insect food.

They are very active birds and may be seen moving rapidly about the branches and foliage of trees for insects. They also indulge in short and rapid aerial pursuits of their prey. Their chief call is a loud whistling 'why-chew why-chew', a pleasant and lively sound to hear each spring in the south as the birds return.

A cup-shaped nest is built of soft green mosses and lined with fine rootlets and sometimes a little hair. The common site is the upright fork of a branch usually at no great height, but occasionally up to thirty feet from the ground.

PEARLY FLYCATCHERS, *M. frater*, somewhat resemble the foregoing species, but are found only in north-eastern Queensland from Cape York to the Claudie River district.

Usually in pairs, these handsome flycatchers inhabit both open forest and thicker jungles. In the jungles they may be seen hawking for insects from perches on the edges of clearings.

SPECTACLED FLYCATCHERS, *M. trivirgata*, are also eastern Australian birds, found from Cape York south to near Sydney, and perhaps occasionally south of that city.

These richly-coloured flycatchers are migrants, moving south during September and departing in February and March after breeding. A whirring or softer trilling 'prree-prree-prree', uttered frequently, is heard throughout their stay in the south.

They have the true flycatcher habit of pursuing insects in

BLACK-FACED FLYCATCHER 6¼ in.

FLYCATCHER 6 in.

WHITE-EARED FLYCATCHER 5¼ in.

SPECTACLED FLYCATCHER 6¼ in.

RUFOUS FANTAIL 6in.

GREY FANTAIL 6in.

NORTHERN FANTAIL 6½in.

WILLY WAGTAIL 7¼ in.

RESTLESS FLYCATCHER 8 in.

mid-air. The birds take up a position on a projecting branch as insects come within range. They also capture a few insects in the foliage of the trees.

A cup-shaped nest is built of bark-strips and moss and lined with various soft materials.

WHITE-EARED FLYCATCHERS, *M. leucotis*, look quite different from the other birds in this genus, being boldly patterned in black and white. They are found from Cape York down to south-eastern Queensland into N.S.W.

Like quite a number of our northern species, not a great deal has been recorded about their habits or life history. They are very active birds, catching most of their food on the wing. Their diet is insects, and they have the habit of hovering to pick insects off the foliage of the high rain-forest trees. The call most frequently heard from these birds is noted as 'ta-ta-taaaa'.

A cup-shaped nest is constructed of moss and spiders' cocoons, felted together with cobwebs and lined with fine vegetable fibres. Usually it is placed in the fork of a low bush at from about five to ten feet from the ground.

WILLIE WAGTAILS, *Rhipidura leucophrys*, are found in most parts of Australia, but are rare in Tasmania where their presence is considered to be accidental.

Their favoured habitats appear to be fairly open areas such as partly cleared farmland, lightly timbered park-like country and the growth bordering watercourses. Wagtails are frequently in the vicinity of water, but there are some records of the bird in arid areas, some having been recorded in dry country three hundred miles north-west of Alice Springs.

Wagtails have become exceptionally tame and appear to have profited by the spread of cultivation in Australia; forest clearing is opening up new territory for them. In gardens and parks they are a familiar sight and they will frequently nest under verandahs or in shrubs growing close to a building.

These little birds often associate themselves with grazing stock and perch upon their backs to await insects. In the tropical north of Australia they have been recorded as perching on the backs of crocodiles and even hopping into the saurians' open mouths to pick amongst the teeth for pieces of meat. Wagtails are vociferous and their chief song is rendered as a rapid 'sweet-pretty-little-creature'. This song is frequently heard at night and especially on moonlit nights. They will also sit and sing for a long time in a tree lit by a street lamp.

Their alarm call is a strange harsh chattering, not unlike the rattle of a half-empty matchbox.

96

The diet of wagtails is insects, most of which are caught in the air, although the bird also flits about on the ground snapping up small low-flying insects.

The nest is a beautifully constructed cup of grass and other vegetable fibres strongly bound and felted together with spider-webbing. It is usually built on to a thin horizontal branch.

GREY FANTAILS, *R. fuliginosa*, are another widely distributed species familiar to many people. In suitable habitats they are found in most parts of the continent and Tasmania.

They are even more erratic in their movements than wagtails. Whilst perched they constantly pivot their bodies about, fanning and closing their tails and being generally restless. They spend a good deal of their time in the air in short but frequent flights in pursuit of insects. As they fly the little birds throw themselves about as rapidly as the eye can follow; twisting and banking, up and down, doubling back on themselves and performing quaint evolutions of all kinds.

Their song has a delicate yet vigorous twittering quality. They sing when disturbed, and if intruded upon at the nest they fly about one's head, singing, and now and then perching in their nest, still twittering as they do so. If disturbed at their nesting before the eggs are laid or before incubation is well advanced they will readily desert the nest.

A neat, cup-shaped nest is built, from the bottom of which hangs a long tail shaped like a wine glass without a base, which gives it a very graceful appearance. It is constructed of plant fibres firmly felted together with spider-webs. Both birds assist in the building of the nest and the rearing of the young.

The usual building site is a thin branch, occasionally over water, and at heights from a few feet to perhaps sixty feet.

NORTHERN FANTAILS, *R. setosa*, found in tropical northern Australia, are similar in habits to Grey Fantails. They have a similar restless nature and capture their insect prey in short erratic flights from a perch. The northern birds, however, are considerably less active than the southern species. Their song is a delicate twittering but quite distinguishable in the field from that of the other fantails.

RUFOUS FANTAILS, *R. rufifrons*, are migrant species on the whole. They are found throughout most of eastern Australia at various seasons but are rarely seen as far west as south-eastern South Australia although they have been found nesting just over the border.

The first Rufous Fantails arrive in south-eastern Australia during September and by October the migration is in full swing. In late February the northward movement begins and few of these fantails remain by the end of April. In a mild year some birds remain south throughout the winter, in which case they generally haunt open forest country.

The migrating birds winter in the north-east of Australia and it may yet be proved that some cross over to New Guinea and back each year. The breeding habitat of these little fantails is dense cover such as ferny gullies, thickly forested mountain slopes and rain-forest.

They are pretty birds and as they flit about catching insects in sunny clearings their rumps and upper tails glow a ruby red. Their song is a delicate twittering and lisping trill. These birds have similarly erratic habits to the other fantails while perched and flying.

RESTLESS FLYCATCHERS, *Seisura inquieta*, are almost as familiar a bird in many places as Willie Wagtails. They are rather similar in colour and pattern, but may immediately be distinguished by their lack of black throat and bib.

Restless Flycatchers are found throughout much of the continent, although they are rare in the arid centre. They do not appear to have suffered from the encroachment of man; perhaps even the contrary may be the case as they

GOLDEN WHISTLER 7 in.

thrive in open, lightly-timbered country such as farmland where there are creeks, dams and swamps.

They are confiding little birds and will often visit gardens in country areas and hunt for insects around houses and farm buildings. The most familiar call of these species is a loud 'pee-pee-pee'. They also have a distinctive churring or grinding call; so metallic is this sound that it has earned for the birds the nickname 'Scissors-grinders'. When uttering this call the birds usually hover near the ground. With their bodies arched and wings beating rapidly, the little birds churr out their strange call. They will also occasionally give vent to this same call when perched.

A neat cup-nest is built of plant fibres bound and felted together with spider-webs.

RUFOUS WHISTLER
6¼in.

♂

♀

PACHYCEPHALINAE (PACHYCEPHALIDAE)

The ten Australian Whistlers are a group of thrush-like birds with fine calls. As a group, they tend to be inhabitants of scrub and forest.

GOLDEN WHISTLERS, *Pachycephala pectoralis*, are the most showy members of the genus, with their livery of gold, green, black and white. The females, as with all the whistlers, are much more soberly coloured.

Golden Whistlers range through eastern and south-eastern Australia from the middle of Queensland to the Eyre Peninsula in South Australia. There is a separate population in south-west Australia and they are also common in Tasmania.

They are birds of the scrub and open forest, where they may be seen in pairs in the breeding season and singly or in loose wandering groups in the winter. During the winter they tend to move out into more open country. They are often seen in suburban gardens in some of our larger cities.

Golden Whistlers have strong voices and a variety of notes, with the males singing a good deal during the breeding season. Various calls have been rendered as 'wi-wi-wi-wit', with the stress on the last syllable, and 'witee-chew-ee'. There is also a single loud, almost whip-like whistle.

Their food is insects, grubs and similar creatures, garnered in low foliage and from the ground. Camping in the bush I have found that Golden and Olive Whistlers are amongst the many species that are bold enough to come hopping into the tent in search of cheese and bread-crumbs.

Golden Whistlers build a shallow cup-nest of grass, shredded bark, rootlets and similar materials, which is usually placed in the upright fork of a low bush. Both birds assist in the nest building and in the incubation and, later, in rearing the young.

Two or sometimes three eggs are laid; these are stone coloured to white, or sometimes pale salmon, speckled with brown and grey. The markings often form a zone around the larger end. Breeding takes place from August to December.

RUFOUS WHISTLERS, *P. rufiventris*, are found in many parts of Australia where suitable open wooded country allows. In some places they are spreading into areas of deforestation where Golden Whistlers are decreasing from the same cause.

In the eastern parts of the continent the birds are nomadic, moving into more open country. There are also reports of the species being migratory to some extent, moving south in the spring to breed and returning northwards at the end of summer and beginning of autumn. Many Rufous Whistlers do, however, remain south all the year. In the west, Rufous Whistlers definitely do not migrate, but some of them appear to be nomadic in winter. Other male birds in the west will defend a territory throughout the year with vigorous singing.

They are fairly common and their loud and joyous song is one of the most pleasant spring and summer sounds. In the spring the song of the whistler develops, and the familiar 'e-chong', a kind of musical whip-crack, rings through the woods. There is also a long whistling, rippling song added to this call, the male birds often indulging in a display of bowing as they sing. The autumn song of Rufous Whistlers is more mellow, and is considered by some observers to be more beautiful.

A fairly fragile nest is constructed of dead twigs, grass and rootlets and is lined with finer materials. It is so loosely made that the eggs can sometimes be seen from below. It is usually placed in the upright forks of a branch in a tree or bush at any height up to twenty feet or so from the ground.

Two or three olive eggs are laid, spotted and blotched with darker browns. Territories may be taken up as early as July or August in some localities but the height of the breeding season is from September to December and January.

98

MOTACILLIDAE

Pipits

The name pipit is derived from the twittering voices of the family, of which there are fifty-four species in the world. The family does not have any relationship to the larks, although they look superficially similar. (See illustration on p. 71.)

PIPITS, *Anthus australis*, are generally distributed in open grassy country throughout the Australian continent and Tasmania.

Singly, in pairs, or in scattered winter flocks, they are found in most grassy habitats from mountain slopes to the seashore. They are active birds, walking and running through the grass in pursuit of insects and in search of seeds. If Pipits are disturbed, they usually run off, stopping frequently with their heads up to view the intruder. If pressed, however, they will rise and fly a short distance, dipping and rising as they go.

Now and then Pipits may be seen perched on a fence-post or a dead branch, from which they will sing their rather twittering warble.

LITTLE WOOD-SWALLOW 6 in.

DUSKY WOOD-SWALLOW 7½ in.

WHITE-BROWED WOOD-SWALLOW 8 in.

ARTAMIDAE

Wood-swallows

WHITE-BROWED WOOD-SWALLOWS, *Artamus superciliosus*, are found in most parts of Australia where the habitat permits, but not in Cape York or in Western Australia south of the Gascoyne River.

They inhabit lightly timbered country and open forest of various kinds, mostly in small flocks. In eastern Australia they are quite a common species but in Western Australia they occur in fewer numbers and only in parts of the interior and the Kimberleys. Quite often, mixed flocks of this species and Masked Wood-swallows are seen.

Their habits are typically 'wood-swallow'. The birds make flights of short duration, although sometimes quite high, in pursuit of insects. On the wing they are buoyant and glide a good deal, and they may be heard uttering a chirruping call as they fly. If disturbed at the nest or alarmed in any way they give a harsh, scolding call.

A slightly-built nest of sticks is made, intertwined with dry grasses. A variety of nest sites are recorded, but it is usually in a forked branch or on a stump.

The two or three eggs laid are whitish to grey-green, spotted and blotched with pale brown over slate-grey markings. The breeding season is October to January.

LITTLE WOOD-SWALLOWS, *A. minor*, are mainly birds of the interior and sub-interior but reach the coast in Queensland. They are distributed across the top of the continent, ranging as far south as the Murchison River in the west, and northern N.S.W. in the east. On rare occasions, Little Wood-swallows come as far south as northern Victoria and adjacent parts of South Australia.

In pairs or small flocks these birds may be seen in open park-like country but are typically a species of rugged range areas. They are graceful, buoyant fliers and procure most of their insect food on the wing.

The nest is often placed on a ledge or in a cavity of a rock-face, but it may also be found in the end of a hollow limb, in a hollow trunk or on a stump. It is a loosely-built structure of twigs, dry leaves and rootlets.

Three dull white eggs are laid, blotched with browns over slate-grey. The breeding season is from October to January.

DUSKY WOOD-SWALLOWS, *A. cyanopterus*, are found well south of the Tropic of Capricorn, and do not extend north of Shark Bay in Western Australia. These are the only wood-swallows common in Tasmania and the Bass Strait; they also inhabit Kangaroo Island, but are absent from Central Australia through lack of their favourite habitat of well-wooded country.

They are nomadic birds, appearing rather spasmodically in the southern parts of their range. Large numbers are seen sometimes in areas where they have been rare, and the reverse also happens.

Dusky Wood-swallows are graceful fliers and often fly high, hawking for insects above the timber. In the main, they tend to favour more heavily wooded country than do some other wood-swallows.

At night they indulge in the typical wood-swallow habit of crowding together to roost, often in a tree-trunk hollow or behind loose sheets of bark. Their insect diet is supplemented with nectar.

A loosely-built nest of twigs and grasses is constructed in the fork of a tree, on a tree-trunk supported by flaking pieces of bark or on a stump. The site may be from about four to forty feet above the ground.

Three or four creamy-white eggs are laid which are marked with shades of brown, black and grey. The breeding season is from September to January.

99

STURNIDAE

Starlings

COMMON STARLINGS, *Sturnus vulgaris*, have become widely distributed in Australia. They are found in Victoria, Tasmania, South Australia (as far west as Ooldea), and have spread north through N.S.W. to at least Innisfail in north-east Queensland.

Starlings were first released in Victoria in 1861. Very adaptable birds, they seem equally at home in cities or in country areas. In some districts their presence is quite beneficial as they destroy numbers of noxious insects. But on the whole they have become pests, frequently raiding orchards and seedlings in freshly-sown paddocks. They are proliferative birds and it seems likely that they will continue to spread and become even more of a nuisance unless some control is undertaken.

Like many starling species they are highly gregarious, especially in winter, when they may sometimes be seen in vast flocks. They feed on the ground or in trees. At dusk they indulge in rather spectacular massed wheeling flights before retiring for the night.

They have loud voices and are given to mimicry, rendering the calls of various birds as well as a variety of other sounds. Most of their own notes are a series of clicking and wheezing whistles, but now and then one does manage to perform quite a song.

An untidy mass of straw, feathers, string, pieces of paper and similar material serve as a nest. This is placed in any kind of a hole or crevice that the bird can find.

Mynahs

INDIAN MYNAHS, *Acridotheres tristis*, are very common birds i South-east Asia, and in Australia they are spreading ou from Adelaide, Melbourne and Sydney. Around Sydne they are encroaching noticeably on country areas. Mynah are also found in portions of the Darling Downs, north eastern Queensland and in northern Tasmania. In Queens land they have become common in the sugar-cane plant ations.

Mynahs were first introduced into Melbourne in 1862 and there, as elsewhere, the birds are thriving, although no equalling the starlings in numbers. They seem to be one o the few introduced species that have not become a nuisance Its strange rolling 'sailor's walk' and clucking, chuckling calls are a rather entertaining addition to suburban bird life

On the whole these birds are considered to be quite useful scavenging about the cities and suburbs and destroying insects in country areas. In 1883 a large number were trapped in Melbourne and released in Queensland, chiefly around Townsville and on the Herbert and Johnstone Rivers, in an effort to combat grasshoppers and cane-beetles.

The nest is an untidy collection of grass, straw and odd pieces of rubbish built into any cavity the birds can discover or in thick vegetation: palm trees are a favourite nesting site.

COMMON STARLING 8½in.

Summer

Winter

INDIAN MYNAH 10in.

E-GAPED HONEYEATER
7 in.

WHITE-EARED HONEYEATER 8 in.

GREY-HEADED
HONEYEATER
7½ in.

SINGING
HONEYEATER
7½ in.

MELIPHAGIDAE

Honeyeaters

There are one hundred and sixty species of honeyeaters and they are confined to Australia, New Zealand and the islands of the South-west Pacific. In Australia we have sixty-nine of these species, so they might be said to constitute our most characteristic family, sharing that distinction, perhaps, with the parrots and cockatoos.

An interesting relationship exists between a number of Australian flower trees and shrubs and various species of honeyeaters. The trees are ornithophilous, which quite literally means 'bird-loving', the tree being entirely dependent on birds (honeyeaters and a few other species) for cross-fertilisation.

As a group, honeyeaters are loud-voiced birds; some have rich or sweet whistling notes, whilst others, such as the wattle-birds, have extraordinarily loud and raucous calls. Most of them are vigorous on the wing and very active amongst the foliage and blossom, where they obtain their diet of honey, sometimes varied with insects.

Physically, they tend to be longish and rather streamlined. Most also have relatively long, down-curved bills adapted to probing into flowers for the nectar. Honeyeaters are also characterised by their extensive tongues which have a brush-tip and the sides of which can be curled up to make a tube for sucking nectar.

SINGING HONEYEATERS, *Meliphaga virescens*, or BLACK-FACED HONEYEATERS, as they are called in some publications, are found throughout most of Australia, although absent from Arnhem Land, Cape York and the east coast of Australia. They are plentiful on the coast west of Port Phillip Bay.

In pairs or in small numbers, they may be met with in almost any kind of habitat except thick forests, and are one of the most widespread of the *Meliphagidae*. The name 'Black-faced' is rather more appropriate than 'Singing' as their voices do not compare in quality with that of many other honeyeaters that really *do* sing, although in Western Australia where the birds were first named, they do have rather better voices.

They are a bold and pugnacious species and are especially quarrelsome towards other honeyeaters. They will seldom allow other honeyeaters to feed in the same tree with them. The diet of the species is fairly wide; they feed on insects, native fruits, honey and also cultivated fruits, having developed a taste for grapes in particular.

An untidy nest is built of grass, rootlets and other plant-matter, woven together with spider-webbing and lined with any soft material such as wool or plant-down. The nest is seldom higher than six or eight feet and is placed in a thick bush of any kind that is available.

WHITE-EARED HONEYEATERS, *Meliphaga leucotis*, are soberly, but handsomely coloured birds, found from southern Queensland down to Victoria and southern South Australia. They also inhabit Kangaroo Island and the south-west of the continent from the mulga-eucalypt line southwards, stopping short of the extreme south-west corner.

In pairs or small parties they frequent heathlands, mallee and open eucalypt forest country. Heavily timbered and thick brush country are usually avoided. Their diet consists of insects and nectar.

They are bold and inquisitive birds and can be called up close with imitations of their voice. Their various calls are loud and clear and carry a long distance. The well-known 'chock' or 'chock-chock' is supplemented by other calls such as 'come-up-come-up, do-it-well-do-it-well'.

WHITE-PLUMED
HONEYEATER
6½ in.

FUSCOUS
HONEYEATER
6 in.

YELLOW-PLUMED
HONEYEATER
6½ in.

They avoid the heavier, damp forests and are found in mallee, lightly timbered sand-dune country and open river flats with a few scattered eucalypts. In some parts of their range they are very common; in Hopetoun (Western Australia), for example, they are frequently met with in the tree-lined streets where they feed on insects and nectar.

Purple-gaped Honeyeaters are active and rather bold birds, particularly during the nesting season. They have a few harsh chattering notes but lack any significant song.

The nest is suspended from a few twigs in a bush or the drooping branch of a tree and is usually only a few feet from the ground. It is made of bark, grass and plant stems bound together with cobwebs. Plant-down and fine grasses are used for lining.

GREY-HEADED HONEYEATERS, *M. keartlandi*, are found from north-western and Central Australia, eastwards to about Cloncurry in Queensland and southwards to the top parts of South Australia. Westwards they extend to the Hamersley Ranges.

In pairs or small gatherings they may be seen in the rocky gullies of the ranges where they frequent the stunted scrub growing about springs and small creeks. They feed on insects and nectar, and utter a 'chip-chip' note as they move through the scrub. They also have a babbling song which, although not very musical, is quite a cheerful sound. There is also another call—a loud, 'chu-toyt'.

The nest usually is built down low with little or no attempt at concealment, suspended in the leafy twigs of a drooping branch. A bush or tree growing in a dry creek-bed or on the bank is frequently chosen to build in. Fine strips of bark, grass stems and plant-down are matted together with cobwebs, and although the nest is not hidden away it usually blends remarkably well with the surrounding foliage.

FUSCOUS HONEYEATERS, *M. fusca*, are found from Cairns in Queensland down through N.S.W. and Victoria to the east of South Australia where they are rare. Throughout most of their range they are common and may be seen in pairs or small flocks.

An open forest species, these birds hunt busily through the foliage of many kinds of trees in search of insects and honey. They also catch flying insects in quick aerial dashes around the tree-tops.

Their alarm call is a loud chattering cry rather similar to that of the more familiar White-plumed Honeyeaters. The normal call of the birds is a bright and cheery whistling that has been described as 'kitty-lin-toff-toff-toff' and also, somewhat conflictingly, as 'arig-arig-a-taw-taw'.

A very neat and well-made nest is constructed of grasses or bark-fibres bound with cobwebs. It is lined with fur, plant-down or any other soft material. Great variations in nesting heights have been recorded, from four feet or so up to the high canopy of the forest.

The clutch is usually three eggs which are a rich yellow or salmon colour, sometimes slightly freckled with brownish-red spots. The breeding season is from July to December.

YELLOW-FACED HONEYEATERS, *M. chrysops*, are eastern birds, found from Cooktown and the Atherton Tableland down to Victoria and south-eastern South Australia. They are quite common in most parts of their range and may be seen in pairs or small parties. There is a definite north-south movement of these honeyeaters in the spring and the autumn often in considerable flocks.

They are very active and inquisitive birds, adapting readily to gardens and other cultivated and domestic land; they cause considerable damage to orchards in some districts.

The song is a sprightly, running series of notes sounding like 'chick-up, chick-up', and other phrases. Their diet consists of insects, honey and various soft fruits.

A neat nest is built of grasses, bark and moss woven

In the nesting season the birds, especially the females, become even bolder, and there are many instances of them having alighted on a human's head to pluck out hairs for nesting material. Various parts of the clothing are also pounced upon for woolly threads.

The deep and well-made nest is constructed of bark, various plant fibres and grass, all bound about with spider-webbing. A lining of wool, fur or hair is added. The nest may be at almost any height, although from four to eight feet from the ground would be typical.

PURPLE-GAPED HONEYEATERS, *M. cratitia*, have a wide distribution through N.S.W., Victoria, South Australia and Kangaroo Island. There is another population in Western Australia where the birds range north to the Wongan Hills, east to Lake Grace and south-west to the Stirling Range.

together with cobwebs. The lining is of plant-down, wool or fine dry grass. As a rule, the nest is not high up; from four to twelve feet is common, but nests may be found in the tree-tops. The birds are bold at the nest, sitting tight on eggs or young, and allowing human intruders to come very close.

Two or sometimes three eggs are laid which vary from pinkish to buff in ground colour. They are speckled and blotched with chestnut and purplish-grey, mostly towards the larger end. The breeding season is influenced in some districts by rains, but otherwise is usually from July to November; it has also been recorded in February in Victoria's Western District.

HELMETED HONEYEATERS, *M. cassidix*, must be one of the most restricted species of bird in the world. They are found in only one small area on the edge of Gippsland in Victoria, along the Woori Yallock and Cardinia Creeks and adjacent areas.

These honeyeaters favour terrain on which the swamp gum (*Eucalyptus ovata*) grows, although they will sometimes also be seen feeding in mixed scrub; their diet consists of nectar and insects. Attention may be drawn to them by a rather sharp trilling note; they will also give vent to a series of 'chure-chure' sounds and a louder, whistling but unmusical 'tooey-t, tooey-t'.

They are a pugnacious species and will frequently attack other birds which trespass on their territory. They will be seen in pairs during the breeding season and small parties in the winter when they tend to move back from the creek-side scrubs into bigger timber.

YELLOW-PLUMED HONEYEATERS, *M. ornata*, named MALLEE HONEYEATERS in some publications, are restricted to the mallee districts at the junction of the borders of South Australiá, Victoria and N.S.W., except for a population in south-western Australia, where these birds are more catholic in their choice of habitat.

They are vigorous, quarrelsome honeyeaters, squabbling amongst themselves and making concerted attacks on any other species that is unfortunate enough to join them in their feeding. They have loud warning calls, which are taken up by the whole flock when a predator is sighted.

All the notes and calls of these honeyeaters are loud and inclined to harshness. They are one of the first birds to be heard announcing the new day, often starting up well before dawn. Yellow-plumed Honeyeaters also have a song-flight in which they dash vertically into the air for twenty or thirty feet, calling loudly at the peak of the rapid climb and as they descend more slowly.

Their diet is largely honey obtained from the blossoms of various eucalypts, but this is supplemented with spiders and insects.

A frail cup-nest is built of grasses and plant-down; it has a lacy look and can often be seen through. It is suspended from a few twigs by means of cobwebbing and is usually below twenty feet in height.

Two or sometimes three eggs are laid which are pale salmon-pink or white marked with small brown and red spots over grey. The breeding season is related to local conditions to some extent; July and March are the extremes but August to November appear to be the main nesting months.

WHITE-PLUMED HONEYEATERS, *M. penicillata*, are found throughout most of the continent except for parts of the far north. Widespread in southern and eastern Australia, they are much more locally distributed in the west. In Adelaide they frequent the street trees and suburban gardens as commonly as in Melbourne. It is noticeable that the western birds are a richer yellow-green colour.

They are typically birds of the coastal scrub and light forest areas, and are also found in the well-watered, lightly wooded country of the interior. They bathe frequently, and may visit the water a number of times a day to splash and drink.

Insects supplement their main diet of nectar which is obtained from many kinds of eucalypt. White-plumed Honeyeaters are vigorous and noisy birds, dashing about in swift erratic flights through the foliage and from tree to tree. They have the habit, particularly in the spring, of dashing high out above the tree-tops or scrub, loudly and even fiercely calling 'chick-o-wee, chick-o-wee-chick-o-wee'. They are also one of the first species to sound the alarm at the appearance of a predator. This alarm call is a high-pitched and very rapid call which sounds something like 'pe-pe-pe-pe-pe'.

The nest is a neatly made cup composed of bark-fibres, grasses and plant-down bound together with cobwebs or occasionally wool or hair. It is a thin-walled structure, and can sometimes be seen through from below. The usual site is in the thin twigs at the end of a leafy branch, at any height from a foot or two up to fifty feet or more.

Two or sometimes three eggs form a clutch and these are white to pale pink, freckled with reddish-brown and grey, usually towards the larger end. The breeding season is from June to December but may sometimes extend further.

WHITE-NAPED HONEYEATERS, *Melithreptus lunatus*, are well known and found from Cairns down through the eastern States to eastern South Australia and Kangaroo Island and the Kent Group in Bass Strait. There is a separate population in south-western Australia, ranging from Moora to Esperance.

The colour of the skin about the eye, known as the orbital band, varies in this species. In Western Australia the more common colour is replaced by grey below the eye, and white around it.

This is a nomadic and even migratory species. North-south movements take place in the spring and autumn, the extent of which have yet to be studied fully. They are common honeyeaters throughout coastal districts and timbered mountain ranges. Chiefly birds of the eucalypt trees, they may be seen, or more often heard, as they busy themselves in

BLACK-CHINNED HONEYEATER 6¼in.

WHITE-NAPED HONEYEATER 5¼in.

the foliage seeking insects and nectar. The usual call is a rather plaintive 'tsip-tsip' or 'tserp-tserp'; the birds also have a single loud whistle.

The cup-shaped nest is rather deep and constructed of rootlets, bark-fibres and grass sometimes matted with cobwebs. It is usually suspended in the drooping twigs of a leafy branch at heights up to thirty feet. Animal hair may be used in the nest, and the honeyeaters can sometimes be seen perching on the backs of horses and cattle plucking out hairs.

BLACK-CHINNED HONEYEATERS, *M. gularis*, are found down through eastern Australia outside the tropics. Apart from their north-eastern Queensland haunts these birds seem to prefer the hotter inland areas.

They frequent open forests seeking nectar and insects amongst the foliage. They are usually seen in small parties. A loud whistling call may be heard at most seasons and in the spring they have a rich and varied song of great volume.

A neat cup of fine bark and other fibres is bound together with cobwebs for a nest. This is suspended from the drooping twigs of a heavy branch. Wool or fur is often used as a lining.

BROWN-HEADED HONEYEATERS, *M. brevirostris*, are found in eastern Australia from southern Queensland to southern South Australia, King Island and Kangaroo Island. There is a separate population in the south-west of Western Australia where they appear to avoid the jarrah forests, making their headquarters in the mallee and salmon-gum country.

Throughout their range these birds are inclined to keep to the drier scrubs or open forested country. They move about the countryside in flocks of up to a dozen or so searching the foliage and blossoms for insects and honey.

Their call is a simple 'chick-chick', although some observers report 'a number of brisk and cheery calls'.

The nest is not often found; it is a firmly woven cup of bark-fibre, grass, cobwebs and hair. The usual nesting site is in the top twigs of a sapling about twenty feet high, but low nests have also been found.

EASTERN SPINEBILLS, *Acanthorhynchus tenuirostris*, are found throughout eastern Australia in areas that are not too dry. They range from Cairns to south-eastern South Australia, then north to the Flinders Ranges. They are also common on Kangaroo Island, Tasmania and islands in Bass Strait.

They favour both heathlands and bush country and have also taken freely to visiting suburban gardens to feed amongst the cultivated shrubs.

Even amongst the active honeyeaters, these birds must be called restless; they flick down on to a bush, quickly probe deep into a bloom or two, and are away again in a flash of their chestnut and curving bill. They also hover in front of the flowers quite frequently like giant humming-birds.

Their most commonly heard call is a shrill whistle, although it has other shrill musical notes. A strange sharp crack can often be heard from a bird's wings as it darts away from the observer.

A cup-shaped nest is built of bark, grass and moss and lined with hair and feathers. As a rule it will not be very high, but nests have been found up to fifty feet aloft. It is suspended from a thin horizontal branch or the drooping, leafy twigs on the outer part of a bush or tree.

TAWNY-CROWNED HONEYEATERS, *Gliciphila melanops*, ear distributed in suitable country throughout most of Australia outside the tropics. They also inhabit Kangaroo Island, Tasmania and the islands of Bass Strait.

These slim, rather long-billed honeyeaters are seen either in pairs or singly in heathlands and light scrub country such as mallee and banksia areas.

They are shy birds and extremely restless, a combination which makes field observation difficult. The sweet, fluting

BROWN-HEADED HONEYEATER 5¼in.

BROWN HONEYEATER 5in.

WHITE-FRONTED HONEYEATER 5½in.

TAWNY-CROWNED HONEYEATER 7in.

whistle of the song has a wistful and somewhat ventriloquial quality and is frequently heard without one catching more than a glimpse of the singer.

They feed in a typical honeyeater manner on honey and insects. They are darting fliers and also indulge in a 'towering' flight in which they soar upwards for fifty or a hundred feet singing as they go. The bird then plunges down vertically into the heath, still singing.

A deep, cup-shaped nest is built of bark and grass and lined with wool or other soft materials. The whole is well matted together with cobwebs and hidden close to the ground in a low bush or tussock.

WHITE-FRONTED HONEYEATERS, *G. albifrons*, are distributed generally throughout Australia except for the tropics. They are rarely seen near the coast in the south and east, although there is one record for Kangaroo Island, and they have been seen in the You Yang Ranges near Geelong in Victoria.

These birds, with their pale faces, narrow heads, and rather scale-patterned plumage, have quite a reptilian appearance as they twist themselves about to reach into the blossoms. They frequent hot dry country as a rule, being typical birds of the mallee and hakea scrub areas.

They have a variety of calls and notes, such as a loud metallic 'chip-chip', a drawn-out 'cree-e-e-e-k' and other more musical phrases, reminiscent to some observers of reed-warblers.

A cup-nest is built of bark-fibres and grass bound together with cobwebs, and usually lined with wool or plant-down. The common site is in the leafy top of a small bush, but the nest is sometimes tucked behind a curling flake of bark on a tree-trunk.

BROWN HONEYEATERS, *G. indistincta*, are found in suitable localities throughout most of Australia except Victoria and South Australia. They are also natives of New Guinea and the Aru Islands. These honeyeaters have been placed by some ornithologists in a separate genus and called *Lichmera indistincta*.

Rather catholic in their choice of habitats, these plainly coloured birds are usually near water and frequent mangroves, and can be seen in the flowering scrub and trees along creeks and rivers and in the more sparsely vegetated areas of the centre and the north-west.

They are beautiful songsters, considered by some observers to be without peer amongst Australian birds. They sing readily, but are particularly vocal in the mornings and evenings.

Their diet consists mainly of honey supplemented with a few insects; the flowers of the callistemons and coral-trees are favoured by the bird.

A small, neat cup-shaped nest is constructed of soft bark-fibres and grass and bound about with cobwebs. It is lined with hair, fibres, grass or plant-down, and placed in the forked branch of a bush or small tree. The nest is usually low down, but may be at heights to twenty feet, and is often overhanging water.

EASTERN SPINEBILL 6¼ in.

105

PAINTED HONEYEATERS, *Grantiella picta*, are distributed from about the Darwin area in the Northern Territory across to the Leichhardt River district in Queensland, and down to northern Victoria.

They are unusual in that they live largely on the berries of mistletoe. They tend to be migrants to the southern parts of their range, arriving in September and departing again during February and March. Their movements are erratic, however, as they follow the fruiting of the mistletoe, which is not always practicable.

A loud and clear 'geor-gie, geor-gie' is the chief call of these honeyeaters as well as a harsh 'chee-haw'.

The nest is a very delicate, although strong, construction of thin strips of bark and bark-fibres bound together with cobweb. The eggs can often be seen from below through the rather lacy construction of the nest. It is built into the outer, drooping twigs of a branch at heights from a few feet up to twenty feet or so from the ground.

REGENT HONEYEATERS, *Zanthomiza phrygia*, are found from southern Queensland down to Victoria, south-eastern South Australia and Kangaroo Island. These striking and handsome honeyeaters become less common at the northern and southern limits of their range.

Open forest country is their chief habitat, and there they may be seen individually or in any number up to quite large parties. They are nomadic birds, following the honey flow and also feeding on insects. In more settled areas their liking for fruit leads them into orchards, where they will sometimes cause a great deal of damage.

Regent Honeyeaters are a pugnacious species, squabbling amongst themselves as well as chasing off other birds.

Their chief call is a metallic, or bell-like 'clink-clink', a bird bowing its head each time it utters the cry; in flight they have a loud chattering call. In some places these honeyeaters have taken well to the encroachment of civilisation; they can still be seen in some Melbourne suburbs, and in Bendigo, for example, they are frequenters of the public gardens.

A cup-shaped nest is built of plant-fibres and bark-strips and lined with soft material such as thistledown. It is usually built into a forked branch of a tree, at various heights, from about three feet to twenty feet from the ground.

CRESCENT HONEYEATERS, *Phylidonyris pyrrhoptera*, are distributed from about the Newcastle area in N.S.W. down to Victoria, South Australia and Tasmania. They also inhabit Flinders Island (and other islands in the Furneaux Group) and Kangaroo Island.

These handsome birds frequent forest, mallee and coastal scrub areas. In Tasmania in particular they are found in high country and they also frequent gardens in various parts of their range. They tend to visit their more domestic haunts in winter, seeking fruits, insects and nectar in the garden shrubs.

Crescent Honeyeaters are loud-voiced birds, with a number of ringing notes which are sometimes strung together to make a song. The best-known and most easily described call is a powerful 'egypt' uttered once, or briskly a number of times. They will often sit for a few moments on some high, exposed dead branch, slimly outlined against the sky, and 'sing' their rich collection of calls and whistles.

They are a sociable species, particularly in the winter; numbers of birds may even be found nesting in a relatively small area. The nest is made up of grasses, bark-strips, wool, and sometimes a few twigs. It is usually placed near the ground in a thick bush.

YELLOW-WINGED HONEYEATERS, *Meliornis novae-hollandiae*, are found from south-eastern Queensland down to southern Victoria, southern South Australia, Kangaroo Island and Tasmania. There is also a population of these birds in Western Australia from the vicinity of Moora down to Israelite Bay on the south coast.

In some publications the Yellow-wings are sometimes given the name NEW HOLLAND HONEYEATERS and elsewhere they are called WHITE-BEARDED HONEYEATERS.

Typical habitats are heathy scrublands, open forest, coastal areas of ti-tree, banksia and similar growth; they also frequent swampy vegetation and sometimes the thicker brush and trees along creeks and rivers. They visit gardens quite freely, especially during the winter, in search of fruits and flowering shrubs. As well as fruit and honey they indulge in flycatcher-like techniques to capture insects.

They are a very active species and strong, swift fliers. Various loud whistles will be heard from them, and a chattering warning call when a cat or other predator appears.

If one intrudes upon their immediate nesting area they become very excited, dashing about with great rapidity and calling loudly. A number of neighbouring Yellow-wings might also be attracted to the scene and between dashing flights the birds land, still shrieking, in the low branches about one's head. As the intruder departs they will accompany him off their 'property', still objecting vehemently.

A nest is built of strips of bark, rootlets, twigs, grass and plant-down. Any or all of these might be used, and I have found that a number of nests in the same vicinity might vary in their materials.

WHITE-CHEEKED HONEYEATERS, *M. niger*, are at first sight very similar to the above species, especially when seen dashing through the scrub in a blur of black, white and golden-yellow. If one can get a look at the eyes, the white irises of the Yellow-winged Honeyeaters immediately serve to distinguish the two species. The pattern of white patches on the heads is also quite different.

White-cheeked Honeyeaters are found from coastal Queensland in the vicinity of Cairns, to south-eastern N.S.W. They also inhabit a portion of Western Australia from the Murchison River district south to Israelite Bay. Heathy country, light coastal scrub and open forest are the typical habitats of this species.

In their general behaviour—their vociferousness and rapid 'hedge-hopping flights'—these birds resemble Yellow-winged Honeyeaters, but one distinctive habit they have is to indulge in rocketing, towering flights above their nesting territory. At the peak of their climb they turn and plummet down with closed wings, flattening out at scrub-level for a short glide to their perch. A rather squeaky, unmusical 'chip-choo-hippy-choo' is the common call.

A low nesting site is usually chosen, in thick foliage or almost on the ground in a tussock. A nest of grass, soft bark and rootlets is built and it is frequently lined with the soft brown 'banksia-fur' from the cones.

BELL-MINERS, *Manorina melanophrys*, are distributed from the McPherson Range in southern Queensland to Victoria, about as far as the Glenelg River in the Western District.

These greenish honeyeaters, known to most people as BELLBIRDS, have the well-known bell-like 'pink-pink' or 'ping-ping' call. They live in colonies, remaining in one particular place throughout the year. When the numbers increase beyond the food resources of the area a number of birds will leave to settle elsewhere.

CRESCENT HONEYEATER 6 in.

Light to medium forest country, scrubby thickets with eucalypt saplings, and the growth along watercourses, are favoured habitats. In fact, most colonies will be found within a short distance of a creek or river.

The diet of these birds is made up mainly of insects, although a little nectar is taken. They are not particularly active by honeyeater standards, and being leafy-green in colour, are surprisingly hard to pick out against the gum leaves. Bell-miners tend to call in unison, so that there floats down from the trees an almost continuous but uneven ping-pinging. At first this is a pleasant rather cool sound, but it can become a little wearing after a few hours.

The species is most pugnacious, usually driving all other honeyeaters from the immediate feeding grounds. Other birds are bullied also. I have watched Bell-miners pestering a kookaburra for half-an-hour at a time; the honeyeaters frequently landing on the larger bird's back or shoulders to give it a quick buffet.

A cup-nest is built of grass, bark, twigs and leaves. Nests vary considerably in construction; some are quite solid structures of leaves and cobweb, whilst others might be almost transparent cradles of cobwebs and plant-down, with a few 'struts' of grass stems.

YELLOW-WINGED HONEYEATER 7in.

WHITE-CHEEKED HONEYEATER 7 in.

107

YELLOW-THROATED MINER 10in.

The nesting site is usually the outer twigs of a thin branch in a sapling or bush and is seldom far off the ground; twenty feet or so would be an unusually high nest. Occasionally nests have even been found in reed-beds.

Two or three rich flesh-coloured to buff-coloured eggs are laid, which are spotted with reds, brown and purplish-grey, usually concentrated towards the larger end. The breeding season is from June to November and sometimes later.

NOISY MINERS, *Myzantha melanocephala*, are found throughout most parts of eastern Australia, South Australia and Tasmania. They are absent from the tropical jungles and rain-forests of Cape York Peninsula.

These solidly-built grey birds are, as their vernacular name suggests, uncommonly noisy. They have harsh calls such as 'quoy-quoy', 'kik-wick' and similarly sharp sounds. Noisy Miners are one of the first birds to give warning calls at the appearance of a cat or hawk or other danger. The species is plentiful, and frequently live near human habitation in country areas. They respond in a highly excited manner to anybody making a squeaking sound. Insects and fruit, rather than nectar, form the bulk of their diet. They can quite frequently be seen feeding on the ground, where, however, they do not linger, rather flying back to the safety of a nearby tree.

A relatively solid nest is built of twigs, coarse grass and strips of bark. It is lined with rootlets and finished off inside with a soft layer of wool, fur or hair. No particular effort seems to be made to conceal the nest, which may be in a low bush, a sapling or a higher tree.

Two, three or sometimes four eggs may constitute a clutch. These are varying shades of pink, well speckled with chestnut and purplish-grey. The breeding season is from June to January.

YELLOW-THROATED MINERS, *M. flavigula*, are found throughout the interior of the continent generally, reaching the coast in north-western Australia. They are also found on Melville Island. Although geographically the ranges of these birds and the Noisy Miners overlap, they are seldom seen together. The yellow-throated birds are found in the drier, hotter parts of the country where their relative does not venture.

108

BELL-MINER 7in.

SPINY-CHEEKED HONEYEATER
10in.

DUSKY MINER
9½ in.

RED WATTLE-BIRD
14 in.

109

In general behaviour the two birds are very similar, although the Yellow-throated Miners are considered to be less noisy and not as bold. They sometimes become fairly tame, however, and visit the gardens and surroundings of homesteads. Blossoms containing a good supply of honey are eagerly visited but a large number of insects are also eaten and some native fruit and garden fruits. The harsh calls of 'quoy-quoy' and 'kwick-wick' are much the same as the Noisy Miners'.

A nest of twigs, plant stems and grass is built in a low bush or higher in a sapling, occasionally up to thirty feet from the ground. The nest is lined with soft material such as fur or wool.

The normal clutch is three eggs, but two or four and more rarely five, are sometimes laid. The eggs are a handsome salmon-pink with darker red spots and grey markings, usually towards the larger end. The breeding season is from July to December.

Yellow-throat is perhaps not a suitable appellation for these birds, as it is about the most difficult diagnostic feature to see in the field. The white rump, which the other two miners lack, is much more apparent and indeed some publications name the birds White-rumped Miners.

LITTLE WATTLE-BIRD
12 in.

DUSKY MINERS, *M. obscura*, are confined in eastern Australia to the mallee country around the junction of N.S.W., Victoria and South Australia. In Western Australia they are more widely distributed, but according to the opinion of Western Australian authorities they are inseparable from Yellow-throated Miners. The *obscura* type, however, are inclined to be south-western birds and the *flavigula* types range over the rest of the State.

The nest and eggs of the Dusky Miner do seem to be inseparable from those of the Yellow-throated Miners. From August to November are the chief breeding months in the south-west, extending to February in the east of Australia.

LITTLE WATTLE-BIRDS, *Anthochaera chrysoptera*, are distributed from southern Queensland down to Victoria and South Australia. They also inhabit Tasmania, Kangaroo Island and the south-west of Western Australia. Various habitats are frequented, such as forest, thick scrub and lighter scrub interspersed with areas of heath. On the whole, they are found along the coast and immediately behind it; there are, however, few records of these wattle-birds further inland.

In pairs and frequently in small gatherings, these honey-eaters move about a good deal, in search of flowering trees and native fruits. Banksias are particularly favoured. Insects supplement their nectar and fruit diet.

They are very pugnacious and indulge in spectacularly fast, twisting and turning flights through the branches in pursuit of other species. Having driven off an interloper, a wattle-bird may land on a branch, and throwing back its head, let out the most extraordinary cacophony of clicking-clacking sounds and rattling cries. They sound like 'kuk-ack-kook-uk-ack-cukack' and variations on this harsh theme. The sounds are rather amusing and one can become quite attached to the garrulous birds, although some observers find the calls unattractive.

At first sight this species might easily be confused with the Red Wattle-birds, even though the latter is considerably larger. They can be distinguished by the rusty colour showing in the open wings of the Little Wattle-birds and their lack of wattle or yellow on the belly.

Their nest is made of thin twigs, with a lining of bark-fibres or grass. The usual site is in the fork of a low tree or bush. The clutch is variable. In Western Australia only one egg is laid, whilst in the east, two eggs are usual. It is interesting that, in many cases, only one of the two hatches (Hindwood). In Tasmania three eggs are sometimes found in a nest. The eggs are pinkish, spotted and blotched with chestnut and purple.

Spring and summer are the peak breeding seasons, but these honeyeaters will breed at almost any time of the year given suitable conditions. They are multi-brooded, sometimes raising consecutive young in the same nest.

RED WATTLE-BIRDS, *A. carunculata*, are found from Queensland, north of Brisbane, to Victoria and South Australia. They also inhabit Kangaroo Island and there is a separate population in the south-west of Australia. These birds are our largest mainland honeyeaters, exceeded only by the Yellow Wattle-birds of Tasmania.

They may be seen in pairs, but often move about in small flocks. It seems clear that they are nomadic, but whether fortuitously following the honey flow or some other seasonal pattern, is not clearly known at the moment. There does not appear to be a winter movement out of the scrub into more open heathlands.

Blossoming eucalypts are eagerly visited and banksias are particularly sought out. The racket made by a party of these birds, feeding and squabbling in a grove of trees, is quite remarkable.

Their hoarse cries sound like 'tobacco-box, tobacco-box',

ften repeated a large number of times. Some observers have claimed that they have occasionally heard a more musical song.

A rather untidy nest is built of twigs and grasses, and lined with bark-fibres, feathers or wool. It is built into an upright ork at maybe four or five feet, or up to forty feet from the round.

Either two or three eggs are laid which are a pinkish-buff, with reddish-brown and purple spots, mainly at the larger nd. The breeding season is from July to December.

SPINY-CHEEKED HONEYEATERS, *Acanthagenys rufogularis*, are ound throughout most of Australia, except that they avoid eavily forested country. They are absent from the extreme outh-west corner of the continent, the Kimberleys and the nore northern parts of the Northern Territory.

They are bold birds and quarrelsome, both amongst them-elves and towards other species. They feed in almost any ype of vegetation, and to their nectar diet is added insects nd fruits of various kinds.

One of the calls of this relative of the wattle-birds, is a ather wattle-bird-like 'quock'; there is also a loud 'challeng-ng' call. A plaintive and rather reedy trilling has also been ecorded. If they are feeding quietly through the foliage the dd clicking sound will be heard.

A nest of grass and rootlets is constructed and bound ogether with cobwebs. It is lined with some soft material ıch as wool or fur. Almost any kind of a bush or tree may be lected and the height of the nest also varies from a foot or vo, up to fifty feet from the ground.

Two, or more rarely three eggs are laid, which are pale live-green, with spots and blotches of brown and purplish-rey. The breeding season is from August to January.

FALCUNCULIDAE

Shriketits and Whipbirds

ASTERN SHRIKETITS, *Falcunculus frontatus*, are found in eastern ustralia from Cairns down to Victoria and then across to delaide. In Western Australia there is another population f shriketits that some ornithologists consider to be a separate ecies. Other opinions have lumped the two together as ontatus. (Serventy and Whittell, *Birds of Western Australia*.)

In pairs or parties, these rather chunky, active birds move about the lighter forest country and scrub. They have taken well to the spread of civilisation and agriculture. In orchard country they are considered to be a beneficial species, as the birds eat good numbers of codlin-moth larvae. They are not shy and will allow a close approach. Shriketits have also taken to freely visiting gardens and tree-lined suburban streets.

They have strong conical, rather finch-like bills, with a hook on the upper mandible. With this efficient digging and tearing instrument they gain a good deal of their insect food by tearing up strips of bark and breaking open rotten wood. The sound of all this industry is sometimes quite loud and can be heard before the birds are seen. They are often nick-named the 'Barktit' because of this habit.

One of their calls has been likened to the phrase 'knock-at-the-door, knock-at-the-door' repeated frequently. They will, however, usually be heard calling in a high-pitched piping, and they also mimic the calls of other species. It is interesting that in southern Queensland the voices of the Eastern Shriketits are quite different from the birds in Victoria. In the far north the calls are even more dissimilar, being less varied and less powerful. This is a phenomenon which may be observed in a number of north-south species.

The nest is beautifully built, and it is unusual in that the bird frequently uses green, living bark which it is able to tear away from the tree with its strong bill. The bark and bark-fibre are matted together with cobwebbing and a lining is added of fine bark-fibres and grass. The usual site is in the thin upright twigs right at the top of a eucalypt. Frequently the leaves above the nest will be nipped off by the birds, and this is presumed to be a method of decreasing wind resistance in the lofty, swaying twigs.

Shriketits are very responsive to imitations of their calls and the nest may often be discovered by calling up a bird and then following it back to its nest. Two or three eggs are laid which are white, marked with dark olive and a paler grey. The breeding season is from August to December.

Whipbirds

EASTERN WHIPBIRDS, *Psophodes olivaceus*, are found from north-eastern Queensland to Victoria, inhabiting brush-filled gullies and big scrub country.

EASTERN SHRIKETIT 7¼ in.

EASTERN WHIPBIRD 10in.

They are extremely shy; I have spent many a long hot afternoon in close proximity to these birds and been rewarded with but a brief glimpse at infrequent intervals. Most of the time whipbirds are on the ground searching through the dead leaves and other debris for insects, spiders and grubs.

The name is, of course, derived from their singular call which is usually a duet. The males utter a rising, extended whistle, which ends sharply and is followed immediately by the females 'choo-choo', or sometimes 'choo-ee'. Early in the breeding season a number of pairs may indulge in concert.

A loose, but well-made cup-shaped nest is constructed of twigs and rootlets and is lined with finer materials. Two pale blue eggs are laid which have irregular markings of black and lavender-grey. The breeding season is from July to November or later.

EPTHIANURIDAE

Chats

WHITE-FACED CHATS, *Epthianura albifrons*, are, no doubt, the best-known of these lively little birds. They are widely distributed, being found wherever habitat permits. From southern Queensland, they range down the eastern States to Victoria, Tasmania, the islands of Bass Strait and Kangaroo Island. In South Australia they are absent only from the north-west. Another population is found in southern Western Australia, north to Point Cloates. Nomadic to a large degree, but also residents in some areas, these birds frequent open country of many kinds; cultivated paddocks, areas of low heathy scrub, and swampy localities both inland and by the sea.

They are seldom still and may be seen in pairs or small flocks hunting on the ground for insects or perched on low bushes and wire fences. Both parent birds, if surprised at the nest, have a dramatic, injury-feigning display, where they flutter, apparently almost helpless, over the ground.

The nest is a neat cup of twigs, grass and fine rootlets, lined with hair or other soft material. It is usually concealed in a low bush within a foot or two of the ground.

Three or four white eggs form the clutch and these are spotted, with reddish-brown, particularly about the broade end. July to December are the usual breeding months but the birds will sometimes continue nesting into a mil autumn.

CRIMSON CHATS, *E. tricolor*, are distributed down easter Australia, generally being found west of the Great Dividin Range. They range south as far as north-western Victori and mid-South Australia. In Western Australia, crimso chats are found from the Kimberleys south to about th Moore River and Kalgoorlie. Occasionally, birds are re ported further south on the Swan River coastal plain.

They tend to be nomadic, travelling in large flocks outsid the breeding season. Sometimes this species mixes wit White-faced Chats.

The flock-call is a metallic 'ting', similar to that of th white-faced birds. Other distinct calls noted are a swee shrill whistle usually uttered three times; a mournful whistl in two syllables uttered by the male in territory establish ment; a low, truculent chatter used in territory defence; an a plaintive hissing uttered in the injury-feigning displa (Serventy and Whittell; S. R. White).

The nest is similar to the White-faced Chats', and is usuall built into the top of a saltbush or a clump of Triodia (i Western Australia) and similar low growth in other places Both sexes share in the nest building, incubation and rearin of the young birds.

Three or, sometimes, four eggs are laid which are white spotted with reddish-purple. The breeding season is fron October to December in the east, and from July to March i the west.

DICAEIDAE

Mistletoe-birds and Pardalotes

SPOTTED PARDALOTES, *Pardalotus punctatus*, are distributed throughout most of eastern Australia down to south-easter South Australia and Tasmania. There is a separate popu- lation in Western Australia from about Moora to the Stirlin Ranges.

WHITE-FACED CHAT 4½in. ♀

♂

♀

CRIMSON CHAT 4¼in. ♂

YELLOW-TIPPED PARDALOTES, *P. striatus*, are distributed from south-eastern Queensland to Victoria, south-eastern South Australia, Tasmania and Bass Strait islands. They are quite common, particularly in Tasmania. They are found in many types of light woodland and partly cleared country, feeding on insects of many kinds, mostly in the higher foliage.

The 'pick-it-up' call is distinctive and is a good way of identifying these small birds which are often very difficult to see clearly. Another common call of this species is 'wit-e-chu'.

The nest is the usual domed construction of bark-fibres and similar materials. It may be placed at the end of a tunnel dug into a bank, or in the side of a rabbit-burrow. More frequently, however, this pardalote nests in a small hollow in a trunk or tree-limb at heights up to about fifty feet from the ground. Four white eggs are laid and the breeding season is from August to December.

STRIATED PARDALOTES, *P. substriatus*, are distributed throughout Australia south of the Tropic of Capricorn where suitable habitats allow. These birds spend most of their time hunting busily for insects in the high foliage, but they may sometimes be seen lower down at scrub-level. The calls 'pick-wick', 'be-quick' and 'witt-a-witta' are often the only way of identifying these tiny birds silhouetted against the sky.

A domed nest is built of bark-fibres and other plant material. It is seldom in a tunnel in the ground, more often being found in a hollow stump or a hole in a tree. Sometimes the birds may be found nesting in the crevices between the stones of buildings, and in thatched roofs.

Usually in pairs, but sometimes in small parties, these tiny birds largely frequent the outer foliage of tall trees. Observation of them is fairly difficult, even through binoculars, as they often appear as little more than silhouettes.

Their varied diet is obtained from the leaves and twigs. Scale-insects are a favourite food; thrips, lerps, spiders, moths and many others are also taken. Thus the pardalotes are useful in taking many insects injurious to the trees.

A somewhat ventriloquial and monotonous call note is uttered, sounding like 'slee-ep, ba-bee', high-pitched on the first two syllables, the second two a semitone lower.

A nest of bark-fibres and similar material is placed at the end of a tunnel which the birds have excavated, usually in a bank but sometimes in the flat ground. Nests may also be found in a stump-hole or a hole in a tree. Both sexes help in the tunnel excavation, which may be up to two feet long, and the subsequent building, brooding and feeding duties are also shared. Four white eggs are laid, and the breeding season is from August to December.

SPOTTED PARDALOTE
3½in.

YELLOW-TIPPED PARDALOTE
4¼in.

STRIATED PARDALOTE
4½in.

113

Mistletoe-birds

MISTLETOE-BIRDS, *Dicaeum hirundinaceum*, are found throughout Australia wherever their staple diet of mistletoe berries is to be found. These handsome navy blue and scarlet birds are more common than many people imagine, but because of their small size and habit of feeding high in the trees, they are frequently overlooked. In addition to mistletoe berries, other native fruits are eaten as well as a few arboreal insects.

The call which might be heard up in the high foliage is 'wit-a, wit-a'. Various other brisk notes might be uttered and in addition they might use a warbling song which sometimes includes mimicry of other birds' calls.

The stomach (more properly the muscular gizzard) which most birds have is, in this species, a simple tube, allowing large numbers of berries to pass directly and rapidly through to the intestine and thence quickly on out of the body. When voided the seeds often stick on the nearby twigs or branches where they frequently germinate and flourish.

MISTLETOE-BIRD 4 in.

The birds are thus largely responsible for the spread of the sixty or so varieties of mistletoe in Australia. There is no mistletoe in Tasmania, and consequently no Mistletoe-bird.

The nest is a very delicate and beautiful pear-shaped structure, with a slit entrance in one side. Soft plant-fibre and plant-down are woven and matted with cobwebs into felt. The dried-out castings of wood-borers or the dead brown heads of small flowers are often worked into the outside of the nest. It is suspended from the thin twigs of a leafy branch at any height from three or four feet up to forty feet from the ground.

ZOSTEROPIDAE

Silvereyes

The most common and widespread species in Australia are the GREY-BREASTED SILVEREYES, *Zosterops lateralis*. They range from the Pascoe River in Queensland down as far as Eyre Peninsula in South Australia.

In pairs in the breeding season, otherwise in large flocks these active little birds may be seen in open forests, scrub, gardens and orchards. They destroy large numbers of crop-damaging insects, although sometimes causing considerable damage themselves amongst ripe fruit.

A delicate but quite musical and sustained song is uttered and the birds are also competent mimics of other bird calls. In winter their flanks take on a much richer, tawny-buff colour than is present in the summer dress.

PLOCEIDAE

Old World Seedeaters

GOLDFINCHES, *Carduelis carduelis*, are well-known European and British birds, which are now found in many parts of Australia. In this country they range from south-eastern Queensland down the eastern States to Victoria and southern South Australia. These pretty finches are also found in Tasmania and there is a separate population in the south-west corner of the continent.

They were originally introduced into N.S.W. and Victoria but have thrived and multiplied to become very common. In the main they have remained in the vicinity of man, frequenting farmlands and orchards of all kinds as well as parks, gardens and areas of waste land in or near the suburbs. They rarely nest in native trees, the ti-tree being a notable exception.

Goldfinches have a delicate twittering flight-call which often seems to be uttered in rhythm with its undulating flight. The birds are not considered harmful, as they are seedeaters with a special liking for thistles and other rough herbage.

A very neat cup-nest is built of plant-fibres well felted together and thickly lined with vegetable-down. The usual site is in the forked branch of a thick, low bush or tree.

TREE SPARROW 5¼in.

HOUSE SPARROW 6in.

GOLDFINCH 5in.

GREENFINCH 6in.

BEAUTIFUL FIRETAIL FINCH 4½in.

PAINTED FINCH 4½in.

RED-EARED FIRETAIL FINCH 4½in.

GREENFINCHES, *Chloris chloris*, are related, but are in a different genus. They have not done so well as the Goldfinches as colonisers of their new country, thus they are not as common nor so widely spread. Their main stronghold is in Victoria, although even there they are not particularly common. From Sydney the birds have spread inland to Bathurst, and in South Australia Greenfinches may be seen in and around Adelaide and in parts of the south-east.

They are shyer than the Goldfinches and tend to be seen singly and in pairs, although small numbers sometimes gather out of the breeding season. A few may occasionally be seen mixing with feeding flocks of Goldfinches.

Their call is a monotonously repeated 'dzweee'; a simple, summery sound, distinctly buzzing, and often preceded by a short rising scale of quick 'tizzing' notes. They also have a harsh twitter sometimes uttered in flight.

Their diet consists of various seeds and insects and they are considered to be a harmless species.

HOUSE SPARROWS, *Passer domesticus*, were introduced from Britain in 1862. They were regarded in a somewhat different light in those days when it was considered a serious offence to shoot a precious sparrow. But by the turn of the century they had prospered to such an extent that they were becoming a pest and spreading rapidly.

The birds are too well known to require much description. Their depredations amongst soft fruits, seedlings and flowers, and the way they usurp the nesting holes of more desirable native species have made sparrows unpopular with many people.

The nest is a shameful piece of housekeeping, being a great untidy bundle of grass, straw, pieces of string, paper and other rubbish, crammed into any available crevice or hole in a tree or building.

TREE SPARROWS, *P. montanus*, are nowhere near as common as House Sparrows and are found, sparingly distributed, in parts of Victoria and southern N.S.W.

Actually they are more numerous than many people suppose, but their close similarity to House Sparrows and their habit of mixing with them, helps the shyer birds to pass unnoticed. They may always be told apart by their brown caps, compared with the grey crowns of the house sparrows. Tree sparrows also have a black spot on each white cheek, which is quite noticeable when the birds are in summer plumage.

FIRETAIL FINCHES or BEAUTIFUL FIRETAILS, *Zonaeginthus bellus*, are found in the coastal areas of N.S.W. as far north as Newcastle, and down into Victoria and south-eastern South Australia. They are also found on Kangaroo Island, 115 and are the only native finches to cross through the Bass Strait islands into Tasmania where they are quite common.

In pairs or small parties they frequent heathy country, swampy terrain, open forests and low scrub. They are rarely seen far from water of some description. In Tasmania they are less confined to coastal areas.

Their flight is direct and when flushed from the ground, where they obtain a good deal of their food, they go off with a whirr of wings like miniature quail. They are not easily put up, however, trying to hide in the grass as a first resort. Their call is a penetrating and mournful 'wee' and a descending call of 'tee-tee-te-te-te-te'.

A nest, shaped like a bottle on its side, is built of fine dry grasses and green grass interwoven with a few leaves. It is built in the thick foliage of a bush or low tree.

RED-EARED FIRETAIL FINCHES, *Z. oculatus*, are restricted to south-western Australia along some of the coastal districts from Esperance westwards, with gaps in their distribution.

They may be found in various habitats such as heavy scrub, forests and paper-bark swamps on the coast. They are territory-conscious birds, and unlike the other native finches tend to remain in pairs even outside the breeding season.

A neat, bottle-shaped nest is built of grass, rootlets and plant-tendrils strongly woven together. The entrance neck may be as much as seven inches long. The sites vary in height from fifteen to fifty feet up, and on an average are higher than the nests of other Australian finches.

PAINTED FINCHES, *Emblema picta*, have penetrated perhaps more than any others into the arid central regions of Australia. They are found from western Queensland across to the southern Kimberleys and down to the mid-western coast of the continent and northern South Australia.

In pairs or in small flocks of up to twenty birds or so they are a typical species of the spinifex country. Stony slopes with a little grass cover are preferred, but they also frequent the spinifex plains.

They are strong fliers, generally travelling close to the ground in an undulating movement. Painted Finches feed on the ground, picking up seeds from around clumps of grass. A loud and harsh call of 'tiik' or 'trut' may be heard from these birds in flight; a similar but quieter call is used between the birds as they feed, and the female has a rather staccato alarm call.

A rather poorly-constructed globular nest is built of small twigs, grasses, spinifex stalks and rootlets. The usual site is in dense clumps of grass one or two feet off the ground. Under the nest the birds first build a foundation of pellets of earth, bark, twigs and a few small stones. Unlike many of the grass-finches, these birds do not build separate sleeping nests; nor do the males share the breeding nest with the females, but roost on the ground nearby.

RED-BROWED FINCHES, *Aegintha temporalis*, are found in coastal districts from Cape York down to Victoria, south-eastern South Australia and Kangaroo Island.

Two main races of these finches are recognised by Keast, the second one being *A. minor*, inhabiting Cape York. In this form the grey of the head, which is paler than in the southern birds, extends down towards the shoulders. The back is also a brighter yellow-olive in contrast to the southern birds which are dark olive-green. The undertail-coverts are blackish in the northern birds, grey in the southern.

These finches feed both on the ground and in the branches of low bushes. The high-pitched calls 'ssitt-ssitt' and 'ssee-ssee' are distinctive, and are almost continuously uttered as the birds move about in search of food consisting mainly of seeds. The song is a rather rhythmical repetition of the call notes.

A bulky, bottle-shaped nest is built with the entrance tunnel to one side. This varies a good deal in length from an inch or two up to six inches.

GOULDIAN FINCHES, *Chloebia gouldiae*, are found in tropical northern Australia from about Derby in the west to the eastern side of the Gulf of Carpentaria and down to about 20° south in inland Queensland. There appears to be some nomadism in these finches, with a southern movement during the wet season. Flocks of up to several hundred of them may be seen out of the breeding season.

There are three phases of these finches during which they have similarly coloured bodies, but may have black, red or yellow heads. Three black-headed birds are found for every single red-headed bird; yellow-headed birds are very rare, being about one in every thousand to five thousand.

These beautiful finches are amongst the least studied of the group in the wild and little is known of their habits. They are never seen far from water and their favoured habitat is open grassy country with scattered timber. Gouldian Finches may also be found along the edges of mangroves and other scrub thickets. They are not particularly terrestrial, preferring to climb about in the grass stems in search of seeding grass-heads and insects.

They are quiet birds, seldom calling, and then only uttering a 'ssitt'. A very high-pitched song audible over a few yards may also be heard. It is a continuous whispering hissing sound interspersed with low clicks.

The nest is very frequently built in a hole, either in a tree or a termite-mound.

BLACK-THROATED FINCHES, *Peophila cincta*, are distributed from Cape York and Normanton down to northern N.S.W. There are, according to Keast, three acceptable forms of this bird.

The form *cincta* is found from N.S.W. to Inkerman in Queensland; BLACK-RUMPED FINCHES, *P. c. atropygialis*, found from the Cairns to Normanton districts, differ mainly in having black upper tail-coverts, a richer fawn on their backs and breasts and a paler grey on their heads; *P. c.*

ZEBRA FINCH 4in.

♀

♂

116

nigrotecta from Cape York have deep brown on their fronts, without the reddish tinge.

Black-throated Finches are very close relatives of the Long-tailed Finches and are similar in habits, although the Black-throats prefer more densely covered habitats as a rule and are usually found in the vicinity of fresh-water. They remain fairly shy birds and have not remained where human habitation has spread to any extent.

Grass seeds and a few insects form their diet and they are largely terrestrial. Their calls are almost identical to the Long-tailed Finches'.

A domed grass nest is built, with a side entrance and a tunnel. Roosting nests, without lining or tunnel, are built for use outside the breeding season.

DOUBLE-BARRED FINCHES, *Stizoptera bichenovii*, are distributed from central-western N.S.W. up to Cape York; westwards they range through Northern Territory to Roebuck Bay on the west coast. They have two distinct colour types which are recognised as geographic races. *Stizoptera bichenovii* are the eastern birds, found in N.S.W., Queensland and Cape York. The western form, *S. b. annulosa*, takes up the western sectors of the distribution and differ in having black instead of white rumps. In parts of Northern Territory there is a hybrid population with some black-rumped birds and others with a variable amount of white feathering (Keast).

Double-barred Finches frequent a wide variety of habitats. Pandanus groves and the rank grass along creeks are a common haunt, but they are also met with on dry, lightly timbered plains, although seldom more than a mile or two from water. They have taken very much to living in the vicinity of man.

They are largely terrestrial, where they obtain most of their food, occasionally moving up into the grass stems and low bushes. Seeds of various grasses and herbaceous plants are taken and also some insects are eaten.

A low 'tat-tat' communication call may be heard and a louder identity call of 'tiaat-tiaat'. Infrequently a low, rather trilling song is uttered during the breeding season.

The nest tends to be globular rather than bottle-shaped, and has only an inch or two of entrance tunnel. It is rather roughly built of dry grasses and grass stalks.

ZEBRA FINCHES, *Taeniopygia guttata*, are found throughout most of Australia except for the wet coastal forest areas. They are by far the most common of our finches and are found in a wide variety of habitats. In pairs during the breeding season, or otherwise in flocks (made up of birds which seem to pair for life), they feed on or near the ground, mainly on seeds, supplementing this diet with insects.

They have a variety of calls. The communication call is a low 'tet-tet' heard almost constantly as the flock moves along. A loud, rather nasal 'tia', is the flight-call and an aggressive call of 'wist', like the sound of tearing cloth, is used when the finches chase other birds. The song is low with somewhat ventriloquial trills being interspersed with the identity call (Immelmann).

A poorly-built nest of grasses is made, sometimes with a few small twigs and rootlets. The egg chamber is lined with soft material of various kinds. Many situations are chosen to breed in. Holes of different kinds, a rabbit burrow, or under the large stick-nests of birds of prey are quite common sites; even the old nests of smaller species will be utilised.

When they build their own nests, they can be in a thick prickly bush or in a tree up to thirty feet from the ground. Outside the nesting season simple roosting nests are constructed.

TIMOR SEA

MELVILLE I.

DARWIN

WEST
ALLIGATOR R.

SOUTH
ALLIGATOR R.

NAPIER BROOME BAY

ADMIRALTY GULF

INDIAN OCEAN

WYNDHAM

KIMBERLEY RANGES

KING SOUND

DERBY

FITZROY R.

HALL'S CREEK

BROOME

FITZROY CROSSING

ROEBUCK BAY

NOR

MUSGRAVE RANGES

TANAMI

TANAMI DESERT

GREAT SANDY DESERT

NICKOL BAY

DAMPIER ARCH.

PORT HEDLAND

TE

MONTEBELLO I.

BARROW I.

FORTESQUE R.

EXMOUTH GULF

Lake Mackay

North West
Cape

ONSLOW

HAMERSLEY RANGES

Point Cloates

ASHBURTON R.

Lake Amadeus

MINILYA R.

GIBSON DESERT

AYERS R

MAC

GASCOYNE R.

Lake Carnegie

SHARK BAY

CARNARVON

DIRK
HARTOGS I.

WILUNA

EVER

MURCHISON R.

WESTERN AUSTRALIA

GREAT VICTORIA DESERT

GERALDTON

NULLARBOR PLAIN

OOLDEA

A U

HOUTMAN
ABROLHOS

MORAWA

KALGOORLIE

NARETHA

MOORA

EUCLA

DARLING RANGES

MOORE R.

NORSEMAN

Lake Dundas

GREAT   AUSTRALIAN   BIG

PERTH
FREMANTLE

Lake Grace

BUNBURY

ESPERANCE

Cape Naturaliste

STIRLING RANGES

ARCHIPELAGO OF THE RECHERCHE

ALBANY

118

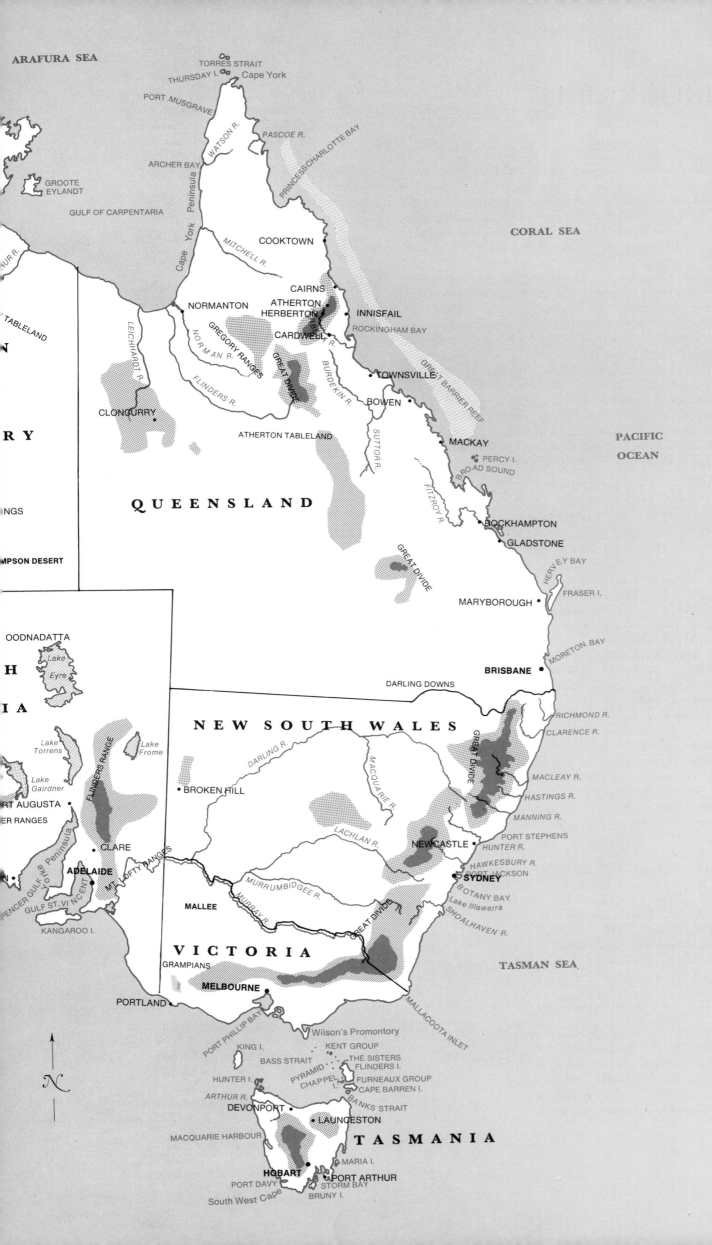

ARAFURA SEA

TORRES STRAIT
THURSDAY I. Cape York
PORT MUSGRAVE

ARCHER BAY

PASCOE R.

PRINCESS CHARLOTTE BAY

GROOTE
EYLANDT

GULF OF CARPENTARIA

WATSON R.

Cape York Peninsula

MITCHELL R.

CORAL SEA

COOKTOWN

TABLELAND

CAIRNS
ATHERTON
HERBERTON
CARDWELL
ROCKINGHAM BAY

NORMANTON

GREGORY RANGES

NORMAN R.

RY

CLONCURRY

LEICHHARDT R.

FLINDERS R.

GREAT DIVIDE

BURDEKIN R.

TOWNSVILLE

BOWEN

GREAT BARRIER REEF

NGS

ATHERTON TABLELAND

SUTTOR R.

MACKAY

PACIFIC

PERCY I.
BROAD SOUND

OCEAN

PSON DESERT

QUEENSLAND

FITZROY R.

ROCKHAMPTON
GLADSTONE

HERVEY BAY
FRASER I.

GREAT DIVIDE

OODNADATTA

Lake
Eyre

MARYBOROUGH

H

Lake
Torrens

IA

Lake
Frome

Lake
Gairdner

RT AUGUSTA

ER RANGES

FLINDERS RANGE

MORETON BAY

BRISBANE

DARLING DOWNS

NEW SOUTH WALES

DARLING R.

BROKEN HILL

MACQUARIE R.

GREAT DIVIDE

RICHMOND R.
CLARENCE R.

MACLEAY R.

HASTINGS R.

MANNING R.

LACHLAN R.

PORT STEPHENS

NEWCASTLE
HUNTER R.

CLARE

MT. LOFTY RANGES

ADELAIDE

Yorke Peninsula

SPENCER GULF

GULF ST. VINCENT

MALLEE

MURRUMBIDGEE R.

MURRAY R.

HAWKESBURY R.
PORT JACKSON
SYDNEY
BOTANY BAY
Lake Illawarra

SHOALHAVEN R.

KANGAROO I.

VICTORIA

GREAT DIVIDE

TASMAN SEA

GRAMPIANS

MELBOURNE

PORTLAND

MALLACOOTA INLET

PORT PHILLIP BAY

KING I.

Wilson's Promontory

KENT GROUP

BASS STRAIT

THE SISTERS
FLINDERS I.

PYRAMID
CHAPPEL

HUNTER I.

ARTHUR R.

FURNEAUX GROUP
CAPE BARREN I.

BANKS' STRAIT

DEVONPORT

LAUNCESTON

MACQUARIE HARBOUR

TASMANIA

MARIA I.

HOBART
PORT DAVY
South West Cape

PORT ARTHUR
STORM BAY
BRUNY I.

BIBLIOGRAPHY

The following bibliography lists all the publications referred to in the course of writing the present volume. Some of these works are of particular importance as they have been the basis for various aspects and sections of *Australian Birds*, and I should also like to take this opportunity of thanking the various authors for whatever use I have made of their books.

The Mallee Fowl by Dr H. J. Frith was the basis of my section on this bird. Brigadier Hugh R. Officer's excellent book on the honeyeaters was of great value in dealing with this group—the notes on nesting and distribution being particularly useful. *Australian Finches* by Klaus Immelmann was largely referred to for the finches. For the waterfowl, the group-monograph *Waterfowl in Australia* by Dr H. J. Frith was used. *The Lyrebirds of Sherbrooke* by Dr L. H. Smith provided a number of facts and anecdotes about these interesting birds. Except for where species have been more thoroughly dealt with in monographs or regional studies N. W. Cayley's *What Bird is That* was taken as a basis for information on distribution and nesting.

GENERAL

Austin, Oliver L. Jr. *Birds of the World.*
  London, Paul Hamlyn, 1961.
Cayley, Neville W. *What Bird is That?*
  A guide to the birds of Australia. 4th edition.
  Sydney, Angus and Robertson, 1966.
Chisholm, Alec H. *Bird Wonders of Australia.* 5th edition.
  Sydney, Angus and Robertson, 1958.
Fisher, James and Peterson, Roger T. *The World of Birds.*
  London, Macdonald, 1964.
Grossman, Mary L. and Hamlet, John.
  Birds of Prey of the World. London, Cassell, 1965.
Hindwood, Keith. *Australian Birds in Colour.*
  Sydney, Reed, 1966.
Lanyon, Wesley E. *Biology of Birds.* London, Nelson, 1964.
Leach, J. A. *An Australian Bird Book.*
  9th edition, revised by P. Crosbie Morrison.
  Melbourne, Whitcombe and Tombs, 1961.
Mathews, Gregory M. *The Birds of Australia.*
  London, Witherby, 1910-1927.
Mayr, Ernst, Linsley, E. Gorton, and Usinger, Robert L.
  Methods and Principles of Systematic Zoology.
  New York, McGraw-Hill Book Co. Inc., 1953.
Peters, James Lee. *A Checklist of Birds of the World.*
  Cambridge, Harvard University Press, 1931-1962.
Peterson, Roger T. and Editors, Life Nature Library.
  The Birds. New York, Time-Life Books, 1964.
Pizzey, Graham. *Animals and Birds in Australia.*
  Melbourne, Cassell, 1966.
Thomson, A. Landsborough. Ed.
  A New Dictionary of Birds. London, Nelson, 1964.

MONOGRAPHS

Barrett, Charles. *Parrots of Australia.*
  Melbourne, N. H. Seward Pty. Ltd., 1949.
Bedford, The Duke of. *Parrots and Parrot-like Birds.*
  New Jersey, All-Pets Books, Inc., 1954.
Cayley, Neville W. *Australian Parrots.*
  Sydney, Angus and Robertson, 1938.

Frith, Dr H. J. *The Mallee Fowl.*
  Sydney, Angus and Robertson, 1962.
Groen, Dr H. D. *Australian Parakeets,*
  Holland. Dr H. D. Groen-Haren, N.D.
Officer, Brigadier Hugh R. *Australian Honeyeaters.*
  Melbourne, Bird Observers' Club, 1965.

REGIONAL

Condon, H. T. *A Handlist of the Birds of South Australia.*
  Adelaide, South Australian Ornithological Association,
  1962.
Serventy, D. L. and Whittell, H. M.
  Birds of Western Australia.
  Perth, Paterson Brokensha Pty. Ltd., 1962
Sharland, Michael. *Tasmanian Birds.* 2nd edition.
  Sydney, Angus and Robertson, 1945.
Wheeler, W. Roy. *A Handlist of the Birds of Victoria.*
  Melbourne, Victorian Ornithological Research Group,
  1967.

PAPERS

As well as using books for reference, I have referred to many papers published in a variety of scientific works. Some of these, in particular, are recommended for further reading on some difficult groups of birds.

For example, the nomenclature and the classification of the whistlers (*Pachycephala*) and the yellow robins (*Eopsaltria*) have been altered a number of times over the past few years. Changes have been as great as moving the Little Yellow Robin out of the *Eopsaltria* altogether and classifying it with the *Microeca* flycatchers.

For further reading on the *Pachycephala* see:
Mayr, Ernst. *Notes on Australian Whistlers.*
American Museum Novitiates. American Museum of Natural History. No. 1653, 1954.

The *Eopsaltria* have been treated in:
Chisholm, A. H. *Yellow Robin (Remarks on Robins).*
Emu, Vol. 60. p. 231.

Certain of the taxonomically difficult pardalotes have been dealt with in:
Hindwood, K. A. and Mayr, Ernst.
A Revision of the Stripe-crowned Pardalotes. Emu, Vol. 46. p. 49.

The two following thorough and valuable papers on classification were used in my section on classification:
Mayr, Ernst and Amadon, Dean.
A Classification of Recent Birds. American Museum Novitiates.
American Museum of Natural History. No. 1496, 1951.

Mayr, E. and Greenway, J. C.
Sequence of Passerine Families (Aves).
Brevoria, Museum of Comparative Zoology, Cambridge, Mass. No. 58, 1956.

The thornbills (*Acanthiza*) are a taxonomically complex group of birds that have been treated thoroughly in the following paper:
Mack, George. *A Systematic Revision of Australian Thornbills.*
Memoirs of the National Museum of Victoria, No. 10, 1936, p. 86.

In addition to the above papers, reference has been made to numerous issues of the R.A.O.U. publication *Emu*.

INDEX

Illustration page numbers are in italics ; references to each bird are in roman.

Albatrosses, *17* ;17
  Black-browed, *17* ;17
APODIFORMES, 65
'Apostle-bird', 83
'Arco', 83
Avocet, Red-necked, *41* ;43

Babblers, *83* ;83,84
  Chestnut-crowned, *83* ;84
  Grey-crowned, 83
  Hall's, *83* ;84
  Red-breasted, *83* ;83
  White-browed, *83* ;83
  White-throated, *83* ;84
'Barktit', 11
Bee-eater, *67* ;68
Bellbird, *108* ;107
Bell-miner, *108* ;107
Betcherrygah, *see* Budgerygah
Birds of Paradise, *80* ;69,80
  Paradise Rifle-bird, *80* ;80
Bitterns, *22* ;20,22
  Black, *22* ;20
  Brown, *22* ;20
  Little, *22* ;20
Blackbird, *86* ;86
Boodgereegar *see* Budgerygah
Bower-birds, *79* ;78,79
  Satin, *79* ;78
  Spotted, *79* ;79
Brolga, *35* ;35
Bronzewing Pigeons, Brush, *47* ;46
  Forest, *47* ;46
Budgerigar *see* Budgerygah
Budgerygah, *56* ;58
Bushlark, *71* ;71
Butcher-birds, *78* ;77,78
  Grey, *78* ;78

'Cackler', 83
CAPRIMULGIFORMES, 63
CASUARIIFORMES, *14* ;15
Catbirds, 83
CHARADRIIFORMES, 37
Chats, Crimson, *113* ;112
  White-faced, *113* ;112
'Chatterer', 83
Chough, White-winged, *76* ;77
CICONIIFORMES, 20
Cockatiel, *56* ;52
Cockatoos, *49,51* ;48,49,50
  Blood-stained, *51* ;50
  Corellas, *51* ;50
  Galah, *49* ;49
  Gang-gang, *49* ;48
  Red-tailed Black, *50* ;48
  Rose-breasted, *see* Galah
  Sulphur-crested, *51* ,49
  White, *51* ;49
'Codlin-moth-eater', 83
COLUMBIFORMES, 46
Coot, *36* ;36
CORACIIFORMES, 66
  Corellas, *51* ;50
Cormorants, *18* ;19
  Black, *18* ;19
  Little Black, *18* ;19
  Little Pied, *18* ;19
Cranes, 35
  Blue, *see* White-faced Heron
Crows, *75* ;76
  Little, *75* ;77
Crow-shrikes, Piping, 77
  see also Magpies
Cuckoos, *59,60* ;59,60,61
  Fantailed, *60* ;60
  Golden Bronze, *60* ;61

Narrow-billed Bronze, *60* ;60
  Pallid, *59* ;59
  Shining Bronze, *60* ;59,60
Cuckoo-shrikes, *73* ;73
  Black-faced, *73* ;73
  Gascoyne, *73* ;73
  Ground, *73* ;73
  Little, *73* ;73
  Papuan, *73* ;73
CUCULIFORMES, 59
Curlews, *40* ;39
Curlew-Sandpiper, *39* ;40

Dollar-bird, *67* ;68
Dotterels, *40* ;37,38
  Black-fronted, *40* ;37
  Double-banded, *40* ;38
  Hooded, *40* ;38
  Red-kneed, *40* ;38
Doves, *46* ;46
  Bar-shouldered, *47* ;46
  Diamond, *47* ;46
  Indian Turtle-dove, *46* ;46
  Peaceful, *47* ;46
  Senegal Turtle-dove, *46* ;46
Drongo, Spangled, *74* ;74
Ducks, *24,25* ;24,25
  Black, *24* ;24
  Blue-billed, *24* ;25
  Chestnut-breasted Shel, *25* ;24
  Grey Teal, *25* ;24
  Musk, *24* ;25
  Perching, 25
  Pink-eared, *25* ;24
  Pochards, 24
  Shoveler, Blue-winged, *25* ;24
  Stiff-tailed, 25
  White-eyed, *25* ;24
  Wood, *25* ;25

Eagles, *30,31* ;27,28
  Red-backed Sea, *30* ;28
  Wedge-tailed, *31* ;27
  Whistling 'Eagle', *30* ;28
Egrets, *21,22* ;20,22
  Cattle, *21* ;22
  Large, *21* ;20
  Little, *22* ;22
  Plumed, *22* ;22
  White, *21* ;20
Emu, *14* ;15

FALCONIFORMES, 27
Falcons, *27,28* ;30
  Black, *37* ;36,46,
  Brown, *28* ;30
  Kestrel, *28* ;30
  Little, *27* ;30
  Peregrine, *27* ;30
Fantails, *96* ;97
  Black and White. *see* Willie Wagtail
  Grey, *96* ;97
  Northern, *96* ;97
  Rufous, *96* ;97
Fantail-warbler, Golden-headed, *87* ;87
Finches, *115,116,117* ;115,116,117
  Beautiful Firetail, *115* ;115
  Black-rumped, *117* ;116
  Black-throated, *117* ;116,117
  Double-barred, *117* ;117
  Firetail, *115* ;115
  Gouldian, *117* ;116
  Painted, *115* ;116
  Red-browed, *117* ;116
  Red-eared Firetail, *115* ;116
  White-rumped Double-bar, *117* ;117
  Zebra, *116* ;117

Firetail, Beautiful, *115* ;115
  Red-eared, *115* ;116
Flycatchers, *93,95* ;93,95
  Black-faced, *95* ;95
  Brown, *93* ;93
  Lemon-breasted, *93* ;93
  Pearly, *95* ;95
  Restless, *96* ;97
  Spectacled, *95* ;95
  White-eared, *95* ;96
Fowl, Jungle, Mallee, *34* ;33
Frogmouths, Tawny, *63* ;63

Galah, *49* ;49
GALLIFORMES, 33
Gannets, Australian, *19* ;19
Golden-headed Fantail-warbler, *87* ;87
Goldfinch, *115* ;114
Goshawks, *29* ;28
  Brown, *29* ;28
  Grey, *29* ;28
Grassbirds, *87* ;88
  Little, *87* ;88
  Tawny, *87* ;88
Grebes, *15,16* ;16
  Crested, *15* ;16
  Little, *16* ;16
Greenfinch, *115* ;115
GRUIFORMES, 35
Gulls, *37* ;43
  Kelp, *42* ;43
  Pacific, *42* ;43
  Silver, *42* ;43

Hall's Babblers, 83,84
'Happy Family Bird', 83
Hawks, *28,29* ;28,30
  Brown, *28* ;30
  Goshawks, *29* ;28
Hens, *36* ;35,36
  Dusky Moor, *36* ;35
  Eastern Swamp, *36* ;35
  Swamp, *36* ;36
  Water, 35
  Western Swamp, *36* ;35,36
Herons, *20,23* ;20
  Nankeen Night, *23* ;20
  White-faced, *20* ;20
Honeyeaters, *104,105,106,107,109* ;101–105,111
  Black-chinned, *104* ;104
  Black-faced, 101
  Brown, *105* ;105
  Brown-headed, *104* ;104
  Crescent, *107* ;106
  Fuscous, *102* ;102
  Grey-headed, *101* ;102
  Helmeted, *103* ;103
  Mallee, 103
  New Holland, 106
  Painted, *106* ;106
  Purple-gaped, *101* ;102
  Regent, *106* ;106
  Singing, *101* ;101
  Spiny-cheeked, *109* ;111
  Tawny-crowned, *105* ;104
  White-bearded, 106
  White-cheeked, *107* ;107
  White-eared, *101* ;101
  White-fronted, *105* ;105
  White-naped, *104* ;103
  White-plumed, *102* ;103
  Yellow-faced, *103* ;102
  Yellow-plumed, *102* ;103
  Yellow-winged, *107* ;106
'Hopper', 83

Ibises, *21*;23
  Glossy, *21*;23
  Straw-necked, *21*;23
  White, *21*;23

Jackass, Laughing, *64*;67
'Jacky Winter', 93
Jungle-fowl, *34*;33

Kestrel, *28*;30
Kingfishers, *65,66*;66,67
  Azure, *65*;66
  Blue, *see* Azure
  Forest, *66*;67
  Sacred, *66*;67
Kookaburras, Laughing, *64*;67

Larks, *71*;71
  Bush, *71*;71
  Magpie, *77*;77
  Sky, *71*;71
Lorikeets, *48*;48
  Rainbow, *48*;48
  Red-collared, *48*;48
Lyrebirds, *70*;69,71
  Prince Albert, *70*;69,71
  Superb, *70*;69,71

Magpie Lark, 77
Magpies, *77*;77
  Lark, 77
  White-backed, 77
Mallee-fowl, *34*;33
Marshbirds, *see* Grassbirds
Martins, *72*;72
  Fairy, *72*;72
  Tree, *72*;72
Miners, *108,109*;107,108,110
  Bell, *108*;107
  Dusky, *109*
  Noisy, *108*;108
  White-rumped, 110
  Yellow-throated, *108*;108
Mistletoe,bird, *114*;112,114
'Mollyhawks', 43
'Mollymawks', 43
Moorhens, *36*;35
Mound-builders, *34*;33
  Jungle-fowl, *34*;33
  Mallee-fowl, *34*;33
Mudlark, Papuan, *76*;77
Mutton-bird, *17*;17
Mynah, Indian, *100*;100

Nightjars, *62*;63,65
  Owlet, *62*;65
  Spotted, *63*;63
Native Companion *see* Brolga

Old World Flycatchers, 93
Old World Warblers, 86
Osprey, *32*;32
Owlet-nightjar, *62*;65
Owls, *61,62*;61,62
  Barking, *61,62*;61,62
  Barn, *61*;61
  Boobook, *61*;62
  Grass, *61*;62
  Masked, *61*;62
  Powerful, *62*;62
  Tasmanian Masked, *61*;62
Oyster-Catchers, Pied, *39*;37

Painted Snipes, *37*;37
Parakeets, Barnard's *see* Ringneck Parrot
  Pennant's, 53
Pardalotes, *113*;112
  Spotted, *113*;112
  Striated, *113*;113
  Yellow-tipped, *113*;113
Parrots, *52,57,58,59*;48,49,52,53,56,57
  Blue-winged, *58*;56
  Elegant, *58*;57

King, *59*;52
Orange-breasted, *58*;57
Red-backed, *57*;56
Red-crowned, 49
Red-winged, *59*;52
Ringneck, *53*;56
Rosella, *see* Rosellas
Scarlet-chested, *58*;57
Superb, *52*;53
PASSERIFORMES, 69
Pelican, Australian, *18*;19
PELECANIFORMES, 19
Penguins, Little, *16*;16
Perching Ducks, 25
Pigeons, 46,47
  Brush Bronzewing, *47*;46
  Crested, *47*;47
  Forest Bronzewing, *47*;46
  Wonga, *47*;47
Pipit, *71*;99
Pittas, Blue-breasted, *69*;69
Plovers, *38,39*;37,38
  Banded, *38*;37
  Golden, *39*;38
  Grey, *39*;38
  Spurwinged, *38*;37
Pochards, 24
PODICIPEDIFORMES, 16
PROCELLARIIFORMES, 17
PSITTACIFORMES, 48

Quails, *33*;34
  Brown, *33*
  King, *33*;34
  Stubble, *33*;34
Quail-thrushes, Spotted, *84*;83,84

Rails, 35
Rainbow-bird, 68
Raven, *75*;76
Reed-warbler, 87,87
Rifle-birds, *80*;69,80
  Paradise, *80*
Ringneck Parrots, 53,56
Robins, *94,95*;94,95
  Dusky, *94*;94
  Hooded, *94*;94
  Northern Yellow, *95*;95
  Red-capped, *94*;94
  Scarlet, *94*;94
  Southern Yellow, *95*;95
Roller, 68
Rosellas, *55*;53,54,55,56
  Adelaide, *55*;54
  Beautiful Lory, 53
  Blue-cheeked, *55*;53,54
  Crimson, *54*;53
  Eastern, *54*;55
  Green, *54*;54
  Moondark, 55
  Northern, *55*;54
  Pale-headed, *55*;53,54
  Smutty, 55
  Western, *55*;56
  Yellow, 55

Sanderling, *39*;40
Sandpipers, *39*;39,40,41
  Broad-billed, *39*;41
  Curlew, *39*;40
  Sharp-tailed, *39*;40
Scrub-wrens, *91*;92,93
  Buff-breasted, *91*;92
  Large-billed, *91*;93
  White-browed, *91*;92
'Seagull', 43
Shearwaters, *17*;17
  Fluttering, *17*
  Short-tailed, *17*;17
  Wedge-tailed, *17*;17
Shelducks, Chestnut-breasted, *25*;24

Shoveler, Blue-winged, *25*;24
Shrikes, *73*;73
  Black-faced Cuckoo, *73*;73
  Gascoyne Cuckoo, *73*;73
  Ground Cuckoo, *73*;73
  Little Cuckoo, *73*;73
  Papuan Cuckoo, *73*;73
Shrike-thrush, 84
Shriketits, Eastern, *111*;111
Silvereyes, Grey-breasted, *114*;11
Sittellas, *82*;81,82
  Black-capped, *82*;82
  Orange-winged, *82*;82
  Striated, *82*;82
Skylark, *71*;71
Snipe, *37*;37,39
  Japanese, 39
  Painted, *37*;37
  Pin-tailed, *37*;39
Songlarks, *86*;86
  Brown, *86*;86
  Rufous, *86*;86
Sparrows, *115*;115
  House, *115*;115
  Tree, *115*;115
SPHENISCIFORMES, 16
Spinebills, Eastern, *105*;104
Spoonbills, *21*;23
  Royal, *21*
  Yellow-billed, *21*;23
Starlings, Common, *100*;100
Stiff-tail Ducks, 25
Stilts, *41*;41
  Banded, *41*;41
  White-headed, *41*;41
Stint, Little, Red-necked, *39*;40
STRIGIFORMES, 61
Swallows, *72*;72,99
  Dusky Wood, *99*;99
  House, *see* Welcome Swallow
  Little Wood, *99*;99
  Welcome, *72*;72
  White-backed, *72*;72
  White-browed Wood, *99*;99
Swamphens, *36*;35,36
  Eastern, *36*;35
  Western, *36*;35,36
Swans, Black, *26*;26
  White, 26
Swifts, *68*;65
  Fork-tailed, *68*;65
  Spine-tailed, *68*;65

Tailor-bird, *87*;87
Teal, Grey, *25*;24
Terns, *44,45*;43,44
  Bridled, *44*;44
  Crested, *45*;43
  'dog', 44
  Fairy, *45*;43
  Gull-billed, *45*;44
  Lesser Crested, *45*;43
  Little, *45*;43
  Roseate, *45*;44
  Sooty, *44*;44
  White-winged Black, *45*;44
Thornbills, *85,91*;91,92
  Brown, 85
  Buff-tailed, *91*;92
  Striated, *91*;91
  Tasmanian, *91*;92
  Yellow-tailed, 91,92
Thrushes, *84,85*;84,85
  Brown, 84
  Grey, *85*;84
  Ground, *85*;85
  Little, *85*;84
  'Port Jackson', 84
  Rufous, *85*;85
  Sandstone, *85*;84

Song, *86*;86
Spotted Quail, *84*;84
Stripe-breasted, *85*;85
Treecreepers, *81*;81,82
Little, *81*;81
Red-browed, *81*;81
White-browed, *81*;82
White-throated, *81*;81
Trillers, *74*;74
Varied, *74*;74
White-winged, *74*;74
Tube Noses, 17
Turtledove, Indian, *46*;46
Senegal, *46*;46

Waders, 37
Wagtail, Willie, *96*;96
Warblers, *87,89,92*;87,90

Black-throated, *89*;90
Brown, *89*;90
Buff-breasted, *89*;90
Fairy, *89*;90
Golden-headed Fantail, *87*;87
Northern, *89*;90
Reed, *87*;87
Speckled, *92*;93
Western, 90
White-tailed, *89*;90
White-throated, *89*;90
Waterhens, Dusky Moorhen, 35
Wattle-birds, Little, *110*;110
Red, *109*;110
Weebills, Brown, *92*;93
Whipbirds, Eastern, *112*;111
Whistlers, *97,98*;98
Golden, *97*;98

Rufous, *98*;98
White-eyes, *see* Silvereyes
Wood-swallows, *99*;99
Dusky, *99*;99
Little, *99*;99
White-browed, *99*;99
Wrens, Banded, *88*;89
Black-and-White, *88*;89
Black-backed, *88*;89
Blue, *88*;88
Blue-and-White, *88*;89
Buff-breasted Scrub, *91*;92
Fairy, 90
Large-billed Scrub, *91*;93
Purple-backed, *88*;90
Variegated, *88*;90
White-backed, *88*;90
White-browed Scrub, *91*;92

INDEX OF SCIENTIFIC NAMES

Acanthiza chrysorrhoa, 92
  ewingi, 92
  lineata, 91
  nana, 91
  reguloides, 92
Acanthorhynchus tenuirostris, 104
Accipiter, 28
  fasciatus, 28
  novae-hollandiae, 28
Acridotheres tristis, 100
Acrocephalus australis, 87
Aegintha minor, 116
  temporalis, 116
Aegotheles cristata, 65
Alauda arvensis, 71
Alaudidae, 71
Alcyone azurea, 66
Anas gibberifrons, 24
  rhynchotis, 24
  superciliosa, 24
Anthochaera, carunculata, 110
  chrysoptera, 110
Anthus australis, 99
APODIFORMES, 65
Aprosmictus erythropterus, 52
  scapularis, 52
Apus pacificus, 65
Aquila audax, 27
Ardea novae-hollandiae, 20
Ardeola ibis, 22
Artamidae, 99
Artamus cyanopterus, 99
  minor, 99
  superciliosus, 99
Aythya australis, 24

Barnardius barnardi, 56
Biziura lobata, 25
Botaurus poiciloptilus, 20

Cacatua, 49
Cacomantis pyrrhophanus, 60
Callocephalon fimbriatum, 48
Campephagidae, 73
CAPRIMULGIFORMES, 63
Carduelis carduelis, 114
Casarca tadornoides, 24
CASUARIIFORMES, 15
Chalcites basalis, 60
  lucidas, 60
  plagosus, 61
CHARADRIIFORMES, 37
Charadrius bicinctus, 38
  cinctus, 38
  cucullatus, 38
  leschenaulti, 63
  melanops, 37
Chenonetta jubata, 25
Cheramoeca leucosterna, 72
Chibea bracteata, 74
Chlamydera maculata, 79
Chlidonias leucoptera, 44
Chloeba gouldiae, 116
Chloris chloris, 115
Chthonicola sagittata, 93
CICONIIFORMES, 20
Cinclorhamphus cruralis, 86
  mathewsi, 86
Cinclosoma punctatum, 84
Cisticola exilis, 87
Cladorhynchus leucocephalus, 41
Climacteridae, 81
Climacteris affinis, 82
  erythrops, 81
  leucophaea, 81
  minor, 81

Colluricincla brunnea, 84
  harmonica, 84
  megarhyncha, 85
  parvula, 84
  woodwardi, 84
COLUMBIFORMES, 46
CORACIIFORMES, 66
Coracina gascoynensis, 73
  novae-hollandiae, 73
  papuensis, 73
  robusta, 73
Corcorax melanorhamphus, 77
Corvidae, 76
Corvus cecilae, 76
  coronoides, 76
Coturnix pectoralis, 34
Cracticidae, 77
Cracticus torquatus, 78
Crocethia alba, 40
CUCULIFORMES, 59
Cuculus pallidus, 59
Cygnus atratus, 26
  olor, 26

Dacelo gigas, 67
Dicaeidae, 112
Dicaeum hirundinaceum, 114
Dicruridae, 74
Diomedea melanophris, 17
Dromaius novae-hollandiae, 15
Dupetor flavicollis, 20

Egretta, 20
  alba, 20
  intermedia, 22
  garzetta, 22
Emblema picta, 116
Eopsaltria australis, 95
  chrysorrhoa, 95
Epthianura albifrons, 112
  tricolor, 112
Epthianuridae, 112
Erolia
  acuminata, 40
  ferruginea, 40
  ruficollis, 40
Eudyptula minor, 16
Eurostopodus guttatus, 63
Eurystomus orientalis, 68
Excalfactoria chinensis, 34

Falco, 30
  berigora, 30
  cenchroides, 30
  longipennis, 30
  peregrinus, 30
FALCONIFORMES, 27
Falcunculidae, 111
Falcunculus frontatus, 111
Fulica atra, 36

GALLIFORMES, 33
Gallinago hardwickii, 39
  megala, 39
Gallinula tenebrosa, 35
Gelochelidon nilotica, 44
Geopelia cuneata, 46
  humeralis, 46
  placida, 46
Gerygone flavida, 90
  fusca, 90
  levigaster, 90
  mouki, 90
  olivacea, 90
  palpebrosa, 90
  richmondi, 90
Gliciphila albifrons, 105
  indistincta, 105
  melanops, 104

Grallina cyanoleuca, 77
Grallinidae, 77
Grantiella picta, 106
GRUIFORMES, 35
Grus rubicunda, 35
Gymnorhina hypoleuca, 77

Haematopus, 37
  ostralegus, 37
Halcyon macleayi, 67
  sanctus, 67
Haliastur indus, 28
  sphenurus, 28
Himantopus leucocephalus, 41
Hirundapus caudacutus, 65
Hirundinidae, 72
Hirundo neoxena, 72
Hylochelidon ariel, 72
  nigricans, 72

Ixobrychus minutus, 20

Kakatoe, 49
  galerita, 49
  roseicapilla, 49
  sanguinea, 50
  tenuirostris, 50

Lalage leucomela, 74
  sueurii, 74
Larus dominicanus, 43
  novae-hollandiae, 43
  pacificus, 43
Leipoa ocellata, 33
Leptolophus hollandicus, 52
Leucosarcia melanoleuca, 47
Limicola falcinella, 41
Lobibyx novae-hollandiae, 37

Malacorhynchus membranaceus, 24
Malurus assimilis, 90
  cyaneus, 88
  cyanotus, 89
  lamberti, 90
  leuconotus, 90
  leucopterus, 89
  melanotus, 89
  splendens, 89
Manorina melanophrys, 107
Megalurus, 88
  gramineus, 88
  timoriensis, 88
Megapodes, 33
Megapodius freycinet, 33
Meliornis niger, 107
  novae-hollandiae, 106
Meliphaga cassidix, 103
  chrysops, 102
  cratitia, 102
  fusca, 102
  keartlandi, 102
  leucotis, 101
  ornata, 103
  penicillata, 103
  virescens, 101
Meliphagidae, 101
Melithreptus brevirostris, 104
  gularis, 104
  lunatus, 103
Melopsittacus undulatus, 58
Menura alberti, 69
  novae-hollandiae, 69
  superba, 69
Menuridae, 69
Merops ornatus, 68
Microeca flavigaster, 93
  leucophaea, 93

Mirafra javanica, 71
Monarcha frater, 95
  leucotis, 96
  melanopsis, 95
  trivirgata, 95
Motacillidae, 99
Muscicapidae, 93
Myzantha flavigula, 108
  melanocephala, 108

Neophema chrysogaster, 57
  chrysostoma, 56
  elegans, 57
  splendida, 57
Neositta chrysoptera, 82
  pileata, 82
  striata, 82
Ninox boobook, 62
  strenua, 62
Numenius madagascariensis, 39
Nycticorax caledonicus, 20

Ocyphaps lophotes, 47
Oreocincla lunulata, 85
Oxyura australis, 25

Pachycephala pectoralis, 98
  rufiventris, 98
Pachycephalidae, 98
Pachycephalinae, 98
Pandian haliaetus, 32
Paradisaeidae, 80
Pardalotus punctatus, 112
  striatus, 113
  substriatus, 113
Passer domesticus, 115
  montanus, 115
PASSERIFORMES, 69
PELECANIFORMES, 19
Pelecanus conspicillatus, 19
Petroica cucullata, 94
  goodenovii, 94
  multicolor, 94
  vittata, 94
Phalacrocorax carbo, 19
  melanoleucus, 19
  sulcirostris, 19
Phaps chalcoptera, 46
  elegans, 46

Phylidonyris pyrrhoptera, 106
Pitta versicolor, 69
Pittidae, 69
Platalea flavipes, 23
  regia, 23
Platycercus adelaidae, 54
  adscitus, 54
  adscitus amathusia, 54
  caledonicus, 54
  elegans, 53
  eximius, 55
  flaveolus, 55
  icterotis, 56
  venustus, 54
Plegadis falcinellus, 23
Ploceidae, 114
Pluvialis dominica, 38
  squatarola, 38
Podargus strigoides, 63
PODICIPEDIFORMES, 16
Podiceps cristatus, 16
  novae-hollandiae, 16
Poephila cincta, 116
  cincta atropygialis, 116
  cincta nigrotecta, 116,117
Polytelis swainsoni, 53
Pomatostomus halli, 84
  rubeculus, 83
  ruficeps, 84
  superciliosus, 83
  temporalis, 83
Porphyrio melanotus, 35
  porphyrio, 36
PROCELLARIIFORMES, 17
Psephotus haematonotus, 56
PSITTACIFORMES, 48
Psophodes olivaceus, 111
Pteropodocys maxima, 73
Ptilonorhynchidae, 78
Ptilonorhynchus violaceus, 78
Ptiloris paradiseus, 80
Puffinus griseus, 17
  pacificus, 17
  tenuirostris, 17

Recurvirostra novae-hollandiae, 43
Rhipidura fuliginosa, 97
  leucophrys, 96

rufifrons, 97
setosa, 97
Rostratula benghalensis, 37

Seisura inquieta, 97
Sericornis frontalis, 92
  laevigaster, 92
  magnirostris, 93
Sittidae, 82
Smicrornis brevirostris, 93
SPHENISCIFORMES, 16
Sterna, 43
  albifrons, 43
  anaetheta, 44
  bengalensis, 43
  bergii, 43
  dougalli, 44
  fuscata, 44
  nereis, 43
Stizoptera bichenovii, 117
  bichenovii annulosa, 117
Streptopelia chinensis, 46
STRIGIFORMES, 61
Sturnidae, 100
Sturnus vulgaris, 100
Sylviidae, 86

Taeniopygia guttata, 117
Threskiornis molucca, 23
  spinicollis, 23
Timaliidae, 83
Trichoglossus molluccanus, 84
  rubritorquis, 48
Turdus merula, 86
  philomelos, 86
Tyto alba, 61
  castanops, 62
  longimembris, 62
  novae-hollandiae, 62

Zanaeginthus bellus, 115
  oculatus, 116
Zanthomiza phrygia, 106
Zonifer tricolor, 37
Zosteropidae, 114

25/12/77.

BANDED PIGEON 14in.

BROWN PIGEON 15in.

ROSE-CROWNED PIGEON 8¾in.

PURPLE-CROWNED PIGEON 8¾in.

RED-CROWNED PIGEON 8¾in.